Oath
of Allegiance
Robert Dietz

To Itza!

Who has experienced
that freedom neither provides
nor does it give,
it demands the utmost
of sacrifices!

[signature]

December 1993

**This book has been produced
without Government Grants**

Edited by Janet Rosenstock
Cover Design: Horst Deppe

Back cover photo: G. Georgakakos

Publisher: Regina Coupar
GAMALIEL PUBLICATIONS
Truro, N.S.

Printed by: Atlantic Systematic Envelopes Ltd.
Truro, N.S.
1992
ISBN 0-9695837-1-0

Acknowledgements

Although my name appears as author of this book, a great many people contributed in the making of it.

These were some who provided me with valuable information, and others pointed out errors, some were concerned with my syntax and others worried about my diet. I am very much indebted to many friends and War Veterans who offered me leaflets, photos, maps and other objects for photographic reproduction.

Barbara MacLeod, Angela Landry, Karen Seaboyer of CML Communications, Halifax, N.S.

Dante Di Mattia
Maria Zavarella, Bianca Liberatore, Maria Zappa
Halifax, N.S.

Michael and Jennifer Start
Saint John, N.B.

Bettina Steinbrenner
Hannover, Germany

Peter Panagiotakos
Halifax, N.S.

Dr. Astrid Brunner
Banff Centre for the Arts
Banff, Alberta

Patrick C. Laurette
Formerly Curator, AGNS
Halifax, N.S.

Christopher Denten, San Fransico, Cal.

LCdr Richard 'Dusty' Miller
Vancouver, B.C.

Major Gail Ross
NDMC National Defense HQ
Ottawa, Ont.

Vincent Englehart Ltd.
Certified Management Consultants,
Halifax, N.S., Moncton, Saint John, N.B.

D B M Canada
Halifax, N.S.

Prof. Duncan Fraser
formerly Capt Cape Breton Highlanders, WW II, Wolfville, N.S.

Nicky Lounsbury, Elma McLeod, Jennifer Thornhill, Tina Bradford, Andrew Langille, Morgan van Horne, Bruce Rands, Lisa Wheeler, David Wareing
Halifax, N.S.

Shimon Walt, Halifax, N.S.

Roberta Harrington, Chester, N.S.

Ulrika Sandblom, West Bay, N.S.

Unni Simensen, Maureen Robb
Dartmouth, N.S.

Amber Brown, David Burton, Sue Fougere
Of TooTon's, Halifax, N.S.

Karl Hanke, Blandford, N.S.

Dr. Earle and Judith Bain
Halifax, N.S.

Captain (N) Steen Jessen
National Defense HQ, Ottawa, Ontario

G.G. Gomery
formerly Major RCASC WW II
Halifax, N.S.

Douglas Thompson
formerly Capt. 9 Battery, RCA
11 Can. Army Field Rgt. WW II
Halifax, N.S.

Laverne Tilley
Bank of Montreal
Halifax, N.S.

I am especially grateful to Dr. W.A.B. Douglas, Director, Directorate of History, Dept. of National Defense H.Q. Ottawa for permitting quotations and reproduction of maps from the 'Official Canadian War History' by Col. G.W.L. Nicholson and the valuable assistance of Bruce F. Ellis, curator of the Army Museum Halifax Citadel.

I appreciate very much the painstaking work done by Alex Chisholm who spent considerable time re-photographing numerous snap shots which were mostly in a deteriorating state. For other photographic work, as always, George Georgakakos, a photographer associated with excellence, stood by. My thanks to Colonel Bruce C. Gilchrist, CD, The RCR, for reading the manuscript and suggesting the assistance of Lt. Col. E.L. Schrader, CD, RCA in finding Canadian (English) 'artilleristic' technical terms.

A valuable contribution was made by by the following students:
Aric Bishop and Drummond Vogan, political science dept. Acadia University, Wolfville, N.S. Also Sinclair Stewart, Dept of English, Dalhousie University, Halifax, N.S. and Jennifer Read of Prince Andrew High School, Dartmouth, N.S. They made, after reading the manuscript, valuable suggestions.

I offer my special thanks to those who encouraged me and insisted that 'Oath of Allegiance' should become a reality: Gary Lajeunesse CD,P.Eng., Dulcie Conrad, Writer & Journalist, Peter J. Power, former Capt. RCASC, Halifax, N.S., Col (ret'd) Ian S. Fraser, OMM CD, Gladys Fraser, Vice Pres. CML Communications, Halifax, N.S. and Jim Lotz, Writer and faithful promoter.

My gratitude to Dr. Lawrence Stokes of Dalhousie University History Department for helping me to stay clear of the Historian's preserve. Of course a thank you to my editor Janet Rosenstock for whom my syntax must have been a nightmare. Also Angela Smith whose task was hunting for last minute 'bugs'.

Also 'vielen Dank' to my publisher, fellow artist and writer Regina Coupar for giving me so much valuable assistance.

It was the insistence and stubbornness of Dorothy Sutherland which not only convinced me to write *Oath of Allegiance*

Last but not least I am very much indebted to Dr. Deborah L. Thompson for her special assistance and to my daughter Patricia Dietz, in musical terms, my Opus I, for her difficult task in typing and re-typing the manuscript and sacrificing her weekends and summer evenings of sailing on the Bras d'Or Lakes for the sake of *Oath of Allegiance*.

Again, thank you to all my friends who had to put up with me during a time of withdrawal and pre-occupation.

R.D. October 1992

Dedicated to
my sister
Waltraud
and Her American Family

Part One

OATH OF ALLEGIANCE

I SWEAR BY GOD THIS HOLY OATH
THAT I WILL FOLLOW THE ORDERS OF THE FÜHRER
OF THE GERMAN REICH AND THE SUPREME COMMANDER
OF THE GERMAN ARMED FORCES, ADOLF HITLER,
WITHOUT CONDITION, AND I AM PREPARED
TO SACRIFICE MY LIFE, AS A BRAVE SOLDIER,
AT ANY TIME.

Oath of the German Armed Forces.
(1934-1945)

PROLOGUE

"Please, come and talk to us!" were the words which began this book.

On a quiet February afternoon - and there are far too many of them when one is involved in the business of selling art in a city with the tempo of a village - the ringing of my telephone awakened me. I was in the initial stages of some kind of transcendental meditation, thinking of how unkindly I had treated a young lady who might have become a customer.

The young lady had been stylishly dressed and wore a pair of sunglasses. I was not quite sure if they were to protect her eyes from the striking colours of Robert Annand's painting of "Suzanna and the Elders", or if they were a part of the latest design of some franchised *Salon des Femmes*.

But it was not her dress nor glasses that put me to sleep, or that later got my blood pressure to rise. I lost my patience, as I often do under such circumstances, after she complained that "...the stuff on your walls is just too modernistic, too abstract for my taste!"

But the stuff on the walls was neither modernistic nor abstract. I explained that if she would remove her sunglasses, perhaps she might be able to see that the style of these paintings has actually been around for the last seven decades. Now, if the lady had been dressed like Queen Victoria, I might have overlooked her remarks. But she walked around the room swinging her long leather gloves like a propeller. No doubt she was the wife of a successful professional.

I ended our conversation by asking, "How is it that one side of your brain is normally developed for the fashion of the 1990s, and the other part remains in the 1880s. She left abruptly without reply.

All this is by way of explaining my mood when the phone rang. The friendly, young voice at the end of the line struck me like a harpist's fingers plucking the strings of this angelic instrument. "This is Cathy."

I immediately wondered what had prompted her to call. What was it going to cost me? What cause will I have to support? What advertising, in which student yearbook? I remember thinking, I damn well wish someone would support me for a change! But there was no need to become angry or excited. She only asked if I would come and talk to her history club.

I said "Yes", without realizing what I would be getting myself into. That is how I came to visit Dalhousie University's Henson College to talk to Cathy's history club about, "Growing up in Germany between the two World Wars and the role art played in Hitler's *Machtergreifung* - Seizure of Power.[1]

When I first met Cathy and her classmates, Renee and Bettina, I was quite astonished by their general knowledge and even more startled by their more specialized knowledge of European history.

They were so well read on the Battle of Stalingrad (now called Volgograd) and battles that took place in Ukraine, I felt embarrassed. As an artillery observer in the German Army, I was not supposed to know any more than what I saw through my telescope. These students, by contrast, were even able to tell me that the Regiment and Division to which I belonged was part of the Army Group under Field Marshal von Manstein.

I quickly realized that I would have to prepare myself well for my upcoming talk. It was the enthusiasm and sincerity of these three students which gave me the inspiration and energy to put my thoughts on paper and to remember what the war was really like.

My father was a stone mason, so were his father and brothers. They made mill stones and cobble stones.

They also happened to be the local town musicians.

They also played on top of the castle tower on New Year's Eve as it was the tradition since the middle ages.

My mother came from a line of artisans mainly wood carvers.

Photo: G. Georgakakos

INTRODUCTION

Scientists who study the human brain are not yet certain how our memory functions or how far back we can recall. It seems clear, however, that events which deeply affect us can leave an impression even if they occur when we are very young. If I dip back into my memory I can recall incidents which took place when I was less than two years old and I believe I remember them because I was born a few years after the end of the Great War into an atmosphere of discontent and violence. Germany suffered under the harsh terms of the Versailles Treaty,2 an occupying army was still in the streets, and new extreme political parties were in the making. I grew up between wine and beer barrels, breathing the thick tobacco smoke exhaled by the customers in my father's tavern and bearing witness to how these events effected everyone around me.

    As a young boy, I loved to play with my toy soldiers of which I had two categories. The important and leading figures, Frederick the Great, *Generalfeldmarschall* von Hindenburg, von Mackensen, Kaiser Wilhelm II, and others of their ilk, were sculpted and made of a mixture of clay and *papier-mâché*. The military bands, cannons, and howitzers fell into the same category. But the foot soldiers were home made with the help of my father. I had several casts which were clamped together. I collected old lead pipes, and when my mother was absent, my father and I melted the lead in a cast-iron pot on the coal stove. It was a difficult and dangerous procedure when we pored the glowing lead into the forms. The burn marks on the floor gave us away each time we did it.

    In later years I would come to think of these soldiers as a kind of metaphor for the reality that came to be. The leading figures were quite unlike the ordinary soldiers - and in the end, it was the sacrifice of the ordinary German - Jew and Gentile - that left its mark on the nation.

Chapter One

I am the result of my father's love for music and my mother's artistic talents.

Mayen, where I was born, is a typical medieval town in the Rhine/Mosel triangle at the foot of the Eifel mountains. Mayen received its charter from Kaiser Rudolf of Habsburg in 1210. Its ancient castle is built on a rock in the middle of the town and is surrounded by a protective wall. Both the castle and part of the wall still exist.

Before he was seriously wounded in World War I, my father was a stone mason. His father and brothers were also stone masons and with only one exception, they were all descended from a line of stone masons. This family of stone masons also happened to be musicians who formed their own brass band. Every New Year's Eve they played on top of the old castle's tower. New Year's Eve chorales have been a tradition in Mayen since the middle ages.

My mother came from a line of artisans, mainly wood carvers who decorated every village church in the region. I am the result of my father's love for music and my mother's artistic talents.

As a result of his wound, my father gave up masonry and became the owner of a *Gasthof* in 1926 - that is the German word for an inn, pub or tavern, or a combination of the three.

In those days, French armoured cars were still parked

on the street. The French troops had taken over from the American occupation forces. I remember people talking about the nice, happy American boys and about ice cream and candies. But when they discussed the French, their description was less complimentary.

I did not personally experience the difference between the American and French occupiers because I had just been born when the Americans left. I know that the German people resented the French and blamed them more than the Americans for the harsh terms of the Versailles Treaty which ended the Great War. The Germans began *Passiver Widerstand* - passive resistance after coal shipments were sent to France as a way of paying reparations. Then Albert Leo Schlageter was executed for blowing up a bridge to interrupt the coal shipments and the situation between the French occupiers and the Germans became even more tense.

But I was only a few years old and I liked the armoured cars parked on the street. To my eyes, they were fascinating monsters and one day when I fell off one, the *poilu* even gave me a piece of his chocolate bar, while my father gave me a kick in the pants. I didn't understand my father's reaction. Why? What had I done wrong?

Only when I was older and I learned about the *Grossen Krieg* - the Great War - did I begin to understand my father's feelings. Then, I learned that my father had received his debilitating wound at the first battle of the Somme in 1916, and that he had lost his brother in the last battle of the Somme in 1918.

I was one of a family of six. I was the eldest child, with a sister Waltraud who was two years younger. We were joined by a brother, Hans Werner, who came 9 years after I was born and another sister, Eva Maria who was born nearly 18 years later.

Our *Gasthof* was a busy place in those days. It was always filled with people, music, and especially cigar smoke. It was a fascinating place for a small, impressionable boy and as I grew older, I liked being there more often.

My father used to entertain his customers with his violin. He had a very special instrument besides his regular violin. He had a jazz violin which he had obtained from one of the American musicians while playing regularly at the U.S. Army officers mess during their occupation (prior to my birth). The jazz violin was a strange instrument. It did not have a real body, it had instead a finger board with an aluminum funnel attached. It produced a sound like that of a mewing cat and the tunes played on it were similar to those played today by Stephan Grappelli.

Listening to the radio became very popular for everyone during my pre-school years. Our radio was an awkward-looking piece of furniture and no one was allowed to touch it after my father positioned the dial on the proper channel. I listened to almost everything that came out of our radio, especially the music. I remember hearing Kurt Weill and Berthold Brecht's *Die Dreigroschenoper* - the Three Penny Opera when it was broadcast.

As soon as I began school, I had to make myself useful by helping my father behind the counter and running last minute errands. I was often sent to the butcher shop for liverwurst or to the bakery for crusty rolls.

The most important day for me, or anyone living in the predominantly Catholic Rhineland, was Sunday when we all attended mass. My father did not attend mass, claiming that war invalids were 'excused.'

I liked the early Mass best because it had no sermon, making it at least fifteen minutes shorter than the other masses. The High Mass started at 10:00 a.m., not only at the nearby church but also in my father's pub. The husbands would deposit their wives safely in the front rows of the church, while they supposedly filled the back pews. Instead, they came to my father's pub.

One of my duties was to run over to the church and report back how far the Mass had proceeded. As I recall, the husbands always seemed to meet their wives at the church exit just as the service ended. The women were usually in a trance from smelling the incense while the men experienced their own euphoria from the schnapps they had just consumed.

I found working in my father's pub even more interesting during the week, when I could watch the card games. These games were often accompanied by heated political and mili-

My father in the Kaiser's Artillery, World War I.

Some of his brothers, the ones too old for front duty, became members of a military band.

Oath of Allegiance

`Zur Linde' was the name of our Pub.

The Card Game

painting by Robert Dietz
Oil on board
Photo: Rob. Roy

from the collection of
Michael and Jennifer Start

tary arguments about battles in the Great War, a war which had ended some ten years previously. These discussions usually led to customers accusing one another of not having been anywhere near the scene they had just described.

As a young boy I was under the impression that all of my father's friends were war heroes. One day I had the courage to ask, "What about you, Papa? Did you not get the Iron Cross?" There was silence. "No", he said with a huff, "I got a piece of iron into my cross!" (os sacrum). With those words he pulled up his left pant leg and showed me his horrible scars. The leg was seven centimeters shorter than the right. That was the only conversation I ever had with my father about his experience in the Great War.

All this education as a young child eventually made me an expert in the military history of The Great War. Naturally, I specialized in military music. That is the reason why my large collection of toy soldiers consisted mainly of military bands. In other words, I had more soldiers marching on parade and playing music than storming the enemy's positions. It was not until ten years later that I learned it should be the other way around.

At the age of six I knew all the military marches composed for every battle Frederick the Great had won. I never missed the Sunday concert at noon in the market square. The program always had the same pattern, so it didn't take me long to figure out how it was arranged. First, the music began with a typical Prussian military march such as, *Preussens Gloria* - The Glory of Prussia.

Then came an overture, 'Poet and Peasant' for example, or everyone's favourite, the 'Light Cavalry' by Franz von Suppé. Near the end, the band played a typical Strauss waltz and eventually, with a Cornet solo, they returned to a military march, 'Old Comrades,' as a finale.

My father quickly recognized that I had an ear for music. I became a drummer - and a good one, too. I participated in and won first prize in every tambour competition in the *Jugend Klasse*. I became a welcome soloist at benefit concerts.

When I was good, my father never said a word. When

I made a mistake, I was called a *Dummkopf* - meaning a dumb head, or a *Schaafskopf* - a sheepshead -, sometimes he screamed, *Du Esel* - "you ass". I managed to please him most of the time. When pleased, he would put a big cigar in his mouth and take some extra deep puffs, walking and puffing away as if he was using his cigar smoke as a propellant. If I had been a *Wunderkind* playing the piano or violin, I might have liked it, but playing the drums? I believed anyone with a sense of rhythm could have been able to play them. In any case, I hated it because it always scared me to go on stage. It made me so nervous that I did not see anybody around me.

My stage fright was caused by a fear of my father. "If you embarrass me, I'll kick you off the stage!" Thirty years later when I tried to play the French horn solo in Flotow's Overture to the opera, 'Martha,' his threatening remarks still rang in my ears.

In school I was taught that by the end of the Great War, four million people had died during the four years of fighting. None of us could imagine that there would be a second, even more profound catastrophe for mankind.

I was now almost six years old and soon became aware of the political scene around me, first in my father's pub and soon afterwards on the streets and in the market square. And for the first time in my life, I became very uncomfortable about what I saw.

I did not understand what was happening, but my memories are vivid and I remember what excited me and how it made me feel.

I witnessed the end of the French occupation of the Rhine and the beginning of violent rallies and street demonstrations. I became aware that there were several political parties all fighting one another either with words, or with their fists, or with both. As a child I simply understood they didn't agree on important matters.

There was a great deal of excitement during the celebrations at the end of the French occupation. One of the weekly rehearsal sessions of the *Stadtkapelle* - the town brass

The Tambour
Competition.

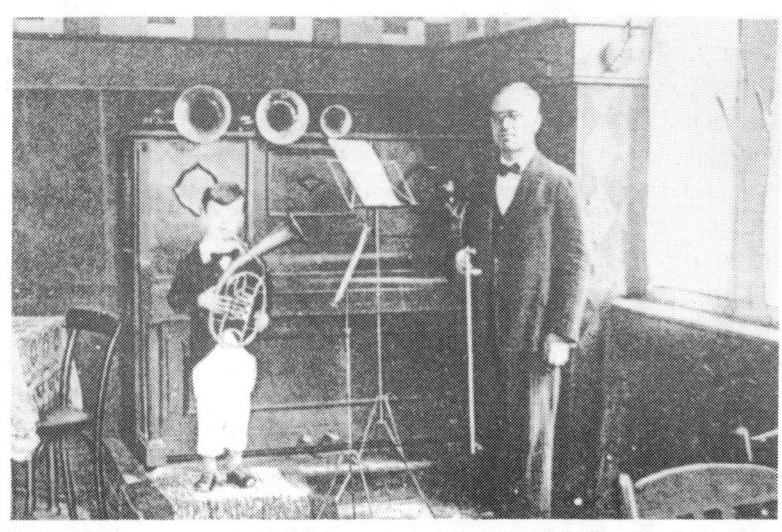

A special attraction in my father's pub.

Anker = Theater
Mayen.

Donnerstag, den 18. Dezember, abends 8,30 Uhr eine musikalische und künstlerische Sensation für Mayen

Wohltätigkeits - Weihnachtskonzert
für die armen Kinder der Stadt Mayen.
25 Mann starkes Orchester!
Leitung Kapellmeister Otto Kastl.

Aus dem Programm:
Prolog aus Bajazzo mit Solo-Gesang und großem Orchester
Wachtparade unter Mitwirkung eines 6jährigen Trommlersolisten.

Köstliche Weihnachts = Tongemälde

Sopran=, Bariton=, Violin= und Klaviersolis usw. usw

Preise der Plätze: Saalseite 0,50, Saalmitte 0,75, Loge 1,50.

Vorverkauf im „Anker".

„Der Aufzug der Wache" wurde hierbei von dem kleinsten Tambour Mayens, dem sechsjährigen Robert Dietz eingeleitet. Wie er stramm auf= und abmarschierte, und die Trommel wirbelte, das war zu köstlich. Er mußte noch einmal herbeigeholt werden und wiederholen. — Die Ge-

A welcome soloist at benefit concerts.

band - took place, as usual, in my father's pub. The musicians were always provided with free beer during their rehearsal. My father used to say, "Beer is the only way to get these guys to come to rehearsal". These sessions began in a side room, the official band quarters, but soon moved into the main room. Here the regular customers, spiritually prepared by the beer and wine, waited to be joined by the musicians for an extended rehearsal session and a slight change of program. The repertoire for the program change did not require sheet music, but instead more *Löwenbräu and Hofbräu*. While the band, by now adopting the instrumentation of a village band, played or at least tried to play, the guests sang Munich beer garden tunes sometimes to the melody of *Wien bleibt Wien*. Finally, late into the night or the early morning hours, each musician played all the way home where he was scolded by his not so happy other half.

At the card game following the weekly rehearsal, I heard the harmless and fun-loving husbands complain about how abusive their wives were after they got home. While the men were having their fun, the women were left at home trying to provide the daily bread for their children with what little money was left over after the night of celebration.

My father did a lot of crazy things with some of his friends from the *Stadtkapelle* (town band). He often got himself in hot water with the bandsmen's wives who objected to his mischievous pranks. For example, when the weather was hot and dry, the consumption of beer would go up, as did his business and his inventiveness for playing jokes on his friends. When it would be time for my father to pay his bills at the brewery in nearby Koblenz, he would gather his friends and the band for a one-hour train ride to this beautiful city on the Rhine. While my father and the brewery director had their friendly bill-paying session and exchanged cigars, the musicians would go on a guided tour through the brewery. Naturally, the tour was conducted by the brewmaster himself who "begged" the men to taste his latest, by-all-the-gods-of-Germania-approved extracts from hops and malt. They, in turn, would pay their compliments by drinking to the old brewmaster's health and shouting, "*Hopfen und Malz, Gott erhalt's!*" (May God keep

hops and malt!)
    The day would end with a short concert in the brewery courtyard, where employers and employees would enjoy the music while the brewmaster and the brewery director took turns conducting the band. At sunset, the musicians, a bit out of step and a lot out of tune, would march to the *Hauptbanhof* (main railway station), where trains would arrive and depart in different directions every 10 minutes. When the station master would call out, "All aboard!", the musicians, still somewhat in a confused state-of-mind, would ask my father if they were boarding the right train home. He usually would tell them to go ahead without him as he would follow later. Needless to say, when the musicians' wives came looking for their husbands the next day, my father, with the most innocent expression, would claim ignorance saying that he could not understand their delay since they all left for home much earlier than he.

    Although there was room for some light-hearted fun during these difficult times, the reality of economic depression in Germany brought about increasingly more violent rallies where fist fights often broke out between supporters of the extreme left and the extreme right parties; that is between the Communists and the National Socialists. I hated these violent rallies especially when women and children were demonstrating. Communist women and children would shout, *"Was haben wir?"* - "What do we have?" The children responded, *"Hunger!"* The women would then ask, *"Was wollen wir?"* - "What do we want?" The response was, *"Arbeit und Brot!"* - "Work and bread!"
    I was not hungry. I was too young to realize that I was better off than the protesters because their husbands and fathers spent what little money they had at my father's pub.

    I was a little boy who kept his toy soldiers in proper parade order, and who liked military precision of marching bands. In my child's mind, I believed that for a demonstration to be successful, it had to have discipline, military precision, and most important, rousing music. I hated the Communist rallies, not for political reasons, but because they were so disorganized and undisciplined. The Communists did not stand properly in line,

They loved to play and loved to drink.

'The General Salute',
the Präsentir-Marsch' for the Reichspräsident

nor did they wear nice uniforms. They did not have bands to play for them as did my tin soldiers. I did, however, often hum their battle song the *Internationale*. It was a good melody.

My child's mind could not figure out the Social Democrats at all, though I thought them better disciplined and better organized than the Communists. At least they did not have women and children screaming on their behalf. However, I felt they could not have been too important because they did not have any proper bands at all to lead the parade. Neither did the other party that stood in the middle of everything. They were called the Zentrum - the Center Party - but according to my father's customers of the 'Round Table' they must have been an incompetent lot. They were in the government and were the Dummköpfe who did everything wrong.

Then there was the *National Sozialistische Deutsche Ar-*

beiter Partei (National Socialist German Worker's Party), N.S.D.A.P. or the Nazis. To my young eyes they were well organized, and properly dressed in their crisp, brown uniforms and polished boots. They had excellent bands, imported from some larger town nearby, to provide the music for their parades and rallies. I was impressed when they stood in the market square in the evenings. Their band, surrounded by torchbearers, played stirring martial music under the light of the burning torches.

Naturally, I would have liked the Nazis better if they had worn gray uniforms like my toy soldiers, or like my favourite real life soldier, Field Marshal von Hindenburg. Von Hindenburg was the new President of the German Reich, of all the German people. He was a hero who in the eyes of many deserved to be the President because he had defeated the Russians in the Battle of Tannenberg in August 1914 and had driven them into the Masurian swamps and lakes.

I cut out von Hindenburg's pictures from the newspaper, the *Illustrierte Zeitung*. I especially liked pictures of him in parade scenes, reviewing the troops with his generals saluting him. I imagined the band played *Deutschland, Deutschland über Alles* as it did when I saw him in the weekly newsreels at the local movie theatre, in what was called *Fox Tönende Wochenschau*.

In those days, I wanted to be a *Stabs Musikmeister* in front of the band or perhaps even a general. But I definitely preferred the thought of being the bandmaster watching with one eye for the signal to start the band playing the *Präsentir Marsch* (a general salute) on the arrival of the field marshal. The *Generalfeldmarschall* was in my collection of toy soldiers standing right next to Frederick the Great with his generals, Ziethen and Dessauer. General Dessauer was not in my collection because he defeated the Saxons at Kesselsdorf, but because of the famous march *Der Alte Dessauer* which is named for him. It has a brilliant trumpet solo. In fact, it was this piece of music that gave rise to my desire to learn to play the trumpet. My mother objected because she believed my lungs would not be strong enough, but in spite of my mother's attempts to stop me, I got my first trumpet the following Christmas.

The most turbulent months of street fighting occurred in 1932 when the Nazi Party began holding more rallies and thus became more visible. They looked smart in the streets, and so did the *Stahlhelm*, - the Steel Helmets - dressed in gray military uniforms. In the main, membership in the *Stahlhelm* consisted of war veterans from the *Deutsch Nationale Volkspartei*. They still looked like soldiers, especially when goose-stepping to the march *Preussens Gloria*. They were impressive looking and I wanted to join them.

It was at this time, when I was eight years old, that I found out that my father was a Socialist, a member of the SPD. The socialist philosophy had no effect on me, for I did not know what it was all about. It did bother me that the SPD never had a band playing for them. To be a musician and a Social Democrat seemed to me nearly impossible. They would not fit together, there would be disharmony. How could I explain this to my friends in school? The only consolation I had was to withdraw to my room where I could play with my toy soldiers.

I remember the winter of 1932 well. It was a very cold winter and, according to my father's card-playing customers, the worst in years. Mothers and children stood in line at soup kitchens while fathers lined up at the employment offices. I saw people, sometimes old couples with a hand carriage, loaded down with lumber they had gathered in the nearby forest. There was not enough coal to burn; most of it was still being shipped to France as reparation payments. I remember my mother adding two or three more sandwiches to my lunch box so I could give them to some of my poorer school friends. Soon I found out that if I would eat a little more at home, I could give my own sandwich away.

I was attending the *Volkschule* - the elementary school. It was around this time that I heard for the first time that Jews were supposed to be bad people. I recall asking my mother, "how is it that my little sister, Waltraud, still goes to a Kindergarten with all the Jewish children? You had better keep her at home." My mother, I'm sure, ignored my comments.

I noticed that more and more of my father's customers gathered around the radio to listen to political speeches. Hitler shouted, *Die bolschewistisch-jüdischen Schweine* - "(the Jews), are the cause of our misery. We will sweep Germany clean as soon as we take over and get rid of this government of weaklings." Most of my father's friends laughed at Hitler's outbursts, but they did so for only a few more months.

One time Hitler shouted over the radio, "The Jews are the cancer that destroys the bloodstream of our pure Nordic Germanic race - and I will guarantee that we will not only liberate the German people from this Jewish pestilence and evil, but the whole world as well!"

My mother would tell us, "Children, it is time to pray for the Jews." When my little sister and I started to argue that the Jews were the ones who had crucified the Lord, my mother finished the argument by saying, "But not our good friends and neighbours, the Treidels and the Gottschalks. They were not there when that happened, when they crucified the Lord."

During the winter of 1932, the media paid more attention to the Nazis. We constantly saw pictures of Hitler in the newspapers. But soon we also became familiar with the faces of the other main figures of the Nazi party: Dr. Goebbels, Hermann Göring, Rudolf Hess and others.

The card games at the 'Round Table' became louder and livelier each day, especially when the players represented a variety of political beliefs. I remember that during one of these arguments my father threw somebody out the door right on to the street. It took all of, perhaps, five seconds. When my father finally calmed down he said, "Hitler is like a louse, when he gets into your fur you can't get him out."

It didn't take long for my father's *Gasthof* to look more as if it were Good Friday than a hall decorated for Easter Sunday. It was empty and I realized why.

One can easily understand that for millions of people hungry and unemployed there seemed to be no light at the end of the tunnel. For most people the end of the Weimar Republic came as a relief. Many voted for their economic interests.

Everything happened fast and with great efficiency.

Oath of Allegiance

Hitler's enforcers and Göring's auxiliary police moved into the Labour Union offices on May 2, arresting the leaders and staff and replacing them with their own people. Some union leaders were sent to Dachau. Henceforth, the institution which controlled all German workers was called the Nationalsozialistische Deutsche Arbeitsfront, (NSDAF) or simply DAF. The first day of May was declared the *Tag der Deutschen Arbeit* - Day of German Labour. We now had a situation against which the German worker no longer demonstrated. Instead they supported the *Neue Bewegung* (New Movement) and demonstrated against the *Jüdisch-Bolshewistischen* reactionaries who were their former leaders.

Many other organizations were taken over in a similar manner. Whether they were student organizations or teachers' unions, all they had to do was put *NS* in front of their name and the new organization was in place. For example, the *Nationalsozialistischer Studentenbund* became the NS Student Federation. The federation of war veterans was taken over as well. *Der Stahlhelm* was now the NS-Frontkämpferbund. They were originally a part of the *Deutschnationale Volkspartei* carrying Hindenburg's banner of black, white, and red.

There was even the *Nationalsozialistischer Deutscher Frauenbund*, the NS Women's Organization. A few years later its members were awarded a medal called the, *Ehrenkreuz der Deutschen Mutter*. They received a bronze medal if they had four children, a silver medal for seven children, and a medal in gold for being the mother of nine children. I do not know if there was a medal for mothers with even larger broods.

It did not take long before I experienced how quickly one could become a member of the 'Movement'. I belonged to a Catholic youth group similar to the Boy Scouts. One evening, during our gym session, the district Hitler Youth Leader appeared. He was decorated with the insignia of his office and had his little adjutant in tow. He gave a short speech, took our oath and that was that.

The Hitler Youth organization had the mandate to educate Germany's young people in the, 'German Spirit'. It was also given the special task of providing pre-military training.

Hitler once said, "Our youth has to become as tough as leather, as hard as Krupp steel, and as fast as a greyhound. They must learn to think German, to feel German and to act German."

At the age of 10 every German boy and girl automatically became a member of the Hitler Youth, but not everybody had the privilege of a public expulsion as did Lothar and I. Lothar was my best friend. We first met in high school where we often studied together, and made and enjoyed music together. Lothar fell on the eastern front as an infantryman in the battle around Smolensk in September 1943.

In those early months of the Nazi regime, I was too young to even suspect what the future would hold. I didn't take life that seriously yet, but enjoyed doing all the things any other boy would do.

My parents owned one of the newer and larger homes in the area. It was a newer house in that others were about 100 years older than ours. We lived in a corner house built in 1903. It allowed me the advantage of being able to see down the streets in all four directions.

During the early morning hours before going to school, and late at night when I should have been asleep, I would sit at my window lookout watching all the traffic along the streets. I saw who went in and out of my father's pub below, and because of the narrow streets, I heard the nearby family disputes before the rest of the town gossiped about them.

On a Saturday or Sunday night, my little sister Waltraud joined me in 'target practice'. We would use peas or beans in our sling shot and aim to hit the rear ends of our father's customers as they left the pub somewhat inebriated after the weekend dances. My sister and I were never discovered in our well-camouflaged position. Perhaps this early experience is the reason why, some 10 years later, I ended up as an artillery observer in the military. However, I did not do as well in Italy's Apennine Mountains. I was bombed out of my observation post.

'The Forward Observer'
Pencil Sketch   R. Deitz

Chapter Two

The year 1934 was particularly eventful for me. I was ten years old. At first I went to the *Gymnasium* - a high school for exercising brains, not muscles. The school was in the humanist tradition; I learned Latin and Greek, and studied other subjects which I did not appreciate at the time. It was only in later years that I reaped the benefits of those studies.

In August, Field Marshal von Hindenburg, who was President of the Weimar Republic, died. I remember how sad I felt at his death. All that day I kept one ear close to the radio and listened to the music which was especially selected for the occasion.

As was my habit, I withdrew to my room and created a model of a state funeral for the Field Marshal with my little toy soldiers. I made a coffin out of some matchboxes but my father pointed out that I needed a gun carriage. He knew these things because he had served in the Horse Artillery and they were the part of the army which looked after state funerals and other events requiring public processions. My father also knew that the coffin was to be placed on top of the gun carriage. He became so involved with my display that he ended up buying a gun carriage, a few more howitzers, and some light and heavy field artillery for my collection. He even bought a recording of Beethoven's Second Movement of the 7th Symphony, the popularly referred to, Funeral March, to play for the occasion. At one point, my father joined my pretend funeral procession blowing his tenor horn *con forza* while I played on a muted drum marching behind him. My mother wasn't very understanding of our musical tribute to mourn the dead Field Marshal. She would cry out, "*Gott im Himmel!* When will he be buried?"

When, in reality, he was buried, it was a sad day not only for me but for the whole nation. From that day on, the Second Movement of Beethoven's 7th Symphony was permanently engraved on my memory.

Before the funeral, I knew that Beethoven had composed the *York'scher Marsch*, one of the most stirring military marches ever written. Now I learned a new Beethoven march and this immortal melody was the Second Movement of the 7th Symphony, a slow march funèbre in 2/4 time.

Even today, when I listen to this movement, I close my eyes and imagine a funeral procession passing by; a steady beat and a solemn rhythm of the lower strings representing my muted drum to which the alto parts introduce a new melody as if complaining about the sad event. That was then the part which father took on, when he tried to play the viola part on his tenor horn.

It was some time after Field Marshal von Hindenburg's death and my pretend funeral procession that I became involved in a real funeral.

Mayen had a population of some 18,000, approximately 82 percent of whom were Catholic. Whenever there was a funeral there was a liturgical service in the church followed by a procession through the streets. The officiating priest, together with the altar boys, joined the procession. One altar boy carried the crucifix; another the container of holy water; and a third swung the incense burner back and forth. It was tradition that the altar boy carrying the cross always walked at the head of the procession. But when there was a funeral for a member of the Nazi Party, it sometimes happened that the altar boy would be told by some Nazi official to go to the rear of the brownshirted honour guard. The Nazis did not want to march behind the crucifix. They had no respect for it.

Naturally, with my strong Catholic religious background, I could not stand by in the face of this lack of respect for the cross. I wanted to do something. One day I visited the parish priest and asked to carry the crucifix in the next funeral - at the head of the procession. I was not really an altar boy, but I became one for the occasion, which was the funeral of a Nazi Party member. As was the tradition, I took my cross and marched to the head of the procession following the official church ceremony. I felt as if I had, "I will show you guys!" written across my face, but it was not that easy.

The stout leader of the Nazi Party Honour Guard told me, "Go back, there will be no crucifix in front of us."

I replied with great conviction and courage, "This is a church funeral and not a political rally. If you don't like it, you can go home!" I was only 10 years old then. He was 30, wearing a brown uniform and high boots. The more we argued, the more people gathered around to watch the fight between 'David and Goliath'. It became rather embarrassing for Goliath.

The funeral procession did not continue until three policemen removed me by force as I kicked and screamed. The parish priest was standing there as scared as a rabbit, wishing he had never granted my request. I handed the cross over to the priest and ran home crying, furious that I lost the battle. Of course, there were a lot of secret congratulations and chocolates from my friends and friends of my family the next week. I was lucky they could not arrest me because of my age.

After Hindenburg's death, Hitler finally, and fully, accomplished his concentration of power. On June 30, 1934, (a little more than a month before Hindenburg's death) Hitler had eliminated almost the entire leadership of the S.A. in his role as the Supreme German Judge. On August 2, the *Deutsche Reichswehr* took the Oath of Allegiance, the text of which represents Hitler's concentration of power.

> I swear by God this holy oath that I will follow the orders of the Führer of the German Reich and the supreme commander of the German Armed Forces,
> ADOLF HITLER, without condition, and I am prepared to
> sacrifice my life, as a brave soldier, at any time!

With Hindenburg's death, there was no longer anyone above Hitler, except God. And even 'God had to become a member of the Party.

I recall the illustrated magazines and newspapers which showed the Papal Nuncio, Cardinal Pacelli, who soon became Pope Pius XII, sitting down with the Nazis to sign the so-called Papal Concordat in July 1933. My aunt always said, "What is good enough for the Pope, should be good enough for us!" She took temporary leave from her otherwise socialist philosophy and allowed her sons to join the Party, too.

I always wondered why she no longer served dried bread and molasses but suddenly had fresh, crusty buns with butter and liverwurst. I then learned that when her sons joined the party, they also found employment and, therefore, a better stocked pantry was the order of the day. She also gave long speeches about the poor Führer who was constantly confronted with an army of six million unemployed young people. The figures seemed to change from visit to visit, sometimes it was seven million.

Whatever the unemployment figures were, even I had to admit that Hitler was successful and popular. He became the topic of conversation during the card games in my father's pub. I often overheard one of the more politically informed customers saying, "If people were to vote now, Hitler would get the 58 percent he did not get on January 30, 1933 when he came to power."

On my way to school, I noticed more and more posters showing the Führer in his new role as the power between 'Us and God'. He concentrated all powers unto himself. He was the Chancellor, the President, the Head of State, and the leader of the German people. He was the Führer, and that was what the people called him. *"Führer befehl, wir folgen!"* "You give the orders, we will follow!"

Although more people found employment towards the end of 1933 and into the new year, I noticed that my father's pub was not keeping pace with the general upswing in the economy. Fewer people came for their usual social gathering and those who did, stayed only for a short while. They no longer engaged in lengthy discussions as they used to do. Instead, I heard more and more stories about arrests.

One of our steady customers asked my father one day, "Where is Johann, I have not seen him for some time?" My father replied, "Don't you know?" And then he whispered into his friend's ear, which he had never done before. I learned later that Johann had been arrested and sent to Dachau.

After that I no longer enjoyed being in my father's pub. I did not like the afternoon card games because there were no more heated political discussions and arguments. And what is a card game without arguments?

I noticed more people whispering into one another's ear or talking in hushed tones. One of my father's customers was a stone mason. I remember trying to tell him it was bad manners

Oath of Allegiance

to whisper into someone's ear. "It's *verboten!*" He replied, "My dear little friend, everything is *verboten* today. It is *verboten* to open your mouth and when you close it, it is *verboten* to think. And if you don't stop thinking and keep your little mouth shut, you are going to be *verboten* one day too!" Then the stone mason ran his heavy hand through my hair and I noticed that his eyes swelled with tears. What was happening to our country?

I was told to keep quiet more often now, not only by my father, but sometimes also by customers who suggested I be kept out of the pub, especially after I embarrassed my father. I had begun reading a lot of newspapers and all the magazines which my mother laid out in our guest room. One day, I discovered a picture in which a general stood at attention in front of Hitler and saluted him. Being a young expert in military matters, I went to my father behind the counter, which was surrounded by customers, and asked him, "Did you not tell me that Hitler was a Lance Corporal? How come a general stands at attention and salutes....?" Well, that was the end of my career in his *Gastwirtschaft.*

After that incident, I went to church with my mother more often. I felt I needed to attend because many people stayed away. They officially left the church for political reasons as it wasn't wise to go to church any more. This disturbed me very much. Had I not taken an Oath of Allegiance in front of the Bishop a few weeks ago on the day of my confirmation? How was this different from the Oath taken by our soldiers to the Führer a few days ago? From then on, I went to church if for no other reason than to demonstrate my loyalty.

The changes in church attendance were obvious to me. Parishioners used to walk down the aisle with their heads held high as if looking for applause before kneeling down to cross themselves. Then they would find themselves a seat near the back of the church which they could have taken in the first place. Now, these same people, if they came at all, remained in the back of the church not wanting to be seen. Civil servants, and others who were dependent on the government for employment, simply stopped attending altogether. Staying away from Church is what people did at the time, especially if it meant personal gain or improvement of one's own economic situation. It was a time when the character of individuals could be judged by their actions.

I soon learned to understand my father's response to my mother's description of Sunday mass. She would describe Mr. X going to communion and how pious and dignified he looked. My father would often say in disgust, "I could never kneel beside a hypocrite like that. I would lose my temper and punch him in the nose. That would cause a disruption in the church service and that is why I can't go to church."

My mother always felt that was a cheap excuse for not going to church. It did not take long, however, until my father's suspicions of hypocrisy were proven right. Mr. X accepted an important job in the government which required official confirmation that the candidate had left the Church.

My old high school teacher, who had a Ph.D. in classical languages, had a Latin quotation for every occasion. He described the situation with, "*Qua mobilis est aurea popularis*" - How fickle is the air of the people. Whenever something went wrong, or when he made a mistake, he used a German quotation which he picked up during his military service. When he was about to use it, he would warn the female students to cover their ears.

"Doch Scheisse im Trompeten - Rohr
Kommt, Gott sei Dank nur selten vor!"

Freely translated it means:

"A shit-blocked trumpet (with your forebearance), is generally, thank God, a rare occurrence!"

As you can see he was very careless with his words and was soon dismissed from his teaching position. Dr. B. was a native of Cologne, the city where the Carnival is the main feast of the year, and where humour was born. He did not end up in a concentration camp. I believe they did not take him seriously enough, perhaps, because he was a Cologner.

Let me give you an example of the humour for which the people of Cologne were known. Cologne was one of the first cities under attack by the Royal Air Force. Their first bombs exploded in the Red Light district. *Fama est*: The Vicar General of the Archdiocese of Cologne was terribly upset with the loss of revenue from the rental payments.

Another more humorous story concerns the Carnival songwriter and comedian, Willy Ostermann, who died just a few weeks before the outbreak of World War II. The story goes that after the first air raid and bombing of Cologne, St. Peter had beckoned to Willy Ostermann. Moving the clouds aside St. Peter pointed his finger towards Cologne to show Willy what had happened. "My God," Willy said amazed, "did they ever celebrate Carnival!"

Chapter Three

*Mayen was a comfortable little town.
It was gemütlich.*

The Jews were a part of us:

During the Great War (W.W. I.), some 63,202 young German men of the Jewish faith fought side-by-side with comrades of different beliefs. They fought in the trenches at Verdun, in the battle of the Somme in the West, and in the Masurian swamps in the East. Nearly 12,000 were killed, many were wounded and many were decorated for bravery.

The small Jewish minority of less than half a million had lived in Germany since the middle ages. They were the most integrated Jewish population in Europe. They had tried to become a part of the German people, and they adopted German culture. In retrospect, one has to ask, "How did it happen so quickly that the Jews suddenly became so isolated and excluded from German society?"

At that time my home town had two Catholic Churches, a Protestant (Lutheran) Church and a Synagogue. There were three Catholic schools, one of which had a Protestant and also a Jewish classroom attached to it. We had a trade school, a business and commerce school, and a humanistic high school. Our town also had a Catholic cemetery with an area for Protestants. The Jewish cemetery was at the other end of the community.

When I was growing up, the stone industry and tourism

were important to our local economy. The Jews of Mayen were engaged primarily in retail businesses selling clothing, shoes, and jewelry as well as trades such as butchering and baking.
    Characteristic of the rural and agricultural neighbourhood, there were several Jewish horse traders.
    We also had a Jewish doctor who was well loved and respected by everyone who knew him. Mayen was a comfortable little town. It was *gemütlich*.

    My father was not the most personable resident of the town. The leg wound he got during the war caused him much suffering. The pain he lived with made him a hard man, and that, in turn, made him a difficult person with whom to live. My mother was the opposite. She was a gentle woman, friendly and helpful to everyone, and above all very religious. She was quite upset with the treatment that her Jewish neighbours received. In spite of the fact that my mother was told to distance herself from her non-Aryan friends, she kept up her relationship with them. She often sent my little sister, Waltraud, to their houses at night with a basket of supplies which they were not able to buy for themselves anymore.

    One day at my first communion, around Easter 1934, she had Frau Treidel, the wife of a Jewish horse trader, do all the cooking for the occasion. I remember enjoying the company of her children who sat with us at the dinner table.
    My Godmother, who gave me a wrist watch for this special occasion, did not sit down at the dinner table with us and our non-Aryan friends. Instead, she left early.
    Our friendship with our Jewish neighbors continued for about a year after the *Machtergreifung*, and after the law which forbade Germans from associating with Jews.
    The situation for the Jews grew more and more difficult. Anti-Semitic posters were not only put on billboards, but also on the doors and display windows of Jewish businesses. To the disgust of many, the Nazis started to harass Jewish children who were playing or walking in the streets. Soon these children were not allowed to attend public schools.
    The whole propaganda machine of the German gov-

ernment was geared to eliminate the Jewish race. Inflammatory movies were produced showing a Jewish banker, broker or butcher raping a 'beautiful, blond, young and innocent girl of the superior Germanic race.' The scenes showed God punishing the evil Jewish rapist - death by hanging. Another infamous example of the same sort of film was *Jud Süss*.[3] I recall that our entire class went to see these so-called 'educational' movies. A few days later we went to the same theatre and listened to an all-Beethoven recital.

Soon I heard my classmates and others calling former playmates names too sickening to repeat here. How painful it must have been for Jewish parents to explain to their children why all these things were happening. Jehovah did not hear their prayers at the supper table. *Terribilis est!* It was terrible, indeed.

My father became depressed about the treatment of Jews in our community. He began going out with his friends and would not come home until the early morning hours. Usually he returned drunk. Then, one night, something happened that shook our entire family.

It must have been sometime after midnight when I woke up startled, hearing my mother screaming with fright. My father was lying in the doorway, covered in blood. We learned that the SS, the black-shirted Nazi Storm Troopers, had been waiting for him. At a regular meeting of innkeepers, my father was reprimanded by his colleagues for continuing to buy his meat from a Jewish butcher even though it has been two years since the *Machtergreifung*. Father was told that, by continuing to buy from a Jew, he was undermining the Führer's program and the fight against the "Jewish disease". They chastized father for his behaviour and reminded him that he had recently received a special medal from the late *Reichspräsident* called the *Verdienstkreuz fur Frontkämpfer* for soldiers who had been at the front during the Great War. My father, who must already have had a few drinks by then, replied, "I buy where I want to buy and nobody is going to tell me where! And as I have done in the past, so I will do in the future. I buy my meat from my Jewish butcher friend and as far as the medal is concerned, you can tell the *Reichspräsident*..." He then added

Donnerstag, 1. August 1935 — Nationalblatt

Aus dem Kreise Mayen

„Ich kaufe nach wie vor beim Juden"!

Kaum ist die Erregung der anständig und nationalsozialistisch denkenden Volksgenossen über den Fall „Doll" etwas abgeebbt, sehen wir uns veranlaßt, einen neuen Fall eines typischen Judenknechtes in aller Oeffentlichkeit anzuprangern.

Es handelt sich um den Gastwirt Peter Dietz, Gasthof „Zur Linde", Mayen, Stehbachstraße. Dieser saubere Volksgenosse, der es im Oktober des Jahres 1933 aus Konjunkturgründen für nötig hielt, sich der Mayener Ortsgruppe des NSDFB anzugliedern, saß vor einigen Abenden in einem hiesigen Café. Man unterhielt sich über Einkaufsmöglichkeiten usw., wobei der Herr Dietz sich der Tatsache brüstete, daß er sein Fleisch bei einem jüdischen Metzger kaufe. Als er von den Tischgästen darauf hingewiesen wurde, daß er als Gastwirt, der auch von der Arbeit des Verkehrsvereins Mayen durch Zuweisung von Essen usw. profitiere, doch zum mindesten die moralische Verpflichtung habe, bei einem deutschen Metzger einzukaufen, erregte er sich gewaltig und behauptete, das könne ihm ganz gleichgültig sein, er werde nach wie vor beim Juden kaufen. Es folgte dann der Hinweis, daß er das von Hindenburg gestiftete und vom Führer verliehene Ehrenkreuz für Frontkämpfer trage und als Kriegsverletzter eine Rente des nationalsozialistischen Staates beziehe. Es sei doch seine selbstverständliche Pflicht, den Kampf der Regierung gegen die Seuche des Judentums auch zu seinem Teil zu unterstützen. Darauf erfolgte die unmißverständliche Antwort: „Ganz Deutschland kann mich ...." (folgt der bekannte Ausspruch aus dem „Götz von Berlichingen").

Wir wissen, daß der Mayener Ortsgruppe des Stahlhelms keinerlei Schuld an diesem geradezu unglaublichen Verhalten eines ihrer auf den Führer und das Hakenkreuz, das Zeichen des antisemitischen Kampfes, vereidigten Mitglieder beigemessen werden kann.

Andererseits ist dieser Vorfall wieder einmal ein Beweis dafür, welchen Gesellen teilweise der „Stahlhelm" als Unterschlupf zur Tarnung ihrer wahren Gesinnung gedient hat. Wir erwarten es als selbstverständlich, daß die Mayener Ortsgruppe des NSDFB augenblicklich die Konsequenzen aus diesem Verhalten des „Kameraden" Dietz ziehen wird.

Dem Herrn Dietz aber können wir flüstern, daß der nationalsozialistische Staat sich diese geradezu ungeheuerliche Beleidigung und diese offen zu Tage tretende sabotierende Gesinnung keineswegs gefallen lassen wird. Konzessionsentzug wird nach unserer Ansicht die geringste Strafe für das sein, was dieser Kumpan sich geleistet hat. Ueber das andere sprechen wir uns an geeigneter Stelle wieder, Herr Dietz.

F. K.

Jewish horse traders outside the town wall.

insult to injury by saying, "All of Germany can kiss my arse." He finished his drink, took his cane and left the meeting.

What he said wasn't much, but it was enough. For my father, it was an Innere *Notwendigkeit*, an inner necessity to speak out. But for our family, his speaking out brought great hardship.

Early that morning, the police came for him. Our business was shut down for a while and I was rushed off by one of our relatives to a school run by the Lazarist Fathers of St. Vincent de Paul about 100 kilometers away from home. I had never been that far away before. I was only 11 years old at the time, and for six weeks I went to sleep crying in my pillow.

Chapter Four

"One has to demand the impossible in order to get the possible accomplished."

— Helmut von Moltke

As it turned out, there was not much time for sleeping or crying at my new school. At 5:30 a.m., in the tradition of the 17th century institution, the Prefect, Father Wilhelm, who was also our supervisor, marched through the dormitories shouting, "Benedicamus Domino!." We jumped into our gym shorts answering, "*Deo Gratias.*" Then everyone raced down the stairs pushing and shoving, until we got outside. The temperature could have been a rigid minus 10 degrees celsius or a comfortable plus 10 degrees. It didn't much matter to Father Wilhelm.

"Attention! Right turn! On the double!" he shouted at us as we ran through the woods, across the fields and brooks, and up and down hills. He roared as if he was storming the enemy's position at the fortress of Verdun during the Great War. He had received the Iron Cross First Class doing just that, while serving as a company commander. When he charged, there were no more soldiers left behind him. He was a war hero, and he expected us to be heroic too.

At least ten times a day he would quote the great Prussian strategist, Helmut von Moltke: "One has to demand the impossible in order to get the possible accomplished." I doubt that Sparta demanded such physical and mental hardship as did Father Wilhelm. None of us argued with him.

It was 1935, and it took a short eight years before I benefited from my Spartan-like education. When I was marching in Ukraine between Poltava and Charkov in February 1943, I was able to take off my shirt. I removed it for the purpose of outdoor delousification, or just hunting for lice, at minus 12 degrees celsius.

I grew used to the school after a few months. In fact, I almost liked it there, especially as there were many cultural and recreational activities such as music, theatre, and sport. In addition, one hour was set aside on fine days for working in the fields during the summer and at harvest time. We also did some construction work, building our own outdoor swimming pool and soccer field.

Every Saturday afternoon was reserved for practicing the Gregorian chant and rehearsing for Sunday high mass which was well attended by outsiders who came to enjoy the performance of the boys' choir.

It was an especially great day for us when Abbot Ildephonsus came to visit from the famous 11th century Benedictine monastery at Maria Laach. He was impressed with our singing during high mass and told us, "I wish that our monks would sing with such great spirit and enthusiasm."

I have to admit that we rehearsed three times more often than usual because we wanted to impress our distinguished visitor.

We had visitors of importance all year round. One was Dom Placidus from the same Benedictine monastery as Abbot Ildephonsus. Dom Placidus was his religious name; in actual fact, he was born *Graf* (Count) von Spee.
As Maria Laach Monastery was only a few miles from my home and I knew the Monastery, I was chosen to look after our visitor, Dom Placidus. I met him at the train station, went on errands for him, and served at mass every morning at six. The purpose of his visit was to write a book about Palestine, the Holy Land, where he had served during the First World War in a German/Turkish unit with one of the fathers of our Order. Dom Placidus - Graf von Spee had been a cavalry officer. He was a very tall man with a white beard. He was tall like a Cavalry

officer should be, according to my theory, but wore the black robes of a Benedictine monk. I walked behind him like a little dog would walk behind its master. What made me prouder still, and somewhat conceited about this situation, was that I could tell everyone that I not only knew Dom Placidus, the Count von Spee, but also that he was the brother of an even more famous man, the naval hero, Admiral Maximilian Graf von Spee. The Admiral went down with his flagship, the *Scharnhorst*, on December 8, 1914, during a naval battle near the Falkland Islands.

Ironically, during the Second World War, a battleship called the *Graf von Spee*, named after the Admiral, fought near the Falkland Islands, where it was badly damaged. Trapped by British ships, it was later scuttled at the entrance of Montevideo Bay. The fact that I knew somebody with the name von Spee made me famous too, or so I presumed.

Eventually, I settled into my 'new life' at the school. I studied the classical languages, Latin and Greek. At the time I cursed and swore because I could not figure out the benefits of reading Gaius Julius Caesar, *De Bello Gallico* and Cicero's speeches in the Roman Senate, Tacitus's *Annales* and a few pages of Livius' translations of Greek dramas. I found these Latin readings too damn difficult until I was able to obtain a miniature pocket translation book. It was a time when we all wrote our tests with the aid of such *Lilliput* translation books. This we did with 'great reluctance' and only after calling upon the Holy Ghost for help, *Veni sancte spiritus....,* but since he did not come to us on his own, we helped ourselves.

During my fourth year of humanist education, I had to study the ancient Greeks. This made my life really miserable. The only practical use I got from it occurred nine years later, just before the end of the war, when the Russians stormed the fortress of Küstrin, the last stronghold before the fall of Berlin.

A 'Gymnasium' (high school) for exercising the brain, not muscles.

«Ὦ ξεῖν', ἀγγέλλειν Λακεδαιμονίοις ὅτι τῇδε κείμεθα, τοῖς κείνων ῥήμασι πειθόμενοι».

Oh, wanderer, when you happen to Sparta,
Tell there that you beheld us lying here,
Following our orders.4

    Though our school was considered a private one, we were also under the jurisdiction of the provincial school authorities who occasionally appeared to check on our activities. I had the impression that Father Wilhelm's authoritarian appearance, and his military decorations displayed proudly on his chest for the Nazi school inspectors, contributed to the shortness of their visits. They were always pleased with our physical fitness program and our knowledge of current events such as the remilitarization policy, the reoccupation of the demilitarized Rhineland in 1935 and the on-going Spanish Civil War which began in July 1936. Of course, when the school inspectors came, we saluted them with "Heil Hitler" which we especially rehearsed for the occasion.
    We were all interested in the Spanish Civil War. We read

magazines to find exciting stories about the progress of Franco's troops, and to see whether Colonel Moscardo was still holding the Alcazar fortress. Every event brought great excitement for us as young and enthusiastic students of history who felt like participating in the war. The main event in 1936 was the Holy War against Communism. It must have been, because the newsreels showed the Princes of the Catholic Church blessing the arms of the Italian Division while embarking on a ship destined for Spain. Germany's contribution was the special unit of the Condor Legion under the command of Major General von Richthofen. It was sent to Spain in November.

Our enthusiasm was so great that we were able to get Father Wilhelm to change our daily *Tischlesung* (table reading). We ate our meal under strict silentium while one of the students sat behind a desk on a podium and read whatever was prescribed. From then on we read, 'The Heroes of Alcazar'. We may not always have looked forward to our meals, but we looked forward to the continuation of the story.

As in all wars, atrocities were committed on all sides. Dive-bombers of the Condor Legion massacred the innocent people of Guernica (1937) and Communist factions of the Loyalists declared nuns and priests enemies of the people and executed them as suspected enemy collaborators.[5]

It was sometime during the first half of 1938 that the German government closed all denominational schools including the one which I attended. It happened shortly after a devastating propaganda campaign by Goebbels which announced that these schools were the breeding grounds for homosexuality and 'other perversities'. The government discovered that one of these so-called perverted activities happened in a few of the schools and that became the excuse to close all the institutions. It was not until a couple of years later that I became aware why the Gestapo was asking so many curious questions during an investigation. I did not grasp what it all meant. Nor did I understand that the slightest innocent mistake could have sent one of our dedicated teachers to the concentration camp at Dachau.

From then on my school was converted into an NS

Schülerheim, a national socialist residence for students. Personally, I was quite happy about the closing since it meant I could return home to my old school, the municipal *Gymnasium*. As I recall, the Austrian *Anschluss* in the spring of 1938 was quite an event for us as high school students. Naturally, we were jubilant and we were happy to see all Germans united in one Reich because we were now part of a greater Germany.

Returning to my old school was not as easy as I had thought it would be. It had not changed much but several of the teachers were no longer there. Some had been forced to retire, others were dismissed, without any pension, for being outspoken about events in their community.

During this time I also felt very insecure and nervous about my 'masculinity', considering the events which had taken place in a school similar to my previous one, and the publicity which followed. I felt I was somehow suspected of something I knew very little about.

One day, a classmate named Hildegard invited me and several other boys and girls to a house party, with her parents' permission of course. As a result of the party I finally experienced 'love'. Thankfully, this affair automatically corrected any doubts I might have had about my masculinity. Now I felt like a 'normal' student with a 'normal' reputation.

I had a special interest in the arts which was not considered abnormal. After all, I was not the only student who played in the orchestra, or helped design the stage for the next play, and who also played soccer. But I did start to ask questions about *Deutsche Kunst und Entartete Kunst* (German Art and Degenerate Art).

I had no problem with music. I felt Bach was the greatest, the most German of composers; his music has bone and marrow, like the Reformation by Martin Luther. And later when I fell in love, I also fell in love with Mozart. I've always thought one needs to be in love in order to play Mozart. A few years later I needed Beethoven to give me the backbone for my revolutionary ideas. I was moved to tears when I first heard the choir in Beethoven's opera, *Fidelio*, when the prisoners crawled

Oath of Allegiance 45

out of the dungeons protecting their eyes against the blinding sunlight they had not seen for so long. 'Oh welche Lust....' There were also Egmont, Coriolan, Symphonies number three, five, seven and, of course, the Ninth Symphony - the 'Ode to Joy'. Whenever I had the chance to listen to Beethoven's music, I felt strong enough to move the Pillars of Hercules.

Musicians like Hindemith and Weill left Germany for the United States because the Nazis considered their music to be decadent. The music heard on the radio and concert stage was considered 'clean' because it was screened by Dr. Goebbels' Propaganda offices. But it was different with the visual arts. In Nazi Germany the visual arts were subject to especially strict censorship as they are in all societies governed by deeply conservative forces.7b

    We had an excellent art teacher who was the object of a certain amount of ridicule by the students. It had something to do with the peculiar hat he wore and the fact that he had six daughters.
    One day he invited me to the studio in his home. I was quite overwhelmed with the things I saw there. It was all so different from the type of art he demonstrated in school - so much more exciting. He even showed me catalogues with pictures by what he called 'real artists'. These artists were condemned by the Nazi regime and not many books featuring their work existed. He was not afraid to show me these books because he knew my father, and he felt comfortable talking to me. He talked a lot.
    I found out why those beautiful sculptures in our Fairy Tale Park were suddenly destroyed one day. It was simply because they did not represent 'good German art'. I spent the whole afternoon with my art teacher and from then on many more hours. He taught me all about Deutsche Kunst und Entartete Kunst.

Haus der Deutschen Kunst.

"No nation lives longer than the documents of its culture." These words by the Führer were engraved in stone above the portal of the *Haus der Deutschen Kunst* - the House of German Art - in Munich. Although I was only a high school student when the building was consecrated, I was quite aware of the fact that it was something special and of great importance. We referred to it as the *Kunstverschiebebahnhof*. A *Verschiebe-Bahnhof* is simply a railway station or a freight-train yard where individual cars are hooked up to the proper trains and directed onto the appropriate tracks. We, as students, felt that was what the Nazis did with art - they manipulated it in the 'right direction'. Naturally, commissions were given to artists whose depictions of the historical events in the life of a nation came closest to the regime's philosophical outlook. According to the regime, art had to be 'uplifting'. Only the beauty and ideals of men and women should be expressed in it.

The regime's philosophy embraced some art and rejected some art. It embraced the great master of Hellenic sculptural art, Praxiteles, who created his works from models of beauty found only in the Aryan races, in people with a heroic history. This interpretation meant that nobody else but *we - the Germans* - were supposed to have any heroic past.

Hitler always spoke of the artifacts of the Germanic past which are rich in symbols of heroic nordic Germanic tribes. Surprisingly, he gave credit to some medieval ecclesiastical art, especially when he referred to sculptures being examples of 'our' heroic past; for example, the sculptures of Magdeburg Cathedral, Otto the Great, the famous *Reiter* of the Bamberg Cathedral, the Lion of Braunschweig and the dignity of the German woman which finds its artistic expression in the sculpture of Uta of Naumburg.

All of these impressive ideals and ideas were stated by the great German poet, Friedrich von Schiller.

Der Menschheit Würde ist in Eure Hand gegeben.
Bewahret sie!
Sie sinkt mit Euch!
Mit Euch wird sie sich heben!
(The dignity of mankind
has been placed into your hands!
Protect it!
It will go down with you!
But also rise with you!)

Friedrich von Schiller also wrote 'Wilhelm Tell' which was, as I remember, taken off the reading list for high schools. It was also dropped from the theatre schedule because of its inflammatory passages. Nor was it advisable for students with revolutionary hypertension.

Chapter Five

*For today Germany is ours
And tomorrow the whole world.*

Shortly after returning to my old school, I became acutely aware of the necessity to join one of the special units of the Hitler Youth. I joined as a general member with a choice of branches.

I certainly did not like the group that scheduled their assemblies to coincide with the school mass and which stood at attention for inspection every Sunday morning on the market square and then marched and sang through town. They always sang that ugly marching song:

> Es zittern die morschen Knochen
> Der Welt vor dem Grossen Krieg.
> Wir haben die Schrecken gebrochen,
> Für uns war's ein grosser Sieg.
> Wir werden weiter marschieren,
> Wenn alles in Scherben fällt,
> Denn heute gehört uns Deutschland.
> Und morgen die ganze Welt.

> The rotten bones of the world
> Tremble before the Great War.
> We have broken the terror -
> A mighty victory for us!
> We will march on
> Though the world will be a shambles:
> For today Germany is ours
> And tomorrow the whole world.

There was also a motor sport division, but the minimum age was sixteen and one required a license. I did not qualify and, besides, my father would not have allowed me to drive what he considered to be, 'one of those hellish machines.' Another choice was to join the *Reiter Hitler Jugend* which was the mounted division of the Hitler Youth.

If I had known in advance how scared I would be on a horse, I would not have tried making a fool of myself. Yet, five years later, after returning to the front from a field hospital, I became temporarily a dispatch rider between the battery and Regimental Headquarters. I was more scared as a dispatch rider than at any other time during my front line experience, and not because of the horse. I was scared because I was always alone in an area behind the lines, an area crawling with partisans. It was a creepy feeling knowing someone could jump you from behind at any minute. I felt greatly relieved when I could return to my unit on an established front line. There, even though one could not always see the enemy, the direction of the enemy line was known. Moreover, the bullets usually came from one direction - from the front.

Since riding proved to be unsatisfactory, my only other choice was to join the orchestra of the Hitler Youth which was in the process of being set up. I did not mind the weekly rehearsals and I participated in concerts here and there.

As the military was preparing for the upcoming manoeuvres in the Eifel region our usual high school routine was frequently interrupted by armoured vehicles parked in the school yard. They were headed towards the Belgian and Luxembourg borders. At first, I had some difficulty getting used to seeing the modern equipment such as a reconnaissance squadron on motor bikes, the use of light armoured cars instead of a cavalry squadron on horses, and mechanized field artillery instead of a horse artillery. Naturally my collection of toy soldiers was still geared to the Great War: a set up where one used four horses for each vehicle of the light field artillery and six for each of the heavy artillery.

I soon found out how drastically things had changed when I saw the infantry on motor vehicles. Previously, the captain would have ridden a horse in front of his marching company.

The infantry was supposed to be on foot - or so I thought. I suddenly realized then that my army of toy soldiers was outdated. I had to do something about it. But when I went to my father requesting an extra allowance for the modernization of my private army, he said, "...first, you are getting too old to play with toy soldiers. And second, it is not **your** army that needs modernization, it is the French and the English who need it." It took me some time to find out what he meant.

Even though everything was mechanized, the music thankfully was still the same. The military bands played my old favourite, *Marschlieder* which the soldiers sang while marching through town. It was always exciting to listen to them.

We talked a lot about the new modern army in school and in our dreams we picked out in which unit we would like to be a lieutenant or even a captain. The bookstores were brimming with new books about heroes of the Great War like, Manfred von Richthofen, the Red Baron, and Admiral Graf von Spee. I was too young to fully grasp the fact that Germany was psychologically being prepared for war.

In spite of my age I was aware of the Austrian *Anschluss* which took place in March, 1938. Hitler used the Roman strategy, *Divide et Impera* - divide and rule. The Nazis first caused fear, confusion, and terror, then they moved in to save the lives of their badly treated followers. The manner in which the *Anschluss* was carried out earned Hitler his reputation. *Deutschland* was now *Gross-Deutschland* (Greater Germany), like Great Britain, and this quest for an even 'Greater' Germany continued until Hitler decided to pause. The Prime Minister of England, Neville Chamberlain, commented on the idea of a Greater Germany. He saw it as a unification of those who spoke the German language (and for a time it was) and felt it was not unlike Britain's United Kingdom of Wales, Scotland, and Northern Ireland. We who were impressionable young students of the Gymnasium, did not think things looked that bad.

The Nazis achieved great success at the 1936 Olympic games in Berlin. It was the same in the auto industry. Porsche

Oath of Allegiance

built the Volkswagen (the peoples car) according to Hitler's instructions. German cars became victorious on every racing track in Europe. Italian as well as English racing drivers drove German cars. Instead of driving Alfa Romeo, Ferrari, Maserati, and Bugatti, they now drove Mercedes Benz, Auto Union, and BMW cars. They also drove DKW and BMW motor bikes. It was actually a flourishing time for Germany and everyone was eager to find excuses for all the flaws - that is, all the criminal things the Nazis did. Most believed it was Divine Providence which sent the Führer to save us from all the misery of the past. Then, once again all the good will and hope for something better was destroyed.

Chapter Six

. . . the bugles called. - Mount your horses comrades, . . .

I used to sleep on the top floor of our building and all year round kept the window open. My mother said that it made me tough and healthy to breathe fresh air. There was hardly any pollution from exhaust fumes in those days.

On November 10, 1938 I woke up around 6 a.m. or 7 a.m. and noticed the sky had a strange red glow. Still only half awake, I saw clouds of smoke and heard glass breaking as if rocks were being thrown through shop windows nearby. I dressed quickly and ran outside making my way towards all the commotion. Others had gathered by that time but were quickly dispersed by the police. Some of the women were screaming at several busy-looking SS men. They were not locals and nobody really knew who they were. One of them had a gasoline cannister in his hand. He laughed as our town Synagogue was set on fire. The town folk stood there in stunned silence. The event was not isolated. Such destruction and burnings took place all over Germany and many Jewish shops were destroyed. The night became infamously known around the world as *Kristallnacht* - the night of broken glass.

A few days earlier in Paris, a 17-year-old Jewish boy by the name of Hershell Gruenspan attempted to assassinate Ernst vom Rath, a German diplomat who later died from his wounds.

Young Hershell tried to avenge his parents who were deported to Poland a few weeks previously.

Many prominent Jews were now arrested and sent to Dachau, their possessions confiscated. The ones who still remained at home were greatly restricted in their movements. There was no more hope for the Jews. Their fate was now being defined by the *Volk der Dichter und Denker*, the people of poets and thinkers. This was the very same nation that produced Bach, Beethoven, Goethe and Schiller.

I realized then that we must be a nation of contradictions. Slowly I learned to understand so many of the cynical remarks I picked up at the card games in my father's pub. I began to think that something must be quite wrong. From now on there were more conferences, more annexations, a more visible military presence, more manoeuvres, and more reserve officers as well as men called up for military exercises. The older people somehow already felt the war in their rheumatic bones.

The Bugles call!

Not too long after the Czechoslovakian invasion the bugles called. *"Wohl auf Kameraden auf's Pferd, auf's Pferd in's Feld in die Freiheit gezogen!"* - Mount your horses comrades, let's move out into the fields and into freedom!. I am not quite sure if I saw tears of fear or tears of excitement around me. My father, expressing some kind of relief said, "Thank God that the war will come now, by the time you are old enough, it will be all over." But when I was old enough to go to war, the war was everywhere and far from over.

Soon everything was in place and reset into the 'war machine'. Ration cards for food, soap, and other important things were already in circulation.

Mayen was only about 100 kilometers from the Belgian border so it was logical that several headquarters should be set up in and around our small town. Our house was converted into the headquarters of the army's Military Police. A guard posted outside our door presented arms when the Major-General arrived and left. We had to use the side entrance; but not my mother. She insisted on using the front entrance and eventually they stood at attention for her, too. Even her kitchen was taken over and she had to hire extra help so the staff cook ended up in her service under her command instead of the other way around.

Whenever my mother had a complaint, she did not see the adjutant, but went directly to the Major General. She was a very feisty woman in her new role. One day when the staff medical officer felt that the amount of calories should be increased she replied, "... then the supply officer should deliver more bacon". She ordered him to stay out of her kitchen and that was the last time he put his nose into her pots.

My father immediately made use of the situation and had his business listed as one which was important for the war effort. He also got permission to keep my sister Waltraud out of school so she could work at home.

Waltraud remained at home, replacing all the help my parents could not get until the war was over. I still remember her wearing my old army boots when I came home almost starved in August 1945. My mother could never understand why my sister did not walk like a lady. How could she with half a pound of spikes under her (my) army boots?

Owing to the increased military presence, we were treated to a concert by the Vienna Philharmonic Orchestra under the direction of Hans Knappertsbusch playing Mozart, Beethoven and Johann Strauss. This performance was enjoyed by many citizens of our small town of 18,000 people along with a large audience of soldiers whose numbers I could not guess.

We also celebrated the German victory over Poland in our high school. The students assembled in the auditorium and the principal gave his usual speech with all the 'pomp and circumstances'. If one would line up all the teachers of that school - of whom at least 40 percent had a Ph.D.- there would have been no difficulty picking out the *Herr Direktor*. He was as much respected by the teaching staff as by the students. He always wore a black cutaway with grey pants, white starched shirts with cuff links and a bow tie. Before he spoke, the school orchestra presented Schubert's *Marche Militaire* in which I played the percussion instruments twice as loud as I

Oath of Allegiance 55

should have done. It was a necessity. It was done to hold the orchestra rhythmically together and to cover any other deficiencies.

The principal's speeches were always very patriotic. He demonstrated his enthusiasm for the system and also displayed his party membership pin in such a visible manner that everybody was under the impression that he was a sincere Nazi with 150 percent convictions. However, I knew that he protected a partially - Jewish female student at the school. Many teachers acted that way, but in doing so they purposely gave a false impression.

Unfortunately, after the war, the victors who also became our judges, did not quite understand that by acting in such a way, the teachers prevented our school from falling into the hands of 'real' Nazis. Had this happened, the damage done to the minds of the students would have been far greater.

There were not many activities during the winter months of 1939/1940. Not even the French made any moves behind their fortifications in the Maginot Line. Why should they? They did not move when they were supposed to do so - when the Germans invaded Poland. They had declared war but were waiting for the war to come to them.

On October 14, 1939, a special announcement came over the radio, a *Sondermeldung* with fanfares, cymbals and drums. We learned that Commander Prien had just penetrated the secure harbour of 'Scapa Flow' and had sunk the battleship 'HMS Royal Oak' right under the noses of the British, a deed still respected today by sailors regardless of the side for which they fought. We also learned about the successes of the German fighter pilots in their *Heinkel* and *Messerschmidt* aircraft, fliers such as Gallant, Mölders, and others. Otherwise, those months were like the calm before the storm.

Then the first announcements of casualties from the Polish *Blitz* dampened spirits. Often the impact of black events are not fully realized until they hit home, when they involve a friend, a cousin, a brother, or even somebody's only son. They all fell for the *Führer, Volk und Vaterland*. We started to engrave the first names on the school's memorial plaque.

Many soldiers came home on special leave, some decorated with the Iron Cross and others bandaged by the Red Cross. All of this created a heightened atmosphere of patriotism. But there were other serious casualties; casualties of a special kind: Colonel-General von Blaskowitz was dismissed when he complained about some bestialic and pathological instincts running berserk behind the lines. He criticized the behaviour of the SS security units responsible for clean-up operations in the rear. They were the murderers and the butchers responsible to the SS High Command. Von Blaskowitz did not know at the time that they were following Hitler's direct orders. This kind of war was not taught in the military academies attended by the Prussian nobility to which the General and several other of his colleagues belonged.6

Although von Blaskowitz was later recalled to take over another command, his name was hardly mentioned in the press except when, as military commander of the western Netherlands, he surrendered to the Canadian Commander, General Foulkes after VE Day in 1945.

It was another quiet winter for the impatient students of my *Gymnasium* who were more interested in who was called up to serve the fatherland than in the identity of the new French teacher. It was not until we had our first class with her, that her anatomical features became the cause of some unusual fainting spells. A few students even claimed that their mental ability was not up to the requirements of the science department and they requested they be switched over to the linguistic department where they were allowed to take French.

Aside from a few announcements about the sinking of merchant ships by our successful U-boats, one can say it was *Im Westen nichts Neues,* - All Quiet on the Western Front. Naturally, Erich Maria Remarque's novel of the same title was banned. The eastern front did not exist anymore except for the Poles whose suffering was the main subject of many whispered conversations. At first most of us found these stories unbelievable.

One day an SS man, a typical braggart home on leave,

had too many drinks at my father's tavern and talked too freely. My father, whose political reputation had already caused him difficulty, could not kick the SS man out. The SS man's bragging confirmed rumours that General von Blaskowitz's complaint concerning the bestialic treatment of the civilian population in Poland by the 'SS Sicherheitsdienst', the SS Security Forces, were justified. I remember very well when the SS man was refused admission to our establishment after the war. My father reminded him of the signs, Juden nicht willkommen - Jews not welcome - which he once held in front of a Jewish store.

In order to find out more about what was going on behind the scenes, we started to listen to the BBC News reports. This too was *verboten*. Listening meant one became a *Volksverräter* - traitor of the people, and as such, one could be arrested if caught. Arrest could mean a one way ticket to Dachau.

The English radio program was heard during lunch hour when I had a break from school. I had to stand outside the entrance of my father's pub and report any suspicious characters who might be walking up the street. If I saw any such people, I was to knock on the door to signal my father to switch the station. The news program always began with the opening bars of Beethoven's Fifth Symphony - ta ta ta, taaa! ta ta ta, taaa! (Much like the knocking on the door.) "London calling!" said the announcer. I was not very happy about having to be the person on watch because I could not listen to the news myself. There was no chance of reaching the BBC on the so called V.E., the *Volksempfänger*[7],- the People's Radio. Only the nearest *Reichsender* was within range.

The war was still on, but without battles it became a lazy sort of war which was not in accordance with National Socialist philosophy. After all, the Nordic race was proclaimed to be a warrior race for whom peace was not the norm. Wealth and peace had a demoralizing affect and caused decadence among the virile Nordics - at least that is what the Nazis said.

But soon the calm before the storm was over and the wind blew again from further north. "In order to protect these countries (Denmark and Norway) from a violation of their neutrality by Britain, no other course was left to the Führer but to take action and invade Denmark and Norway." This occurred in April 1940.

The campaign, however, was much more difficult than we had been told by the Propaganda Ministery's official news releases. From now on, I followed my Latin teacher's advice, *Altera pars audiatur* - the other side has to be heard also. I listened to the BBC for the views from the British side.

It was relatively easy for Hitler to conquer Denmark. Danish resistance against a country the size of Germany would have been suicidal. How else could they have handled the situation? But the German invasion of Norway was a different story. There were many physical obstacles - coastlines, fjords, mountains and long, dangerous naval supply lines.

Although no one told us exactly how many German naval vessels were destroyed, the loss of some ships, especially the huge battleship, *Blücher*, could not be hidden. Luckily for us, the loss of lives was not too high since most naval engagements took place close to shore and even in the fjords.

The German war correspondent, Heinz Laubenthal, described the Blücher's last moment as he had allegedly heard it from a colonel witnessing the incident from the shore. "…..suddenly the stern of the ship went up, perhaps seven to nine meters, straight into the air. We see it clearly, there stands a man upright and erect, his arm lifted in the salute. I have seen statues, medieval knights of shining metal, carved figureheads of legendary fame, but I shall never forget this living symbol of a German sailor standing like this in his hour of death …. a German who knows how to die. A hurrah broke loose and our fervent hearts welled over in the song: *Deutschland, Deutschland über alles, über alles in der Welt.*"

Not too many people took such verbal portraits of patriotism seriously. I remember when Laubenthal's report was broadcast. I was watching a card game around the *Stammtisch* when one of the customers lifted up his beer stein, pinched his nose and said, "Oh my, doesn't that stink!" " Somebody must have farted," replied another customer.

Oath of Allegiance

I had seen a similar patriotic war scene years ago. It was an overly exposed commercial print, a picture of a German sailor during the Great War standing on an overturned vessel waving the Kaiser's flag while going down with the ship. As a little boy, I was quite impressed by that, but it also made me decide never to join the Navy. Dr. Goebbels always understood how to make something out of any event. Our land forces met heavy resistance at Narvik, (June 8, 1940) and a few months later we saw a 'great' movie, *Die Helden von Narvik* - The Heroes of Narvik.

The whole Nordic operation was over in three weeks. It was another Blitzkrieg and a warning for those countries who were still neutral as to what they could expect. It appeared as if Hitler was taking Europe by installments.

After the Scandinavian invasion it became obvious to those in Mayen that preparations for the next strike were already under way. My hometown became a beehive. Our school had to be relocated approximately two kilometers outside of Mayen because the building was suddenly converted into headquarters for an army group. Vehicles moved toward the Belgian border mainly during the night. A nearby railway tunnel was closed and became the headquarters of the *Luftwaffe*. A large converted train was parked outside the tunnel but if an air raid had occurred, the train, occupied by Hermann Göring and his general staff, would have moved inside.

We soon also noticed infantry battalions and horse artillery regiments coming into our town. They came along the side roads while the mechanized troops used the highways and some of the new Autobahns that were especially built for the speedier movement of troops. Although I watched the units on foot occasionally exercising their air raid routines, on the whole they marched quite freely. It was as if they were going on another manoeuvre. They had done this in previous years, marching, singing, and whistling through the land. And why should they not be joyous? There were no enemy reconnaissance planes and General Gamelin did not take any actions except for staffing the 'Maginot Line' with guns pointed towards the east, across the Rhine.

May 10, 1940 was the day that German troops pushed across the borders of Holland and Belgium. There was no use doing so in the upper Rhine area, thereby facing the guns and cannons installed by General Gamelin. No strategist, not even Hitler, would deliver his divisions to such a field of slaughter.

The French campaign created more excitement and attention than any previous campaign. We discussed it all the time in school. People on the street stopped and talked to one another. Women at the vegetable market showed each other the latest letters from their sons. Even the veterans of the Great War became lively. At times one had the impression that they might still march again even without the limbs they had lost during previous battles in France some 24 years earlier. Through open tavern windows came the smell of alcohol and tobacco smoke along with the sounds of *Siegreich wollen wir Frankreich schlagen* - Victoriously we'll beat France - a pre-1914 marching song.

I went with my friends to the movies mainly so that I could watch the *Wochenschau* - weekly news reels. We saw our tank brigades in dust clouds fanning out in the fields between the Somme, and the Oise and Aisne rivers, as they neared the French cities of Cambrai, Valenciennes, and Arras. It was exciting to watch Colonel General (soon to be promoted) von Reichenau marching with his infantrymen along the dusty roads.

One report showed one of the younger Panzer Brigade Commanders pushing far ahead of his front line as he moved toward the English Channel. He was cutting off the retreating Allied troops in order to prevent their escape across the water. In all, 45 divisions were cut off but most of the English were able to make it back by leaving all their heavy equipment behind and boarding thousands of privately owned small vessels summoned by the British for an impromptu rescue operation. (May 26, 1940). I remember saying to my father at the time, "Hitler can't be all wrong, and in any case we should be proud of our victorious troops in France." Even the exiled former Kaiser Wilhelm II who lived in Holland sent a telegram of congratulation

Oath of Allegiance

to Hitler and the German Army for a: ".... God delivered Victory."

Success made it really difficult to convince people of the evil deeds the Nazis had committed and were committing; even my aunt switched her sympathies from the Socialists to the Nazis. After all, she had three sons in uniform somewhere in France.

My mother's reaction was, "Don't forget to go to church and pray for those who do not return." She had lost two brothers in the Great War; one of them died two days after it began in August 1914 near Liège in Belgium, and the second brother in March 1915. (See photo with her third brother standing at the grave.) We were taught in history class that the French

Uncle Peter fell in August 1914, Uncle Johann fell in March 1915 with uncle Fritz on his grave.

did not show any enthusiasm or patriotic spirit in defense of their fatherland; neither did the French learn from their strategical mistakes during the Great War. We concluded our lessons by establishing that the French had become victims of decadence and that was why there was no resistance.

When Marshal Petain took over the newly formed Vichy government (June 16,1940), I had great sympathy for him in his new position. I felt that he was for the French what President von Hindenburg had been for the Germans, not because of what Petain had accomplished, but because he looked so much like him and was almost as old. The 'Hero of Tannenberg' thus resembled the 'Hero of Verdun'.

With great ceremony Hitler reviewed his troops in Paris (June 21, 1940) during a march past at the 'Arc du Triumph' with a regiment from the *Ostmark* (Austria) leading the parade. I really enjoyed seeing the *Trompeter Korps* of an artillery regiment on horseback in the movies. Such a group was usually led by a tympanist twirling his sticks around his head and then striking them on the Kettledrums which were fastened on each side of the horse. They played the *Pariser Einzugsmarsch* - Entrance into Paris - from the 1871 victory parade. I had never before seen a mounted military band perform while moving at a trot.

For the French military, the 'Armistice at Compiègne' was a humiliation while for Hitler it became an act of jubilation. In Hitler's official victory speech at least a half-dozen generals were promoted to field marshals and Göring became *Reichsmarschall*. With great emotion, the Führer painted a picture as if all his field marshals were gathering at *Walhalla* for a banquet with Göring at the head table right beside him. The implication was that the divine providence, God almighty, wanted it that way.

The director of our high school gave a special *Feierstunde* - hour of celebration speech - in a similar, emotional tone.

"....no Alexander the Great, no Caesar, no Frederick the Great, no Napoleon can match the genius, the strategical mastery of the Führer."

Oath of Allegiance

As had happened after the Polish campaign, so it was after the French campaign that certain incidents gave us a black mark. We knew through our own information services about the bombing of Rotterdam. But we found out only through the BBC that the attack by German Stuka bombers was staged one hour after the surrender of Holland (May 14, 1940) was in effect. The raid killed 940 people and destroyed 20,000 buildings.

Chapter Seven

*"We are not allowed to! He is a Jew!"
He whispered these last words looking cautiously around the room to make sure no one was nearby.*

Shortly after the French Campaign was over, our summer vacation also came to an end. The school authorities had shortened the summer holidays to make it easier for the farmers to get help for the potato harvest in the fall. This was fine with us; it meant another four weeks vacation at the end of September. It was some kind of voluntary service in which one was forced to participate.

I looked forward to picking potatoes but did not quite realize that doing it eight hours a day was not the greatest pleasure for my *columna vertebralis*, neither was it a joy to carry 50 kilogram bags on my shoulders. Without realizing it, this was my preparation for carrying 50 kilogram shells two years later. This was the first time, however, I was paid for my work.

We were a team of 10 on the farm. The farmer's wife did the cooking. I am sure she cooked all day long and brought the meals out into the fields. The farmer with his horse and little machine turned the soil for seven of us to pick the potatoes. There was also Maurice, a French prisoner of war and an experienced farmer himself. We were not supposed to associate with him, but we did. He helped by showing us how to do things. Maurice came from the Bretagne. He had a farm and a family of four. He was 42 and far too old to be a soldier and a prisoner of war.

We had great fun with Maurice. We learned more French and he learned the German dialect of our area. When I asked him how he was captured, he said he couldn't remember because he had drunk too much Cognac. His humour certainly made our days on the farm more enjoyable. But as soon as Maurice saw somebody coming our way, he immediately put on a serious face and kept his distance from us. He was very cautious and did not want to get us in trouble. Talking to a prisoner of war was verboten. One day, when I came to work after a weekend at home, I brought Maurice a bottle of schnapps, 48 percent rye which my mother 'illegally' obtained from my father's stock. Maurice became so excited that he kissed me three or four times on both cheeks as is the French custom.

Although Maurice started out as a Prisoner of War, he practically became one of the farm family. I found out after the war that Maurice stayed with the farm until the very end in order to protect the local German farmers from any harassment by the occupying forces which might have occurred with the transition. The farmer's wife told me later, "We treated Maurice as well as we could but he nearly died of *Heimweh* - homesickness." She wrote to Maurice later to let him know that four of the seven boys helping during the 1940 harvest did not return home after the war. They lay buried in the fields of Russia, Italy, and France.

After my weeks of potato picking I returned to school, but I did not enjoy it any more. I was still interested in music and art. I enjoyed my history classes, at least up to the time of Napoleon and the Battle of Waterloo which Wellington won according to English history books but which Blücher won according to German history. I lost my interest in the subject when matters became too complicated after the revolution of 1848.

There were no new battles going on in any of our theatres of war so I went to movies and theatre halls, and to concerts and recitals. I also went regularly to piano lessons. My piano teacher was also the music teacher at the Gymnasium and the organist at the Church. He lived on the top floor of the

Rathaus - the Town Hall - where he also had his music studio. The Rathaus had been built in 1717 and was a masterpiece of Baroque architecture.

"In this building one should only be allowed to play Bach, Haydn, and Mozart", I once told my teacher. He replied, "In this building one should only be allowed to play well. And did you practice the Czerny and the other finger exercises? If you didn't, don't even take off your coat."

One day while we were going through a book of music, I noticed he skipped one particular page. When I brought it to his attention he said, "That is all right, the piece is too difficult for you anyway. We'll play it later."

After I came home I looked at the piece, tried it and liked it. A wonderful lyrical tune. I intended to show my teacher what I could do on my own. At my next lesson when I proudly tried to play the music. My teacher anxiously covered the book with his hands and said, "Oh no, no, no, my friend, we can't play that! We are not allowed to! He is a Jew!" He whispered these last words looking cautiously around the room to make sure no one was nearby. I remember the piece was one of Felix Mendelssohn's *Lieder ohne Worte* - Songs without words.

It was my music teacher who taught me to understand and to love music. He was the first who played J.S. Bach's D Minor Toccata, *the Grosse Fuge,* and all the many other fugues and preludes for me. He played the 'Schübler Chorale' and delighted me with the most simple minuets and gavottes from the little *Notenbüchlein* which Bach wrote for his wife, Anna Magdalena. I thought one of the most beautiful pieces ever written by Bach was his love song for his wife. *Willst Du Dein Herz mir schenken, so fang es heimlich an* - While you send me your heart, so do it secretly.

What moved me most in Bach's music was the experience of hearing the final chorus of 'Saint Matthew's Passion' in one of the Cathedrals on the Rhine. *Nun trocknet Eure Tränen* - Now it is time to dry your tears. I became convinced that music had to be the greatest of all art forms.

About once a month Herr W. invited me, my friend Lothar

and whoever wanted to come, to a symphony concert or opera performance in the nearby city of Koblenz. Participating in such activities caused some of us, including my friend Lothar, to become isolated from our classmates.

Lothar Rosenbaum was a very special friend. He was the most stubborn and inflexible character I had ever known. The expression, *in medias res* did not exist for him. It was either left or right, black or white. There was no grey area. He came from a deeply religious Catholic family. Both his father and mother (before marriage) were school teachers. Naturally, my mother admired Lothar's parents and she approved of our friendship.

When the Nazis took over, Herr Rosenbaum, Lothar's father, was forced into retirement, not because of his Jewish sounding name, but because of his previous affiliation with the Zentrum Party which was in power before Hitler took over. Herr Rosenbaum's affiliation with the Zentrum Party caused my father to also approve of our friendship.

Lothar's was not the only family with a Jewish sounding name, or a different kind of name. Our area was an area well mixed by history.[8]

As we learned from Caesar's *de bello gallico* his soldiers built a bridge across the Rhine a few miles below Koblenz which the Romans called, *Confluentia*. It is where the Mosel and Rhine are joined. The bridge allowed Caesar's army to move more quickly from the Celtic settlements west of the Rhine to bring relief to his field commanders who were constantly being attacked by the Teutonic tribes further north on the east side of the Rhine. The bridge also helped people to mingle. Later, most of the activities in building the Holy Roman Empire beyond the Alps, took place in the Rhine and Mosel regions.

In the 1700s the French army of Louis XIV moved through the land plundering and burning down every castle and fortified settlement in the Rhine and Mosel valleys. Their object was the domination of Europe. A hundred years later Napoleon's army left their mark socially and culturally on the region. Many French words invaded the German language. The Rhinelander has many Roman and French physical characteristics. They are seldom blond haired and are not an example of the so-called, pure 'Nordic Germanic' race.

In any case, Lothar and I were close friends whose other activities, such as religious and philosophical discussions, also tended to isolate us from others because religion was no longer taught in our schools. But we were rebellious so that alone was a good enough reason to participate. We met a few times with a young Chaplain who was about to be drafted into the medical corps. Our meetings usually ended in one of my parent's guest rooms or in another *Weinstube* in town called the *Ratskeller*. We were a group of five or six boys with a habit of drinking four or more bottles of good quality wine, which helped us see the philosophy more in a theological light and theology more in a philosophical light.

At one point, we walked during the night into the forests surrounding the hills of Schloss Bürresheim, a castle hidden in the valley just outside Mayen. We each buried a scroll written by hand and signed by us all. It was our own 'Oath of Allegiance' to someone higher than Hitler. We lit candles and sang, *Wenn alle untreu werden, so bleiben wir doch Treu,* - If all others lose their faith, we'll remain true. The same melody is used in the Dutch national anthem. We then buried our statements, letters and all kinds of things and went home. That was the beginning of 'our group' - a group in which my friend, Lothar, and I became the more radically-minded members. If we had been caught by the authorities doing what we did, we could have hanged at the end of a rope in the market square. But we continued to go to the regular Hitler Youth meetings because it meant that Lothar and I could play in the orchestra. We were quite safe during the coming winter months, though, from then on, we followed political events more closely.

Chapter Eight

. . . he almost believed that the Greeks had blond hair and blue eyes and belonged to the nordic Germanic race.

The winter was soon over and when March came, the first signs of spring came with it. The year was 1941 and I was seventeen years old.

Passing the Volkschule - the elementary school - one could hear the children singing through the open windows.

Im Märzen der Bauer die Rösslein einspannt.
Er setzt seine Felder und Wiesen instand.
Er ackert, er egget, er pflüget und sät
Und rührt seine Hände früh morgens bis spät.

(When March comes, the farmer harnesses his horses and prepares his fields. He plows, he rakes, he sows and keeps busy from early morning until late at night.)

My own awareness of the arrival of spring came when I opened the windows of my room on the top floor. I could smell it. There was a blacksmith in our neighbourhood with a line-up of horses to be shoed. Naturally, before the farmers could work their fields with rakes and plows, and before they could sow seeds, they had to prepare their horses. The fitting of the hot iron shoes and the burning of the hoof was what caused the distinctive smell that wafted through my open window. On a more romantic note, the first flowers, the snow bells, and the sound of the cuckoo in the forest made the arrival of spring official.

But mine was not the kind of spring the people of Yugoslavia, Greece, and the rest of the Balkans were about to experience. On April 6, 1941, German motorized divisions launched coordinated attacks against Yugoslavia from Bulgaria, Hungary, Rumania, and Austria, which they already controlled. They had received the green light for another invasion, another *Blitzkrieg*.

Other Balkan countries, specifically Albania and Greece, also had to be conquered, if for no other reason than to save face for Il Duce and the Italian army. Mussolini's crack fighting force was rapidly becoming an embarrassment for Hitler.

King Boris of Bulgaria fared better than the rulers of Yugoslavia and Greece. He believed in Hitler's *Endsieg* - final victory. He permitted the German army to pass through his country in exchange for access to the Aegean Sea. Of course, he probably understood that had he refused, the German tanks and armoured cars would have pushed their way through anyway. Moreover, they might also have used the strong arms of the Wehrmacht to put on a display of fireworks and other pyrotechnics and aerobatics, à la Rotterdam, over the capital city, Sophia.

As students of history, we learned that the Germans praised the Greeks for their gallantry against the enemy. Such praise reached back into classical history when King Leonidas, with only a handful of Spartans, bravely defended the pass of Thermopylis against a superior Persian force.

Our history teacher got so worked up that he almost believed that the Greeks had blond hair and blue eyes and belonged to the nordic Germanic race. In any case, it was felt that they should have fought on our side, which would have been in harmony with the philosophy of the National Socialist Party.

There was one student who asked a question, "But *Herr Doktor*, if the Greeks had fought on our side, how could the

Führer have found out the truth about the capability and strength of the Italian army?" Since the bell had just rung, Dr. B. said a quick, "Heil Hitler" and left the classroom.

In spite of the German-Russian non-aggression pact signed by Molotov and von Ribbentrop on August 23, 1939, Hitler had prepared for the invasion of Russia for some time - at least according to what he wrote in his book *Mein Kampf*. Many of his speeches talked about *Lebensraum* - the need for more space for the German people - and the necessity of expansion to the East. But the actual invasion of Russia was unprovoked. Perhaps he did it only to show the British how fast he could conquer the Soviet Union. After all, Marshal Mannerheim, with his small but brave Finnish army, did not have any problems, so we were told. Besides, he knew that England was not strong enough as yet to do anything to help Russia. So on June 22, 1941, operation *Barbarossa*, which had been discussed with Mannerheim's general staff since July 1940 and decided upon since December 18, became a reality.

I do not remember what I did or where I was when the announcement of the invasion came, but one could not miss it. I heard the fanfares, the tympani and the cymbals of Liszt's Les Préludes, followed by the announcer presenting the *Sondermeldung*. He gave such a glowing report of events that one had the impression King Barbarossa himself was directing the show from his headquarters at Walhalla.

There were many events to discuss in our history class concerning the war. We learned that tens of thousands of prisoners were being taken by our armed forces. We were told that Field Marshal Ritter von Leeb was in charge of Army Group North and ordered to advance against Leningrad. Field Marshal von Bock was commanding the largest group in the centre with the objective of capturing Moscow, while Field Marshal von Rundstedt was the Commander of Army Group South with its intention of reaching Kiev in Ukraine.

It is difficult to establish correct numbers of people involved in the battle of Russia. What I remember was that approximately two million men with close to one million horses were engaged in one of the largest military campaigns the world had experienced to date. Of course, there were a few thousand tanks, cannons, light and heavy artillery, and thousands of vehicles involved as well.9

Some people had difficulty understanding why, with all the motorized divisions, so many horses were needed. At one time the Russian front extended more than 3000 kilometers. Therefore, the production of vehicles for 35 mechanized divisions was not enough to cover the territory. Moreover, the new *Wehrmacht* only began to build tanks and armoured cars in the mid-1930s, and the small number of car manufacturers at the time were not as productive as the American factories. As a result, our Infantry divisions, with their horse artillery regiments, had to fill the gap.

The Russian campaign was supposed to be another Blitzkrieg and, in the beginning, that is how it appeared. The Russians retreated, often burning everything as they went. When the rains came too soon, many vehicles got stuck in the muddy roads. After the short rain-fall, an unusually early winter arrived. The German troops were completely unprepared for the Russian winters. The Germans might not have been caught with their pants down, but nevertheless, they were caught without heavy winter coats, boots, and suitable underwear. They were also on scorched earth with long supply lines.10

Without horses, our troops would have started a Napoleonic retreat at a much earlier stage. It was so cold that even the brake fluid in the cannons froze. It must have been extremely cold because our Propaganda Ministry announced that fact and people were asked to contribute winter clothing for our soldiers. We started to collect scarves, socks, gloves, furs, and so on while the women and even the children knitted clothing hoping that their own loved ones would receive them too.

I remember seeing the women sitting at home knitting while tears streamed down their cheeks. There was hardly a family that did not have at least one member involved in some kind of casualty from the winter campaign of 1941. A medal was awarded to soldiers who participated in the campaign.

Oath of Allegiance

The medal was simply called the *Gefrierfleischorden* - the frozen meat medal of 1941/1942. This was because so many German soldiers died frozen or had to have limbs amputated because of severe frostbite.

As the historians see it, what happened on the Russian Front was the turning point of the war. It gave the Allies precious time and may have prevented an actual invasion of England. Many saw Germany's Declaration of War on the United States as an attempt to focus attention elsewhere, as a mere distraction.

The only activity I really enjoyed during the following winter months was going to the movies with a girl I greatly admired. We enjoyed seeing the propaganda films together. These films had the best actors playing the role of Frederick the Great and Ohm Krüger, the Dutch leader of the Africaaners. Actors like Emil Jannings, Heinrich George, Werner Krauss and Otto Gebühr, the latter being almost synonymous with the role of Frederick. While the *Alte Fritz* films stimulated our love for the Fatherland, the Krüger film was designed to create hatred against everything English and sympathy for the Dutch Africaans.

During this period, I also became a great fan of the Swedish singer, Zarah Leander and Austria's Marikka Rökk. Rökk would sing and dance in films designed to re-create the Austro-Hungarian fairy-tale environment of the old monarchy. Of course, the music greatly enhanced that atmosphere. Who else would be a more suitable composer than Emmerich Kalmann creating the 'Czardas Princess', 'Countess Maritza', 'Countess of Luxembourg', or 'Ungarische Hochzeit' - Hungarian Wedding to name a few. My favourite lyric was sung by the sensual Marikka Rökk:

> Die Julischka, die Julischka aus Buda-, Buda-pest
> Sie hat ein Herz von Paprika
> Und hält die Männer fest. Ya, Ya.
> Julischka, Julischka from Buda-, Buda-pest
> Her heart is made of Paprika
> And holds on to her men tight. Ya, Ya.

Marikka was not only a real fire-ball herself but a very acrobatic dancer. One can safely say that her body was made of paprika too. She was often the subject of conversation during our break periods. We used to say, *Sie hat feuer und Paprika in den Hosen* - she has fire and paprika in her pants.

Zarah Leander's attraction was her unusually low and deep tone. Her wide range included both the alto and the tenor voice. Just hearing her sing tunes like *Der Wind hat mir ein Lied erzählt...* - The wind has told me a song..., - caused goose bumps to rise on my skin.

The good news for students was the announcement by the Minister of Education that, in case of a draft order during the final school year, graduation certificates would automatically be granted. The decree also applied to anyone who volunteered their services to the military. It was of no surprise when many joined the armed services just to get out of school. Some, who might have completed school, were guided by romantic illusions rather than a desire to escape study. They envisaged themselves dressed in brand new uniforms walking proudly along a busy street accompanied by their girlfriend. She, naturally would be the envy of all the other girls.

This scenario reminds me of one pompous, little major walking along a busy downtown street with his *Quartierwirtin* - landlady/hostess - whose husband was somewhere on the Eastern Front. I and some of my friends from school walked some distance behind them. I recall thinking that his tight fitting uniform made him look like a freshly boiled knockwurst. My friend Lothar also had an opinion of the major. "He walks like a stork in a salad bowl," Lothar commented sarcastically at the time.

While the lady carried all sorts of shopping bags, he, quite convinced of his importance, regularly adjusted his monocle to prepare himself to return the many salutes he received from every young soldier who passed. As we walked behind the couple we watched how his rear-end moved to the beat of an imaginary bass drum. Lothar joked, "Just look at him, all he needs now is a peacock's feather in his arse."

Our jokes dealt with the surface changes in our lives and

Oath of Allegiance 75

the atmosphere in our town, but there were other important, and more profound reminders of the time in which we lived. One day, Hildegard, our *Klassenkameradin* - class mate -, showed me an odd letter. I do not remember where it came from or who signed it, but it was an official invitation to make a 'Gift to the Führer.' It asked the young woman to whom it was sent to spend a vacation with a young SS officer. It included payment of all medical expenses with everything guaranteed including placement in a state-run institution for the baby expected as a result of the liaison. Perhaps our class mate, Hildegard was invited because she was young, healthy, and blond. She did not, however, take advantage of the invitation.

At first we laughed and joked about it as we had about other manifestations of the time. We thought the whole idea was absolutely unbelievable. But it wasn't funny at all. It was a program to help revitalize the Nordic race - the so-called *Lebensborn* program, and when we came to understand it more fully, we worked against it.11 While we could not change anything with respect to the so-called rabbit farms, *Kaninchenzuchtanstalten*, we made sure that the reality of this scheme became known to every decent family in town. We started a real campaign, passing on information embarrassing to the government. At least we learned something from Dr. Goebbels.12

In our last group meeting one of the new members, a former newspaper editor, Michel G., gave us a few good pointers. For example, I recall that he told us, "If you are a worker in a motor factory and want to sabotage the plant, then don't come with heavy equipment to try and smash everything. It would only get you to the nearest tree where they would hang you. Just take sand from your pocket and throw it into the wheels of a machine and soon every thing will stop and you still will be alive." This was pretty serious stuff, but we all agreed to pursue a policy of sabotage of information and misinformation.

One of the students who was on duty in the district Hitler Youth Office came one day in an attempt to give me good advice. He told me that he saw my name and Lothar's on a list of *besonders zu beobachten* - those under special observation. People were to report any *staatsfeindliches Verhalten* - behaviour against the state - directly to the *Bannführer*, the highest ranking district youth leader, who apparently got some wind of our activities. Instead of being cautious, our youthful enthusiasm made us quite the opposite. One day on our way home from school Lothar and I passed the *Bannführer* on the street. We ignored the protocol of saluting him and when he questioned us about our discretion, we apologized by saying that the sun had blinded our eyes. We were then ordered to report to his office where we received a verbal reprimand.

A more serious incident happened a few weeks later during German class. Our teacher, Dr. K., who was not on very good terms with the school's administration because of his former political affiliation with the *Zentrum* Party, discussed the works of the German dramatist, Lessing. He asked us to recite some of Lessing's essays. Dr. K. made us memorize poems, drama dialogues, and sections of prose. We were not too happy about this because memorization was time consuming. Only a few years later, during the many long nights standing watch on the banks of the Donets River, I wrote many of these verses in my diary, but at the time I could not imagine what use such memorization could have. When my turn came to recite some of Lessing's essays, I stood up, faced the class and pointed with my left thumb to the wall behind me where the crucifix once hung. It had recently been replaced with a picture of Hitler and one of Göring. Then I said the following:

"Die Ähnlichkeit ist unbestritten,
es fehlt nur Christus in der Mitten."

Dr. K turned white and left the class.

What I said was, "If the crucifix were still there, the scene of Calvary would be perfect with Christ in the centre and the two criminals hanging on either side." I knew exactly what I had said, but I did not realize the consequences would be so serious.

Oath of Allegiance

Two days later the *Hausmeister* knocked at the door and stood there with a very serious expression. During school hours, he was the principal's official messenger and he felt this role made him extremely important. He would usually begin his announcement by saying, "I and the Herr Direktor have decided that ....." which often caused us to laugh in class because in reality, he was the janitor.

There was no laughter from me this time. He announced that the principal requested my immediate appearance in his office. I had an idea of what was likely to happen. When I arrived at his door, I saw a police officer and two civilians waiting to accompany me to police headquarters. I must admit I was pretty scared. It was my first encounter with the Gestapo. This was the real thing and I was alone. There were no friends to cheer me.

I was interrogated for almost two hours about things which had nothing to do with my now infamous class recitation. They wanted to know all about the chaplain we visited regularly and the newspaper editor who had joined our group. The subject of their questions dealt with homosexuality or implied homosexuality. I was really pushed into the corner and could not answer their questions because, at the time, I did not understand what they were trying to do. I was asked to sign a statement because others had already signed and admitted that the chaplain and newspaper editor had exhibited deviant behaviour. But in fact, this was not true, and no one had signed anything.

They told me if I signed, I would be released immediately, but if I didn't sign, they would take me away. Where? I wondered with terror. Of course, I refused to sign anything that was not true. Then they hounded me about my recitation of Lessing's essay and about why I had pointed to the classroom picture of the Führer. They told me they would turn my case over to the Hitler Youth law department and that I would be notified of my arrest.

For the next two weeks I was rather subdued. Quite honestly, I was scared. But in the third week I became tired of being scared. I was encouraged by a letter of the well respected Bishop of Münster, the Count of Galen, who was once accused of collaborating. He wrote a fiery pastoral letter

3 Gs.50/42

Der für den 20.Juni 1942 angesetzte Wochenendkarzer des Robert Dietz wird in eine für ** die Zeit vom 2.Juli nachmittags 6 Uhr bis zum 4.Juli 1942 vormittags 6 Uhr zu verbüßenden Kurzarrest umgewandelt.

          M a y e n, den 1.Juli 1942.
          Das Amtsgericht.
          gez.Dr.Kentenich
          Oberamtsrichter.
          Ausgefertigt

An
Herrn Robert Dietz
in
M a y e n.
Töpferstraße 30.

        Justizangestellter
   als Urkundsbeamter der Geschäftsstelle
        des Amtsgerichts.

      A b s c h r i f t.

Staatliches Gesundheitsamt
Tagebuch Nr.A 1106   M a y e n, den 1.Juli 1942.

  An
   die Nationalsozialistische Deutsche Arbeiterpartei
   Hitler-Jugend, Bann Maifeld (68)
    in M a y e n

  Betrifft: Vollstreckung des gegen den Jg.Robert Dietz,
      Mayen.Töpferstraße 30 verhängten Jugenddienst-
      arrestes.
  Vorgang: Ihr Schreiben vom 25.Juni 1942.
     Amtsärztliche Bescheinigung.
  Der Robert D i e t z, geb.am 9.3.1924 in Mayen, wohnhaft
Mayen, Töpferstraße 30, wurde hier amtsärztlich untersucht.
   Auf Grund des erhobenen Befundes ist der Unter-
   suchte haftfähig.
         Der Amtsarzt
          Dr.Jennen
         Medizinalrat.

Nationalsozialistische Deutsche Arbeiterpartei
Hitler-Jugend, Bann Maifeld (68)

Briefanschrift:
Mayen, Im Hombrich 20
Fernruf 233

Postscheckkonto Köln 37502
Bankkonto Kreissparkasse Mayen 1089

Der Hauptstammführer
Att.-3.: I P - 1159

Mayen, ben 27. Juli 1942

Aufforderung.

Du wirst hiermit aufgefordert, Dich am Dienstag, ben 28.7.1942 um 16 Uhr, bei der Bannführung, Zimmer 6, zu melden.

Deine sämtlichen Hitler-Jugend-Ausweise sind mitzubringen.

Heil Hitler!

An den
3g. Robert Dietz
geb. 9.3.1924
Mayen
Töpferstr. 30

(Unterschrift / Rangstellung.)
Oberscharführer

Das Amtsgericht

3 Gs.50/42

M a y e n, den 1. Juli 1942.

Sie werden hiermit zur Verbüßung des Ihnen durch die NSDAP, Hitler-Jugend, Gebiet Moselland auferlegten Jugenddienstarrestes von einem Wochenende auf den 2. Juli nachmittags 6 Uhr bis zum 4. Juli 1942 vormittags 6 Uhr xxxxxxxxxxxxxxxxxxxxxxxxxxxxxxxxx auf das hiesige Amtsgericht, Eingang Privatwohnung des Justizoberwachtmeisters Herzheim geladen. Bei Ausbleiben erfolgt polizeiliche Vorführung. Sie werden aufgefordert: 1150 Gr. Brotmarken, 50 Gr. nahrmittelkarte und 10 Gr. Fettkarte mitzubringen.

gez. Dr. Küntenich, Oberamtsrichter.
Beglaubigt

An
Herrn Robert Dietz
geb. am 9.3.1924
in
M a y e n,
Töpferstraße 30.

Justizangestellter
als Urkundsbeamter der Geschäftsstelle des Amtsgerichts.

against the killings of mentally retarded people. Hitler encouraged such killings because it was his belief that unproductive elements of our society had no right to exist since they consumed valuable food destined for our fighting men at the front.

When I finally received my *Haftbefehl* - order of arrest - I immediately had to report to the Justice Department. The *Justizwachtmeister*, Herr Harzheim, was actually a very kind man. He was one of the civil servants who received the position after 12 years of service in the Reichswehr. Many retired soldiers, especially NCO's, took similar positions. After years of service for the fatherland, Herr Harzheim was not too thrilled about becoming a jailer for boys who committed teenage pranks. However, that was certainly not the reason that I was there.

The jail for young offenders was on the top floor of the Magistrates Court and there were only four cells. It did not look too bad when the door opened up, but when it was closed behind me and I heard the cold, harsh sound of the iron bar sliding across the latch, I suddenly felt claustrophobic.

What was to be my home for the next three days had a small window with bars on the outside overlooking a cemetery and a park. On one side of the room was an old wooden bench with a blanket to sleep on and another to cover me up. A chair and a small table stood in one corner by the window. On the table was a candle and a book. At least I thought I would have something interesting to read. As I picked it up I saw the words, *Mein Kampf*, the Führer's bible, a book that Hitler wrote in 1924 when he was in jail in the Bavarian fortress of Landshut. Of course, I must not forget to mention the other chair in the cell, the one with a hole in the seat and a bucket underneath. Presumably I was all set, I had about everything that I needed.

There were no prisoners in the other cells so it was very quiet. I did not sleep much during my first night because as yet my body was not used to sleeping on such a hard bed. Most of my waking hours were spent flipping through the pages of *Mein Kampf*, a book with which I was already familiar. When Herr Harzheim made his rounds I asked him for another book. He promised to bring one only if I kept my mouth shut. On his way out the door, he noticed that I had deposited Hitler's book on the chair with the hole and the bucket underneath. He took it and put it back on the table saying, "The Bannführer will be coming tomorrow. If he sees how you treat the Führer's book you will definitely be here for an extended vacation." He warned me not to be such an idiot and left. He was concerned and I realized that he was no Nazi.

When I returned to school, I discovered that the Leaders of the Hitler Youth had it in for my friend, Lothar. He became the next young guest at Herr Harzheim's 'lodge'.

Chapter Nine

Her smile gave me the final push. Coffee, hazelnut torte, natürlich.

Once back in school I became a troubled spirit with the two souls in my breast fighting with one another. At the time, we were studying the ethical aspects of dualism in our history class, about the recognition of the independent and opposing principles of good and evil. Our history teacher thought that this subject should be taught in religion class rather than in history class. Clearly, he was annoyed that religion was no longer taught.

But he thought the subject was important, and asked us to study *Zoroastrianism* and *Manichaeism* in our spare time. We did not expect that we would have to put that extra load on our brain, and so tried to forget about his request. The history teacher, however, kept on asking questions just in passing during the next few weeks, and in order to keep up our marks and standards, we made sure that the names of Ahura Mazda (the Wise Lord and giver of the vision) and Spitama Zarathustra (the founder of the ancient Persian religion) ended up in our mental storage room for good.

Then one of my two souls must have temporarily triumphed. I don't quite remember what the reason was, but I suddenly volunteered for the *Luftwaffe* - the Air Force. I guess I was impressed with the publicity the Luftwaffe received. It was the time when Gallant, Mölders, and others received their

'Knight Crosses with Oak Leaves, Swords and Brilliants'. They had each more than one hundred victories and their pictures were constantly in the news media. Was I really impressed by the 'Glitzen and Blitzen' of the events or was it my longing to shake off the heavy burden of school and the political problems that had made my life miserable? Perhaps both factors motivated my actions at the time. I became a young man, *am Scheideweg* - at the cross roads.

> "Two souls, alas dwell in my breast,
> each seeks to rule without the other.
> The one with robust love desires
> Clings to the world with all his might.
> The other fiercely rises from the dust
> to reach sublime ancestral regions."
> Goethe, Faust I

Eventually, I went to the Air Force Headquarters in Wiesbaden to fill out my application to become a pilot. Wiesbaden was, and still is, the Capital City of Hesse, not too far from Frankfurt and closer to the Rhine River. The city is also known as a resort and health spa which reflects the history and culture of the past thousand years. The Luftwaffe was the newest branch of the armed forces and therefore it deserved the best, and I talked myself into believing I had made the right decision without knowing what was involved. I had my medical and psychological examinations. Then I was told there was a long waiting list and so much interest that Heinkel, Messerschmidt, and Junkers (the major manufacturers) could not keep up with the production of new aircraft. Even the medical branch of the Luftwaffe was filled and closed to applications. I was told, however, that I was fit for parachute training. I said, "No thank you." Being a paratrooper was certainly not on my mind and if I were to end up in the infantry anyway, I decided to wait another few months till I was drafted. At least I would not have to jump out of the plane first.

Feeling almost sorry for myself, I walked on the boulevards of the fashionable city towards the famous *Kurpark*. The sidewalks were filled with people but I felt like a lonely man in the crowd. There were twice as many women as men, and I walked among them - I don't remember if the vogue for ladies was below or above the knees. As I came closer to the park, I heard music coming from the pavilion. The sound made the other soul in my breast speak, and I thought about the fact that Frederick II, King of Prussia, was as great a flautist as he was a soldier.13

The music was a bit 'schmalzy' but most fitting for the spa atmosphere with Kur-guests walking around sipping on glasses of water from the hot mineral springs while planning the evening entertainments. At night the guests would drink *Henkel Trocken* and other wines in an atmosphere where *Eau de Cologne* and the perfumes of Paris (sent to many ladies from their husbands in occupied France) mixed with heavy cigar smoke.

I enjoyed watching the colonels and generals - the type just recalled out of retirement - as they moved around conversing with their ladies while adjusting their monocles to better observe the rear view of those walking in front of them.

My attention was directed to the Band Shell and specifically to the conductor. I wondered if his over-pronounced movements were inspired by the music or whether the music was the result of his movements.

However interesting the conductor was, the real reason for my interest was the voice and beauty of the soprano soloist who sang a Mozart Aria, *Sag ist es Liebe was hier so brennt* - tell me, is it love that burns inside of me? Following the soprano was a tenor soloist with another Mozart Aria, *Dies Bildnis is bezaubernd schön* - this face is intriguingly beautiful...

This did it for me.

    I spotted a lovely young woman sitting alone on a bench.
    "Pardon me, gracious maiden, would you permit..."
    "Certainly, Sir."
    "What did you say your name was?"
    "Helga."
    I was so nervous I did not ask her last name. While the orchestra played von Flotow's, *Letzte Rose* from the opera,

Oath of Allegiance

Martha, I sat down a bit too close to Fräulein Helga. She must not have objected because she did not move away, not one centimeter.

Then Helga made a suggestion which scared me in spite of the fact that I was fit for parachute training. But I regained my courage when she mentioned that her mother had baked a hazelnut torte and we could have coffee together. Her smile gave me the final push. Coffee, hazelnut torte, *natürlich*. On the way to her home she explained to me that joining her mother for coffee would brighten her mother's day since she was still mourning her father's death. He had fallen in Russia at the beginning of the Russian campaign.

Helga's mother was a pale, but otherwise beautiful woman who invited me in. I saw the photograph of a tank unit commander with a vase of flowers nearby. I walked to the piano to check the music on the music stand. Obviously it was the tradition that the daughter of the house studied the piano. I listened to Helga play Bach and I almost lost my shyness. I even admitted that she played better than I did. Helga's mother became quite talkative and suggested that I should go with her daughter to tonight's symphony concert at the *Grosse Kursaal*. It was a special concert with Fidemaro Konoye as guest conductor. Fidemaro Konoye was a member of the famous Japanese Fujiwara clan. Prince Konoye was, at the time, the Japanese prime minister, and partly responsible for the formation of the Berlin-Rome-Tokyo Axis.

All of this did not make Fidemaro a better musician but, for me, attending a concert given by such a famous personality was an unforgettable experience. And he had personality. As soon as he stepped onto the podium all whispering and coughing stopped and the five foot two inch Fidemaro with his black rimmed glasses seemed to have already electrified the audience. Then, with a sudden downward beat of his right arm, while opening his left fist, he set the whole bass section in movement. The Wiesbaden State Orchestra gave its all in the opening bars of Gluck's overture, 'Iphigenia in Aulis'.

This opening scene has never left my audio visual memory. Beethoven's Symphony no. 7 was the main feature of the first half of the program. In the second part of the concert, the orchestra played 'Etenraku', Japanese Court Music of the 8th Century. The applause for the Japanese piece was out of politeness because the music was strange to us. Although Helga and I may not have been mature enough to appreciate Richard Strauss', 'Death and Transfiguration' we found it overwhelming and the applause was likewise for the conductor and the 103 musicians on stage. I was most grateful to Helga's mother for having given me this great and unforgettable experience on which I dwelled during all the years of the war and many times after. Whenever I hear Mozart's Aria, 'This face is Intriguingly Beautiful', I think of Helga.

I took the early train from Wiesbaden via Mainz and Koblenz home to Mayen. The weather was misty and sad and so was I. I did not tell anyone in school how unsuccessful I had been with my military affairs. I certainly did not tell them about Helga. All they would have said: was that all?

In spite of trying to join the air force - a romantic attempt by a part of my personality, one of my two souls - I was deeply concerned about what was going on in my town and in my country. I was determined to make others see Hitler realistically.

The Bishop of Münster, Count von Galen, was a thorn in the side of the Nazi authorities. He wrote a Pastoral letter expressing his concern for treatment of retarded people.

Dressed in our Hitler Youth uniforms, Lothar and I with the rest of our friends rode our bikes throughout the countryside and with a smart salute of *Heil Hitler!* handed over copies of the Bishop's now confiscated (by the Gestapo) letter in a sealed envelope. The parish priests would accept with their own *Heil Hitler!* even though they knew what was in the envelope. We saw to it that it was distributed to every rectory door in the Mayen area.

My father began to worry about our safety. My mother did not worry because she did not know what we were doing. Did we know? I guess it was the 'inner necessity' that made us do it, and our conscience gave us the strength to do it

Oath of Allegiance

and the courage to resist. "Wachet auf, ruft uns die Stunde" became our battle cry.

However, it did not take long for the police to come looking for me at the school. The school principal told them to leave me alone because I had received my draft order for the *Reichsarbeitsdienst* - labour duty for the coming month - and had volunteered for the Air Force. He made me look like a patriotic youth. The police agreed that I might get straightened out with some good training, but the Hitler Youth leadership recognized what was behind the whole affair. They arrested me once again.

I recall that from my cell I could hear singing in the park across the street, *Wenn alle untreu werden.....* and *Wachet auf, ruft uns die Stunde* - Sleepers awake, the hour is calling. My friends were taking another 'Oath of Allegiance' in the form of a serenade.

Approximately three weeks later I got my marching orders to the *Reichsarbeitsdienstlager* - the Reich Labour Duty Camp - in the south of the Taunus mountain range not too far from Wiesbaden.

It did not take long before I was doing all sorts of drills. This was kind of a pre-military training camp where I learned how to handle a pick and shovel. We constructed a few air raid shelters and a road to a nearby ammunition depot.

After my discharge, I was happy to be able to run around in civilian clothes feeling light and free without those hobnailed army boots. For three weeks I felt like jumping over fences and hedges, but then I received my draft order. I was to report to the *Ersatzabteilung* - reserve division - of the heavy field artillery at Nancy, a historic city in Alsace Lorrain, a much disputed French province.

Chapter Ten

... to tell a German not to sing the Lorelei would be the same as telling North American children to stop reciting Baa Baa Black Sheep.

It was a beautiful, sunny afternoon in early October, 1942 when we who had been drafted left home. I was just 18 years old.

Of the many boys who left our town, only four of us had a draft order for the artillery in Nancy. The others went to the various infantry regiments in the south of Germany for their training. Our families followed us to the railway station to say good-bye. There was crying as well as words of encouragement. It was difficult for me to hold back my tears, and Rainer, one of my friends also destined for Nancy, tried all kinds of jokes to cheer us up. When the station master blew his whistle and shouted "All aboard", mothers embraced their sons and murmured, "God be with you." As the train pulled away, there was not a dry eye onboard or on the station platform.

In the distant evening sunset, the waving of shawls and handkerchiefs slowly faded. We fell back into our seats and swallowed our tears. There was a long silence: I was feeling the cruelty of war, not so much for us who were leaving, but for those who were left behind. We did not think about ourselves at the time.

During that long silence I also thought of my father. He must have felt something there on the platform after we said good-bye to each other. I remember him lighting his stubby old cigar and moving away from the crowded area. He did not turn around again. It made me think of the time when he said to me, "When you are old enough, the war will be over." Perhaps that is why he did not look back at me when I left. He always hated to be wrong.

Once we arrived in Koblenz, the coaches carrying the draftees were hooked up to a train coming from Cologne. We headed southbound along the Rhine valley passing Bacharach, Bingen and the famous Lorelei rock.

"Ich weiss nicht was soll es bedeuten,
Dass ich so traurig bin.
Ein Märchen aus Uralten Zeiten,
Das kommt mir nicht aus dem Sinn."

I do not know why this confronts me,
This sadness, this echo of pain;
A curious legend still haunts me,
Still haunts and obssesses my brain:

The air is cool and it darkles;
Softly the Rhine flows by.
The mountain peak still sparkles
In the fading flush of the sky.
And on one peak, half-dreaming
She sits, enthroned and fair;
Like a goddess, dazzling and gleaming,
She combs her golden hair.

The boatman had heard; it has bound him
in the throes of a strange, wild love.
He is blind to the reefs that surround him;
He sees but the vision above.
And lo, the wild waters are springing -
The boat and the boatman are gone...
And this with her poignant singing,
The Lorelei has done.

The Lorelei is one of the most loved folk songs in Germany. We began to sing it and I thought how mixed up everything seemed. Here we were, German soldiers with a Nazi education that placed Hitler before God, and engraved on our belt buckles were the words, *Gott mit uns* - God with us, singing the song for which the Jewish poet Heinrich Heine wrote the words. Naturally, to tell a German not to sing the Lorelei would be the same as telling North American children to stop reciting Baa Baa Black Sheep. The Nazis realized this, and so the *Kulturministerium* let it be known that the originator of the Lorelei poem was anonymous and that Heine had simply published it under his name. This, they claimed, was, 'typically Jewish.'

The train rolled along the tracks throughout the night with a monotonous beat - ta tam, ta tam, ta tam.... Only once in awhile did we stop or slow down at a large city. We reached Nancy, the capital city of Lorrain in the early morning hours. There we were received by a group of sergeants from the artillery garrison. After our baggage was loaded onto a truck, we marched to the garrison, located in the outskirts of the town.

It took about two days before we got our uniforms and other necessary clothing. We were assessed according to size, educational and professional background, and physical condition. This procedure was necessary since there were various different positions to be filled. For example, for the boys who had to handle the horses, a farm background was very helpful, while for the men delegated to observation posts, a background in high school math was ideal. Gunners were required to handle the howitzers while others were needed for the communication troops to serve as wireless operators and such. Office and kitchen personnel were required too. I was trained for two positions - observer and gunner one. A gunner one handles the optical instrument and focuses the target in sight.

Whatever I did not know about the army, artillery, recruitment training, treatment and mistreatment, I certainly learned very quickly. There was no room for sentimentality, homesickness or other unsoldierly like matters. After all, there was a war going on.

The Prussian idea of military obedience was that a soldier had to be broken down to a stage whereby he had the *Cadaver Gehorsam* - obedience of a dead body. Achieving that obedience was the mandate of the drill sergeant and the best drill sergeants that the German army had were those who had slaved on the estates of east Prussian landowners. They regarded professional soldiering as an escape from their former state of servitude. As drill sergeants they had certain powers and could give orders to those who used to give them orders. There were drill sergeants who could drive young people to desperation, even to suicide. Some were merely sadists who received great satisfaction from making someone with more education than they jump around the drill hall with bent knees and carrying 50 kilogram howitzer shells in their arms until completely exhausted. Collapse brought the poor soldier a punishment - perhaps a week of cleaning the stable. The best way of surviving this kind of treatment which I myself experienced, was to accept it, make fun of it and sing:

Es geht alles vorüber, es geht alles vorbei,
nach jedem Dezember folgt wieder ein Mai

- Everything passes by, after each December follows May.

To go through recruitment training is much more difficult than most people presume. Those who voluntarily join a military institution usually have some idea of what to expect and they are somehow psychologically prepared. Others who are drafted and don't want to be in the military, who have never heard of discipline, obedience, and all the other requirements necessary for the proper function of a military unit, have a difficult time subordinating themselves. One has to become a cog in the machine rather than an individual.

The drill sergeant usually gave up as soon as he saw that his methods had no more effect on the recruit. Of course, after one has had experience at the Front, one can understand the necessity of being properly drilled and trained even in the Prussian way. Once when I drilled recruits for a short time, I, myself was strict and demanding, but that came after experience under fire. As a young recruit I did not always see

Recruitment training at Nancy, France.
Drill sergeant and recruits from the same town.

Ready to go.

the reason for the methods used.

Our basic training was finished after six weeks, a much shorter period than usual, and there was a rumour that the battery would be moved to the southwest of France, near Nantes, for field training.

Our drill sergeants gave us a hard time, but we tried to make the best of it and made fun of things. For example, whenever I had duty watch and made my rounds during the night, it really bothered me to see the words, *Für Offiziere* placed on the left part of the building in question, while on the right part the sign read, *Für Unteroffiziere und Mannschaften* -for NCO's and enlisted men. My partner commented, "I guess the French Revolution did not include the *Scheisshaus.*"

While the sign for the latter remained untouched, during the night we altered the former sign to read, "For the other arseholes". It was not a prank without ramifications.

When the army chaplain came to hear our confessions I told him and apologized for all the confusion and extra drill and hardship I had caused during the previous week. The field chaplain lost his composure and burst out laughing. Although he was an officer, I had the impression that he liked what I did. After confession, some of the other soldiers who stood in line asked me if I had told the chaplain a dirty joke.

Towards the end of my training in France, there was a *Scheisshausgeflüster*[14] - rumour - that we would be transported to the Gulf of Biscay to be used as coastal artillery.

There was a mixed reaction to this announcement. Some thought that it was great. Others thought of it as an embarrassment. Without any Front line experience, we were to retire down to the southwest coast of France and play coastal artillery with no war activity around us. Some asked, "How can we face our former classmates when on leave at home? We won't even be able to go out in uniform. Everyone will point at us saying, "He has never had the smell of gun powder around his nose."

Had I the choice, I would have preferred the coastal artillery. In fact, my comrades agreed. As one of the older comrades said after an argument with a recent high school graduate whose brown Hitler Youth uniform had not turned field grey as yet, "That is okay with me, you go to Russia to defend your fatherland and receive the Iron Cross, or iron in your cross, and I will defend the French coast and all its whore houses from guys like you and get the Legion of Honour."

But soon we did not have to worry about whether we would laze about on the beaches of France or gain battle experience.

By the time I awoke from my dreams, we were already in the middle of our infantry training. It was quite an awakening for many of us, especially when we used live ammunition in our rifles. The drill sergeant gave us hell when our rifle butt was not pressed firmly against our shoulders. How fast did we understand the sergeant's shouting? "You will end up on your arse!"

We had to jump on a tank, crawl on our stomachs using elbows to move forward to the enemy position. While the drill sergeant shouted the most comical vulgarities, a lance corporal operated a machine gun, emptying a whole belt of live ammunition over our heads. They no longer needed to tell us to keep our heads down and flatten our heels. We flattened everything after that.

At the end of the day, one of us had a bullet hole in his gas mask container. He did not get any sympathy but received punishment for his stupidity. He almost got killed. I too was picked up for a repeat performance, I had slipped and fallen off a tank.

Fix bayonets: "Sprung auf marsch, marsch!", the platoon leader shouted, and behind us the drill sergeant screamed, especially at me, "Are you trying to pull a girl's pants off or are you tearing the guts out of Ivan's stomach, you, you..!" He got so angry he could not even find words vulgar enough to use. So I had to do it over and over again until I displayed real rage and the fury of a tiger jumping at his prey. As punishment I was given the title, *Oberscheisshaussanitätsrat* - chief shit-house sanitary consultant, or, in other words, I was put in charge of cleaning the latrines until we left.

Our artillery regiment was on its way to Russia from the

French coast near St. Nazaire, about the time Stalingrad fell in January of 1943. With the loss of the 6th Army, a large gap had to be filled in order to stop the Russian Divisions from pushing the defeated German forces behind the Denjepr River. When we left our idyllic French village not too far from the City of Nantes and the harbour of St. Nazaire on the Gulf of Biscay, we encountered spring-like weather in January. Our horses were in good shape, especially the heavy Belgian Brewery horses. You see, heavy artillery needs heavy horses and they, in turn, need strong men to handle them, especially during shoeing. I was grateful that I was trained as an artillery observer and a gunner. I preferred that position to the possibility of being kicked across the stable by a horse.

Of course, we had a lot of riding horses for the officers and for special sections such as communications, dispatch riders and observation post personnel. Aside from our heavy field howitzers (four of them) a battery had almost as many horses as men. It meant that one battery filled a large transport train. We traveled for the next 18 days.

On my last short leave at home, my father gave me some good advice about traveling on a train with horses in winter. His advice came from his own experiences of the Great War. "Make sure," he said, "that you travel in a box car with the horses. They will keep you warm no matter how cold it is outside."

Chapter Eleven

The blow to our heads and faces at least woke us up before it knocked us out.

The further east we traveled toward Germany, Poland, and Ukraine, the more I appreciated having followed my father's advice.

There were six horses in a box car, three on each side facing one another. There was straw for the hind legs and hay in the centre for the horses to eat and for the six men to sleep on. Sometimes we had to pull blankets over our heads to protect us from being sneezed at by the horses when they had a cold. I think the horses had greater difficulty adjusting to the cold than we did. When we left the French coast, it was a mild 12 degrees Celsius and when we arrived in Russia, the temperature was a frigid minus 22 degrees.

The train stopped every second day for the purpose of moving the horses around to keep their legs in shape and for us who already smelt like horses, to wash somewhere with water or even with snow. We felt that the horses were more important than the men. Michel, my older and more experienced *Kamerad*, who had participated in the previous campaign during the winter of 1941/42, put it this way, "It's not that they are more important than we, they are more helpless. So be nice to them now, because one day you will appreciate them much more when you find them in your soup." Michel was an East

Prussian farmer. He was killed soon after in an artillery bombardment. About two years later when I was eating a bowl of soup, I thought of Michel and his prediction.

    I know that our train passed the city of Kiev in Ukraine. I remember the name Poltawa being called out by the conductor. We were quickly unloaded, I believe near Kharkov. I recall it was a cold and windy day and a column of Red Cross vehicles full of wounded soldiers was waiting to take our place for transport westward. I wondered, what would our fate be?

    We began our march to the front over barren, icy fields where a strong wind always seemed to be blowing in our faces. Even the horses tried to avoid the oncoming winds as they turned their heads and looked back as if they wanted to say, "Lord, have mercy on us." No one was allowed to ride on a horse, they all had to be led. Walking was not only for the benefit of the horses but to prevent the men from ending up

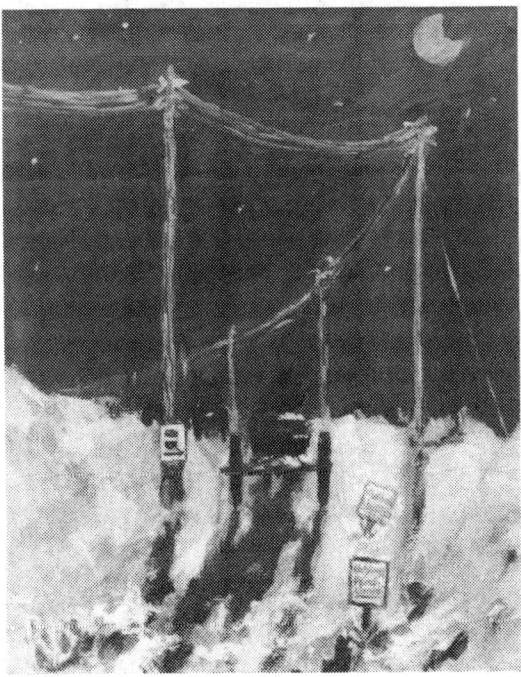

'Ammunition to the Front'
Poster colour   R. Dietz

with frozen limbs.

My place was to march behind my gun carriage. I was the Gunner One, which means when under combat I had to operate the optical instrument and announce, "ready to fire". 15 However, while marching, I had to operate the brakes with the Gunner Two. At least we tried to do this while we were awake but most of the time we marched half asleep in a trance-like state.

I used to tie a rope around my hand on one end and hook the other to the gun carriage. On the order of "Battery March", the horses pulled the cannon and the gun carriage and, in turn, the carriage would pull me. We kept on going until the horses stopped the carriage and a bump on the head stopped us as we ran into the heavy metal plates and other pieces of our cannon. The blow to our heads and faces at least woke us up before it knocked us out. We had some nasty accidents that way and it did not take long till our Battery Commander screamed, "If you want to be knocked out, let Ivan do it." We did not tie ourselves to the cannons any more.

And so we moved along in our heavy overcoats, our ears and noses covered, with just a crack left open to breath through. I noticed troops on the other side of the road; infantrymen moving back with a heavy drag on their feet as they pulled some of their wounded men in carriages with the help of Russian horses (ponies). We looked into their faces by moonlight, and saw their expressions of despair. They seemed to wonder why our reinforcements didn't help them yesterday. We realized we were heading right to the place from which they were departing.

By sunrise we had our battery in position. We fired our first salvos, which consisted of a couple of rounds. Suddenly, we were ordered to stop firing. We were accidentally firing on our retreating infantry. Our new, and as of yet inexperienced observation officer saw troops running toward our position, and since they were camouflaged like the snow, he was not sure if they were Russian soldiers or our own troops. Unfortunately, mistakes like this were not a rare occurrence.

Next, our battery moved deeper into the snow. We experienced cold, hunger, and attacks by Russian bombers. Now we were in a "real" Russian war. I thought of Napoleon's words, "To conquer Russia, one must be prepared to die."

The situation eventually improved when we moved into a new position up in the area between the rivers Don and Donets (near Isjum and Slaviansk). We started to dig in to form a new defensive line along the Donets River. Each howitzer was set up in such a way that even the smallest crew could swing it around 360 degrees without difficulty, in order to face the attacking enemy from every direction. As Gunner One, I practiced the routine with my crew a few times a day before the enemy turned our practice to reality.

The ammunition columns moved in during the night and we carried 50 kilogram shells a distance of some 100 meters into a secure place. Each of us carried 20 shells which was exercise we didn't need. I collapsed into my dug-out and I was still half dead when, four hours later, a gunner shook me awake for duty watch. We had to keep our vehicles far enough away from our position to avoid any air reconnaissance during the day when the tracks could be spotted. We didn't realize how much the enemy could see from their planes. Thank God the Russians did not have a very effective air force. When they dove down, our 8.8 Flak dispersed them very quickly. Only once in a while did they manage to land a few bombs into the middle of our gun post.

One day, an engineering troop arrived to lay a minefield around the position. We knew that we would be there for awhile. Mines certainly made it more difficult for the enemy to overrun our position, but it also made it impossible for us to get out in case of an enemy attack. That is what the Supreme Command of the Armed Forces (OKW) wanted, especially after Stalingrad. The order was, "No more retreats" and that, for us, meant ultimate disaster.

The reality was to escape by whatever means we could. We retreated in panic, to find a new position. Digging in overnight, soldiers waited while half asleep for a new attack from a superior enemy. That enemy, supported by tanks and artillery,

Gunner I with gun carriage

Heavy field howitzer in action.

appeared on the horizon with the rising sun. Then, if we were lucky, our troops escaped at sunset, accompanied by the "roaring Stalin organ" (the truck-borne *katyusha* rockets) until there were no units left. New positions were never well prepared. According to the OKW orders, they were not supposed to be there in the first place. "No retreat!"

At times I thought of one of my typical Prussian drill sergeants shouting at me, after I tried to explain to him an easier way of doing things. "The thinking has to be left to the horses," he told me, "They have bigger heads." He then showed his gratitude by chasing me around the parade square.

I was now becoming a useless soldier. I did too much thinking but was not able to change anything. A good soldier receives and follows orders; he lives up to his 'Oath of Allegiance'. But since Stalingrad+, a lot had changed. The whole attitude of the German soldier - at least on the Russian Front - had changed. Even camaraderie was slowly disappearing. The last comrade fell in Stalingrad+, so they said.

From now on, no matter what situation I was in, my first concern was, "How in hell do I get out of here alive?" When I saw the sunrise and the glowing sky in the east, I hoped to be alive to witness the sunset in the west. But I did not believe I would ever again see a sunset 1000 kilometers further to the west, in the hills and mountains of the Eifel countryside, my home.

I soon was ordered to an observation post at the infantry line on a hill overlooking the Donets River at a spot where the river was about 70 meters wide. I always had the same strange feeling approaching the frontline positions, the every day fighting area, where one had to be constantly prepared for everything. First, there was a kind of shiver, but then, after a deep breath, one thinks of it as just another rendezvous with death. The more dangerous the spot, the more careless one gets - the jumping up and taking cover becomes routine. It does not affect you anymore who drops to the left or who falls to the right, or over whose body you crawl.

Because the new spot was under enemy observation, I crawled into my foxhole before daybreak and remained there till after dark when someone else took over. There was no chance at all of escaping during the day. It was a mouse trap; during the night there was constant danger from Russian patrols which could sneak up and cut your throat. That had indeed happened to a comrade nearby and to my predecessor. That, was the reason why I was sent there. One calls it 'replacement'.

Our army received heavy losses at Stalingrad. I remember hearing the Propaganda Ministry speaking about "defeat" on the radio for the first time. But as they put it, it was a heroic defeat such as King Leonidas showed us 2500 years earlier when he defended the pass of Thermopylis. However, this fact did not console the many families who lost their fathers, husbands and sons.

Replacement forces, after the Stalingrad disaster, had to be found not from new conscripts who needed to be trained but from older professional men. Some of these replacements came from factories. People who were employed in important defence industries were called to the Front. Many workers thought that their valuable jobs would keep them at home for the duration of the war. Woman were being used more and more to fill in for the men in these factories. I was glad that Waltraud was able to stay at home and work in our parents' business. Other girls with whom we went to school had to leave home and work wherever they were needed. Many of the women who were drafted to the air force communication section and the anti-aircraft and air-protection units, ended up in prison camps. Some did not return home. The last memory we had of them was seeing them leaning out of the train windows waving good-bye to their loved ones.

Chapter Twelve

All hell broke loose in the early morning of July 17.

We soldiers were quite naive about what was really going on in the battle fields. Most of the time we didn't even know who our field commander was, much less who was successful in battle. We didn't know if the battles were won by our Field Marshal von Manstein or by the other side, Marshal Budjenny, or Timochenko, or whoever was in command.

June, 1943 was a quiet, gloomy period. We expected something drastic would happen at any time. Some of us received our first promotion - lance corporal, and corporal for the older, more experienced boys of the 10th Battery. I also became a *Fahnenjunker* which in the old Prussian military tradition, simply means a soldier and officers cadet who accompanies the flag or ensign and who, in the later stage, actually carries the ensign in ceremonial parades, though not in combat.

We received a few replacements for the men we lost either in battle or who were hospitalized because of illness. As far as I was concerned most of them were too young or too old for front line service. The older men were NCOs, about 37 years of age having an average of 18 years of service as professional soldiers. They were very good soldiers and had, till now, been considered irreplaceable and so remained in the garrisons to train young recruits. Some of these men had previously been decorated for bravery and were respected and revered by the young recruits. They were able to teach by utilizing their own experience which was often more realistic and informative than learning only from the *Heeresdienstvorschrift* - the army instruction manual. Speaking of army instruction books - that was the first thing I got rid of, but not until I memorized most of it.

We received several senior NCOs who were transferred from various units which had been dissolved. We also got people from transport units, railway or guard duty personnel. Problems occurred when the older NCOs took over positions held temporarily by our young men who had lots of frontline experience but were not officially qualified because of their rank. Those who were willing to learn from us managed quite well, but when they were sent to the B-Stelle - observation post, there was a lot of friction. It was just too difficult to train them under the noses of the enemy.

One of the new people to join our depleted ranks was a *Stabswachtmeister* with many years of military service but no frontline experience. Unfortunately, this Warrant Officer First Class, an apprentice for front line duty, did not last too long. He was a bit too slow taking cover when a Russian tank's cannon blasted into our 'summer residence' down by the Donets River.

Eventually we were sent an artillery apprentice, an Oberwachtmeister (W.O. 2) who had 16 years of service in the air force. He was a typical *Salon Soldat* with polished boots. We told him to stop worrying about his footwear. We teased him that with the glaring reflection caused by his shiny boots, he would most certainly give away our position to the enemy. That sure fixed him. It didn't take long for me to realize that he was of no use to us for he spent too much time reading letters from home and becoming homesick. Unfortunately, he did not last with us either. He too did not take cover fast enough when the Russian artillery bombarded our position. As much as he annoyed me at times, I was sad when I had to send his personal belongings back to the battery sergeant major. The dead officer carried pictures of his wife and three children in his pocket.

Oath of Allegiance

Two days later, another new replacement joined our battery. He was a young lieutenant whose decorations indicated he had lots of frontline experience. The battery commander accompanied him and told me to get ready for a two-day course at the regiment's headquarters to learn about the Russian T-34 tank which they had captured. We were not taught how to drive the tank but how to destroy it. I had hoped that I would never have the chance to face such a monster because the T-34 tank was the best on the battlefield at the time. Our own new German tanks were supposed to be there, too, but I had not seen one yet.

When I returned to my group, they had moved a few hundred meters down river and closer to the water. One night while we were in this position, the infantry platoon next to us returned from patrol with two prisoners. They were Turkmeni, an Asiatic tribe more familiar with knives than with rifles. The Turkmeni were sneaking up on our men and slitting their throats with knives. Our bayonets were designed more for spearing than for cutting but we hoped that a sharp bayonet would match the knives of the Turkmeni.

The place by the river gave me the creeps. There were no sounds at night except for the wind blowing through the trees and the occasional flare ejected from some fox hole nearby, indicating that someone discovered a Russian patrol on a raft. Whenever I heard whispering, I imagined seeing a Turkmeni crawling through the grass with his knife clenched between his tobacco-stained teeth. I really doubted we were a match for those cut-throats, but looking at the faces of my comrades, with their hardened lines, I realized none of them looked like boys anymore. It made me wonder what I looked like. I suppose I had lost my youth long ago too. Maybe we were ready for any kind of cruelty after all. We were soon to find out.

All hell broke loose in the early morning of July 17. I was looking through my field glasses about to admire the rising sun when I saw this flash of light shoot across the entire frontline. Seconds later we heard the explosion of artillery shells all around us. The entire ground seemed to be shaking as if we were experiencing an earthquake. The Russians must have had a dozen batteries with tons of ammunition hailing down on one square kilometer. The salvos firing out in quick succession reminded me of the fireworks I used to enjoy as a boy in Mayen. But the subsequent explosions on one side of us and the other side of us was certainly no fun. We called it *Trommelfeuer* - drum fire - because the explosions felt like a sustained tympani roll. The bombardment lasted, uninterrupted, for a few hours. The whole front line was thundering and the earth was trembling.

We quickly moved our observation post a few hundred meters back to an elevation where we hoped to have a better view. At the same time, the forward observer was ordered down to the infantry battalion commander to provide support. I did not like our new location since it was still under enemy fire and who wants mortars exploding right above their heads? Besides, there were too many trees. But then, if we couldn't see the enemy very well, perhaps they couldn't see us. I remembered what my old Latin teacher would have said in such a confused situation, *Doch Scheisse im Trompetenrohr, Kommt Gott sei Dank nur selten vor!*

Suddenly, the first mortar shells exploded right on top of us into a row of trees. It hit the battery commander and a corporal. When we cautiously moved over to them we found the commander laying face down, bleeding from his mouth and head. He was obviously dead. As we carefully removed his body, I wondered why officers always had this habit of wearing their field caps in this iron-clad environment. I was convinced that a steel helmet would have saved his life, at least on this occasion.

The sergeant in charge of communication searched for the interruption in the telephone line. I was alone now with the newly arrived lieutenant who automatically became the new battery commander. He had no contact with the *Feuerstellung* - the location of our howitzers and the forward observer. Since our battery was still firing one round after another, we were sure that our forward observer had contact with us and that he was directing the artillery fire onto the attacking Russian tanks.

The lieutenant, assuming his new responsibility, ordered me to stay at the telescope while he checked the situation at the forward observation post. I couldn't understand his need to go down there since he could see the disaster from where we were. I guess he wanted the men to know that he had taken over the 10th Battery of the Artillery Regiment of the 333rd Division. He never got the chance to direct the 10th Battery because there was a direct hit by a T-34 tank while the infantry battalion commander was briefing him. I felt totally helpless as I observed the movements of the Russian tanks, but I had no way of contacting the battery to direct the howitzers to fire upon them. I took possession of the dead captain's automatic pistol and waited for things to happen. But what came were the remnants of an infantry company of 38 men, two corporals and a staff-sergeant. The original company had a captain, two or three lieutenants, a dozen NCOs and about 160 soldiers. These starving, worn-out men started to dig their fox-holes right next to me, hoping that I would soon make contact for artillery support. They didn't look as if they would be able to survive another attack. I asked them if they knew the whereabouts of our forward post. They told me the post was overrun by the Russians and the soldiers were either killed or taken prisoner. In other words, they were all killed because there was no such thing as taking prisoners after bitter fighting, especially when food, supplies and manpower were as scarce as they were in such a situation.

While we were talking, a hail of bullets shot right through the trees over our heads. I tightened the leather strap of my helmet and settled down with the boys of our leaderless infantry. We were completely demoralized when several T-34 tanks passed to the south of us. Although it would be awhile before sunset, we prayed for nightfall to come so we could try to sneak away. Our new observation officer, who was also in charge of the battery, arrived with a couple of pale looking radio operators who were shaking with fear. These two looked as if they were more afraid than I of what was going on which made me feel rather courageous. I guess I was better adjusted to the situation.

Mortar shells started exploding all around us. I could clearly hear the screaming of the boys who got hit followed by more cannons firing from the tanks and artillery. One learns quickly how to distinguish between explosions, so that it is possible to tell if the shells are delivered by mortars, tanks, cannons or howitzers.

The new lieutenant tried to find out from which direction a tank was shooting, so he asked me if I could see anything through my telescope. From my position, I could see nothing as yet for I lay hidden below the surface of the ground looking through my rabbit ear telescope protected from enemy fire. However, my lieutenant felt that if I was to target the enemy position I had better stand up and take a better look. He was annoyed at what he thought was my supposed cowardice and became anxious to find the tank. At the very moment I shouted a warning to him on the tank's position, an explosion squeezed me between the rocks.

I suddenly felt a heavy weight over my body. Too frightened to move, I noticed blood running down my face and uniform. I soon realized it was the young officer lying on top of me but I didn't know that it was he who had been hit, and that the blood was his, not mine. He was dead, full of shrapnel from his waist up.

I heard the communication sergeant calling me from a distance, wondering if I was all right. Together we escaped into the hills leaving everything behind but our weapons. We remained there, well camouflaged, until nightfall, then we withdrew under cover of darkness. We found our battery in a state of preparation for an expected early morning attack by Russian tank units. The order for the night was to dig out trenches with our picks and shovels. I kept myself close to the communication sergeant with whom I escaped from the battered observation post. At least he would be the likely person to know when it was time to run.

I guess I was fortunate not to be on duty as a Gunner One at that time. A Gunner One would have been tied to a howitzer without possibility of escape. The enemy troops and tanks would keep on coming no matter how many of them were killed and destroyed. They would come until they reached our positions with us on the points of their bayonets. Our infantry men stood up in the face of battle again and again to fight off a far superior enemy who would eventually run them into the ground with their tanks.

Looking east toward the rising sun, I shivered not from the cold of the dawn, but from the shadows of all the tanks and troops now moving slowly toward our position. I just wanted to close my eyes and sleep an hour before the end of my miserable existence when suddenly I felt a heavy boot on my chest. It was the sergeant. "*Es geht los, auf marsch, marsch!*" he shouted.

Drumfire, Stalin organ. It was a repetition of the previous day with gunfire directed into all our infantry lines and our field artillery positions. As soon as it stopped, we saw, far away in the distance, men running around. But we could not make out if they were our infantry retreating, or the Russians attacking. Our battery officer shouted the order to prepare for shooting. At that point it did not seem to matter whether the target was those retreating or those attacking us. He held back the order as long as he could, until he identified the men in the distance as Russians. He ordered a delayed fuse and then shouted, "Batteryyyyyy.....Fire!" After that each howitzer was on its own.

There were an awful lot of shells shooting at our enemies, but apparently not enough to stop Ivan from penetrating our position. Gunners were mowed down and stabbed with bayonets as they were still trying to reload their guns. Again, I thanked God I was not a Gunner One that day.[1a]

Our sergeant moved us closer to some kind of escape route on which some of our wounded were carried away by horse-drawn vehicles. Dispatch riders drove in between us on motorbikes. Some Russians were heading toward us led by one of their officers who shouted davay, davay (move on, move on). We tried desperately to shield the vehicle loaded with our wounded men. Then suddenly I got hit. I found myself lying in a field, with hand grenade shrapnel in my legs. It was only after I saw the blood that I realized how badly I was hurt.

I crawled on my stomach using my elbows to paddle ahead, while my left wrist was immobile from other shrapnel wounds. I felt hopeless and afraid.

There were still two hand grenades hanging from my belt and the thought of suicide ran through my mind - I couldn't face a Russian bayonet and I thought nobody would pick me up while machine gun bullets flew all around us.

Then suddenly, I heard the familiar sound of a DKW motor bike approaching. I realized that this would be my last chance for survival so with what little strength I had left, I threw myself onto the road. The dispatch rider, furious that I was in his way, headed right for me. I pointed my pistol at his head and shouted, "You'll have to die right here with me unless you take me with you!"

There was no argument. I climbed on and as I grasped him, he cursed and swore at me under his breath as we took off in a cloud of dust and a hail of bullets. Unfortunately, he did not escape unharmed, but at least I didn't have to persuade him to get us to the nearest casualty collection post.

After a preliminary diagnosis, I was told by a medic that the medical officer had just announced that everybody capable of walking had to march on while the rest of the wounded had to wait for ambulances to get through the lines. At that point, I had to turn over my weapons as the Red Cross didn't allow them within their posts. This upset me as well as the other wounded men. It meant we couldn't even kill ourselves if the Russians made it to our Red Cross station.

All I could think about was my family. My parents, my sister who always cared for me, my much younger brother Hans and finally, my little sister Eva Maria filled my thoughts. I did not really worry about myself, but I hoped that my family would never know how I actually died, laying among bleeding soldiers all of whom had taken their Oath of Allegiance. I wondered what our Latin teacher would say, the one who made us memorize the words: *dulce et decorum est pro patria mori*. Would he ever again think that death for one's country was sweet? But he could say, ...*legibus obsequimur*. They died following orders. The reality was, orders or not, there was no choice about who lived and who died.

While I was thinking and praying, a truck and an ambulance stopped at the Red Cross station. The ambulance driver opened the door to his vehicle and in no time it was full. I first thought that the more serious cases would get preferential treatment, but that was not the case. It appeared that the soldiers who were almost dead, would be left behind to die.

I blinked in disbelief. "My God, is that not - yes, it is Johann!" Johann was the ambulance driver from Mayen's municipal hospital. He was standing not more than a few meters from me, piling the wounded into his ambulance. I called his name again and again. He finally looked up and came over to where I was laying. He looked at me puzzled as I said his name again. He obviously did not recognize me. When he asked me who I was, I began to choke. I could not answer him and started to cry. He then looked at my tag and shook his head. "Oh my God, is that you?"

He bundled me up in a blanket, and carried me to his overburdened ambulance. It seemed like a fairy tale to stumble on Johann who drove the ambulance in my home town - to find him here, here in the middle of nowhere, in the middle of Russia. A preferred customer of my father's pub and now he gave me preferential treatment.

The ambulance normally held eight stretchers, three on each side and two in the middle. On this trip there were 12 bodies crammed in the tiny vehicle. As a result, our journey to the field hospital was long and very painful for some of the wounded. It was hot and smelly as well.

When we arrived at our destination it was discovered that one of the wounded had already died. In spite of the real stench, and after the experiences of the past few days, everything smelled as good as *Eau du Cologne's 4711* to me.

All I could do was think about how Johann, who had seen me at least once a week in my father's pub, had not recognized me. He wrote to his wife and asked her to let my parents know that I was safe. I found out later that he himself did not return home from the war; his name is listed in the memorial chapel among the soldiers missing in action.

I finally ended up in a field hospital near Gorlovka in

eastern Ukraine. After spending 147 days in snow, mud, rain, and misery, I had a bed of my own with fresh smelling, white linen sheets and a soft pillow. I was still under the influence of chloroform and other anaesthetics, when I heard some female voices in the distance. I had been dreaming that my bed was surrounded by the angels of Hänsel and Gretel playing the harp as they floated me into the air. It was *wunderbar*, but when I opened my eyes, I looked straight into the face of a stern and very resolute Red Cross nurse. She gave me strict orders not to touch the sand bags placed on my left leg to immobilize it.

She told me that one of five bits of shrapnel in my body was situated very close to the "arteria femoralis" and that any movement could cause the sharp iron edges to rip open the artery. It is still in my leg today.

I have no recollection of how long I was in that hospital room. I shared it with three other wounded soldiers much older than my 19 years. We were a strange mixture, indeed, - a Saxon from Dresden, a Hanoverian, a Stuttgarter and I, the Rhinelander. I spent most of my time talking to the fellow with the wounded leg from Stuttgart who was in the bed next to mine. I enjoyed our conversations because Hans-Dieter was a music student who promised to play Mozart's 'A Major Sonata', the *Frühlings Sonate* - Spring Sonata as soon as he could get out of bed. And he really did, too. During the last week before he was discharged and sent back to his unit, he gave a recital for the patients and staff of the field hospital. Everyone was moved into the recreation room to hear him play Bach's Italian Concerto, my favourite Mozart piece which he promised me, Beethoven's Waldstein Sonata and as an encore, the Hungarian Dance No.5 by Brahms. It was truly an unforgettable evening for all of us in spite of the old upright piano which was slightly out of tune.

I thought a lot about Hans-Dieter. What a great talent and a fine person he was. I prayed that nothing would ever happen to his hands. It greatly saddened me when Hans-Dieter was discharged. I had never asked him in which unit he served, I had been interested only in his musical talents and that he studied at the University of Freiburg in the Black Forest.

I remained in the field hospital about another two weeks after Hans Dieter left. During this time I attended church services which the hospital chaplain held in the recreation room. I had no objection to the recreation room, but I did not like the murals on the wall. As the chaplain lifted up the chalice during mass I looked up and saw in the background a mural depicting a *Landser* - a land soldier - lifting his left leg showing that he had just farted. The exhaust fumes were visually expressed in the form of a cloud floating around his nose. Underneath was written, *Einem jeden riechen seine eigenen Winde wohl* - One always finds one's own wind pleasant. I found this mural very embarrassing and in bad taste, but the chaplain did not seem to mind it because he never made an attempt to correct the situation.

Before my own discharge, I had a chance to attend a cabaret in Stalino produced by a Ukrainian company from Kiev for the entertainment of the German troops. I don't know if it had any effect on the troops, but it certainly did not give me much inspiration. I found it, perhaps, as boring as the others may have found it interesting.

As my injury was not considered to be too serious, I was not on the list of those to be sent to a *Heimat Lazarett*, a hospital at home, and soon I was on the way to my old unit or whatever there was left of it. I made my return trip by rail. A group of us boarded the overcrowded train to either Gorlovka or Stalino, I can't remember where now for certain, but the stench was incredible. I sat in a couch with old Russian men and women all of whom smoked that disgusting smelling tobacco called, *Machorka*[16] - the people's tobacco. I was glad to have survived the trip, barely, and I reported on arrival to the station officer who gave me information on how and where to find my division, regiment and finally, the 10th Battery. This took at least two more days of hitch-hiking and marching.

When I arrived at my post I was shocked. It was no longer my battery with familiar faces. The new sergeant major told me to report to the battery commander in the B-Stelle.

So I went to the observation post via the *Feuerstellung* where I nearly lost my speech. There were no more howitzers but, instead, 35 centimeter French mortars made at the end of World War I. They were engraved with the words, "Le Creusot, 1918." They were big and clumsy and made a terrible noise when fired, and a more terrible hole when the shells landed and exploded.

I intended to let the battery sergeant major know that I still had difficulties with running because of my leg injury. But then I learned we had heavy short-range mortars. We called them 'Big Bertas' because of the caliber, but the real 'Big Bertas' of W.W. I, were long-range cannons named for Berta Krupp, heiress to the vast Krupp steel and armaments empire.

I just did not want to get stuck with something like the mortars which had to be placed close to the frontline because of their short range. Our new captain referred to them as *die verdammten Scheiss Kanonen* - those damn shit cannons. They were even less mobile than the howitzers, but thank God they weren't horse drawn. Anyway, I finally arrived at the B-post with our field kitchen and took my rations for the next day.

I usually got into the habit of eating my next day's rations early for two reasons. I had seen many soldiers with stomach wounds who had no chance for survival because their bellies were full. Those who had empty stomachs seemed to survive much better. The other reason was rather more selfish; I had seen too many soldiers taking the rations from their dead comrades. I felt uneasy about it.

Our B-Stelle was perfectly located along the side of a hill where one would not suspect a post. Small bushes and a few trees were scattered around our site except for one spot which we set up for the latrine. By the way, we had no separate compartments now and officers were welcome.

Captain Müller was not a bad guy. He was a reservist in his late thirties, not too fond of war. He had more respect for the regiment's commander than anyone of us had here at the B-Stelle. Whenever he came to our observation post, he got into long conversations. I had the impression that he would rather be a coward alive, than a war hero dead. Quite often he would ask me to brief him on the situation at hand.

One day Captain Müller appeared with the regiment's commander who asked me to explain the present situation. I reported that our engineers were demolishing the railway tracks. But when I asked the Colonel why they were doing something so unusual, I was told that he came to get a report and not to give one. Then he asked me what I would do and where I would go if the enemy suddenly appeared in front of me. I told him there would be no chance to escape. I said I would direct the battery to fire into our own position and I would remain in my hole. I must have said the right thing because he turned to Captain Müller and said, "That's the spirit!" and they both left. I later wondered to myself if I would really do that.

There was a *Latrinengerücht*[14] - rumour running rampant that our division would be moving out of the front section. I did not know where we were going, nor did I care as long as we got out. As it happened, we did get out, but only because the frontline was constantly moving as opposed to the previous fixed line. I saw that we were facing the same situation as in July. Once again, the Russians started to press on with their artillery and tanks. This time there was even air force action, I mean the Russian air force not the German Luftwaffe. In fact, with the exception of the two-rump observation plane, I had never seen any German planes since coming to Ukraine.

Chapter Thirteen

There was one special attraction for me. Her name was Wanda, and she was a medical student.

We moved in and out of position for several days. It became a demoralizing affair. Even our captain lost his nerve when, at one point, he blew up his French mortars too soon, before the Russians penetrated the position. When our infantry beat them back, the battery was blown up. Captain Müller was later court martialled. (It was the battery officer's job to destroy the guns before they would fall into the hands of the enemy.) I was wounded again, though this time I ended up on a hospital train. I followed all the events and news of the eastern front from my hospital bed at the Reserve Hospital near Lodz in Poland.

I have only a sketchy recollection of how I actually got to the *Kriegslazarett* - war hospital - in Poland. I remember I was exhausted, sitting by a tank trap on the side of a road when suddenly a staff car stopped by me. The driver jumped out, dragged me over to the car and pushed me into the front seat. A medic sergeant was in the back seat, holding the wounded commander of an infantry regiment. The lieutenant colonel was badly wounded. His whole face was bandaged. The sergeant indicated to me that the lieutenant colonel had lost his eyesight. It happened when grenade shrapnel from a tank gun penetrated his face. The colonel was obviously in a lot of pain, and during his delirious state he

Oath of Allegiance

pleaded, "Why don't you just shoot me right here so that I can be buried here with the rest of my regiment?"

The medic bandaged me up while we drove to the nearest field ambulance. But when we arrived, the post had already moved further back. At one point, we were attacked by some low flying Russian planes, but fortunately they only took the time to make one fly-pass though they showered us with their bullets. They must have been on a mission to some other place since they made no attempt to turn around and strafe us again.

We soon arrived in Poltava where a hospital train was loading for transport somewhere westward. The medical sergeant asked me to keep an eye on the wounded commander while he spoke to the medical officer in charge of the transport. The commander was later taken off the train at Kiev and rerouted by air to Germany while I continued on my journey through Ukraine and Poland. Most of the time I was half asleep but in the background I could hear the monotonous rumble of the wheels rolling over the tracks. Any second I expected to hear an explosion and feel the train derail, a result of partisan tactics. They constantly sabotaged our supply lines.

The hospital to which I was taken was near Görnau which before the German occupation was called Zgierz. It was near Lodz. The latter community was also renamed by the Germans, and called, Litzmannstadt.

Once again, I felt as if I were in heaven, lying in a bed with clean, white linen sheets. My left arm was now in a cast and my right foot was heavily bandaged. What more could I ask for? The male staff were cheerful and helpful, and the smiles of the female staff made me feel as if I were floating in the clouds. There was one special attraction for me. Her name was Wanda, and she was a medical student.

Her family had recently been repatriated from Rumania and she was assigned to the surgical ward in the hospital. She spent a lot of time changing my bandages and talking to me about her 'spiritual' interests. She spent so much time with me that at one point Sister Leonidas, the head nurse, had to tell Wanda to divide her time equally among the other patients. This embarrassed her terribly. However, when the Sister noticed that both of us attended mass in the hospital chapel together,

Wanda became her favourite nurse and I, her favourite patient. All in all, Sister Leonidas, who came from a convent in Upper Silesia, was a very kind person; she was in her late fifties and a mother-figure to all of us. She was always there when needed. I often wondered why she chose the name Leonidas. She was not at all like a lion, nor was she like the Spartan King Leonidas.

One day, Sister Leonidas suggested that I take Wanda into Lodz for her birthday, perhaps to a fine café or a concert. The Sister gave me a few extra food coupons so that we could get an extra fine meal and have a good time. She even obtained a special pass so that I could stay out late with Wanda after the normal curfew of 10:00 p.m. I took Wanda to a very prestigious café where the guests were entertained by a salon orchestra of the highest quality. The leader of the orchestra was a rather eccentric looking woman who played the violin. She had the temperament of a gypsy, but when they started to play, I was impressed by their precision and overall musicality. I enjoyed listening to them but I think Wanda had the feeling that I was neglecting her. At one point she said, "I hope that violinist has to use the toilet soon so that you will pay some attention to me. After all, it is my birthday."

In spite of the fact that Wanda was not too happy with me that evening, I continued to take her there often. Wanda's eyes would water, especially after the orchestra played a medley of Rumanian Gypsy melodies. On other visits to Lodz, we attended a symphony concert and an opera, 'The Merry Wives of Windsor' by Otto Nicolay. It was performed by most of the staff of the Cologne Opera House. The opera house had been closed because of the air raids and the staff was relocated to other areas not threatened by attack.

No matter how much I enjoyed my time in Lodz, there was one aspect of my stay that served as a stark reminder of what Hitler had created.

On my first trip into town, I was warned about what I would see. I did not know that the town was infamous for its ghetto which, like the Warsaw Ghetto, had been turned into a camp with high fencing. All vehicles, including streetcars,

Oath of Allegiance

had to travel without stopping through the ghetto which was located on both sides of the road leading from Zgierz to Lodz.

As we drove through the ghetto zone, my curiosity led me to ask the driver to slow down as much as he could. What I could see were two rows of fencing, probably electrically charged and parallel to one another. I saw hundreds of people, including children, behind these fences. They stared at us with large, pleading eyes. They looked as if to ask, "What did we do to you that you put us in here?" At one point, I saw men swinging police batons and beating up on others. What was strange to me was that both the men with the batons and those being beaten were wearing the emblem of the Star of David on their shirts. Long before, the Nazis had decreed that all Jews had to wear the emblem as identification. Those who did the beating also had the *Lager Polizei* - camp police insignia marked on their left arms. It would be years before I understood that some Jews bought survival for themselves and their families by keeping order for the Nazis.

I was absolutely shocked and horrified at the sight of civilians in such a state. The driver noticed my reaction and said that this sight was even too much for a soldier from the front. I fully agreed with him and we hurried off to do our duties in town. I hoped that I would never have to drive by there again, though of course there was no other route by which to return to the hospital.

I was soon ready to be discharged from the hospital and to have my first leave for home. The doctor examined my arm and foot which were both healing very nicely. Just when I was ready to leave his office after being declared fit, he abruptly called me back. He examined me more closely, moving my eyelid back, checking my skin and palpating my liver area. I started to get a little nervous when he asked me for a urine sample. As he examined its colour he called out to his secretary, "No discharge yet for this young man. Transfer him to internal medicine, he has *hepatitis epidemica!*" I had jaundice. That assured me another six weeks in the hospital. I did not feel really sick, but warmth, a special diet, and regular injections of glucose were required. Sister Leonidas, always looking on the bright side of things, reassured me that I would be home for Christmas.

My father arrived at the hospital quite unexpectedly one day. I asked my father how he managed to get from the far western border of Germany to the east of Poland. "With two suitcases of wine," he answered. He used one case of wine to get to the hospital and he was going to use the other to bribe the hospital staff, so that I would be transferred to the hospital closer to Mayen.

I felt embarrassed when he took the doctor out every night. My father left a few days later with no apparent luck. I was still upset with my father but Sister Leonidas tried to calm me down by making me understand that he only meant well.

About a week later my mother and sister arrived. I am happy to say they did not cause me any embarrassment. They did not come to take anybody else out but me. Waltraud and I talked a lot about all the news at home, about the Church choir and who was home on leave. My mother got along quite well with Sister Leonidas. I guess they were on the same wave-length, both being religious. In our conversations together, my mother and sister mentioned their street car ride past the ghetto where they too saw the cruel beatings of the Jews by their own kind. Waltraud was terribly shocked by what she saw. Remembering well the treatment that our Jewish neighbours received, she made up her mind that the devil in hell could not be more evil than the devil in Berlin.

Waltraud usually came to visit me during the early afternoons. Sometimes, when I was half asleep, I could tell when Waltraud was on her way to my bedside because the boys in the next room would whistle when she walked by. In the beginning I felt a bit uneasy about their behaviour but then I thought, "What the hell, why should they not whistle? I have a nice looking sister."

When my mother and sister left to go back home after their short stay, I felt very much alone. I thought a lot about my dear friend Lothar who died of wounds he received in the fierce battle of Smolensk. Why him, I asked myself? I also

Lothar Rosenbaum

> **Jesus!** **Maria!** **Josef!**
> Herr, Dein Wille geschehe!
> †
> Betet für die Seele
> unseres lieben Sohnes, Bruders, Neffen
> und Vetters des
> Gefr. in einem Grenad.-Regt.
> **Lothar Rosenbaum**
> Mitglied des Cäcilienchores.
>
> Unser Lothar war am 22. Juni 1924 in Schönberg geboren, wo er auch seine ersten Jugendjahre verlebte. Schon früh war er begeistert für seinen Kath. Glauben und schloß sich überall, wo er hin kam, Kameraden an, die wie er, ihren kath. Glauben hoch hielten. Es war nicht immer leicht für ihn. Für seine Überzeugung nahm er manche Unbill in Kauf, wofür Gott ihn gnädig in die Schar seiner Getreuen aufnehmen möge.
>
> Er starb nach Vollendung seiner Gimnasialstudien an den Folgen einer schweren Gehirnverletzung, die er in den harten Kämpfen bei Smolensk am 22. Sept. erlitten hatte in einem Lazarett in Warschau am 3. Nov. 1943.
>
> Ihr alle seine Freunden und Bekannten betet mit uns, damit er um so eher ruhe im Frieden Gottes.
>
> In christlicher Trauer:
> Seine Eltern, Geschwister und Anverwandten.
> Mayen, den 10. November 1943.

Death announcement, Lothar R. He died of injuries to his head following the fierce battle of Smolensk.

longed to see my school mate Heinz Theo who was drafted into the artillery in Nancy as I had been. But Heinz got sick and was in the hospital when we were ready to move out to war. He was later transferred to the infantry.

I remember the good advice his father gave to us draftees at the railway station. He spoke with a very coarse voice. "Boys," he shouted quite loudly, sounding as if he had looked too deeply into the bottle. "Boys, remember what I always told you. You must learn how to handle the bayonet if you want to survive." He then grabbed my father's cane and showed us how to pierce it into somebody's stomach. Several months later the mailman came to Heinz' house and handed his father the message of his son's death. It is said he spoke only one sentence, "He did not know how to use his bayonet."

After that his drinking problem grew worse. Heinz was his only child.

I now thought of all the other boys I had left behind at the Front in Kremenchug, a city in Ukraine. I felt guilty because I was still alive. Every time I turned on the radio I became upset by the bad news from the *Ostfront*. Another good school friend, Heinz S. was a math genius. He was the only son, as a matter of fact, the only child in the family. When he got drafted, he ended up in the Panzer Elite Regiment, *Gross Deutschland*. I was told he was officially declared, *Vermisst an der Ostfront* - missing on the eastern front. I wondered how was I going to wish his parents a Merry Christmas?

Twenty years later, when I went to visit his home, I found Heinz' bedroom still unoccupied. His mother, who was now a widow, still waited for Heinz to come home.

As Sister Leonidas predicted, I was able to go home in time for Christmas. It was the most wonderful Christmas I could ever have imagined, in spite of all the bad news about my friends. I was again able to listen to the choir singing Haydn's 'Missa Cellensis'. It did not even bother me that there were far too few male singers. They were all drafted and fighting in the war. As always, spirit and enthusiasm made up for the technical imperfections. The most difficult task for me was to visit the parents of my fallen friends. I just could not wish them a *Fröhliche Weihnacht* and a Happy New Year. It was more difficult to visit them than any assault on an enemy position.

Home on leave with my sister Waltraud.

Officer Cadet training at the Artillery School in Küstrin.

Last home leave before departure to Italy.

Chapter Fourteen

The Americans did not fire with pea shooters, the Tommies did not run away when they saw us and the Canucks certainly did not change their underwear when they met us.

All too soon, I had to return to the *Ersatz Regiment* in Küstrin on the Oder River east of Berlin. This was where Frederick the Great was once kept a prisoner. I now started my training as an officer cadet which was more 'infantristic' than 'artilleristic'. This worried me a little because I thought I would end up in the infantry. But even an artillery officer, especially an observation officer, often has to storm an enemy position.

What seemed ridiculous to me was our weekly official dinner in the officer's mess with the *Kommandeur* of the regiment present. The training officer and the commander's adjutant walked around observing our table manners while we ate with knife and fork and on fish days with a fish knife. It was a joke as only a few weeks ago we had slurped our watery soup from a beaten up mess tin. We were also given riding and fencing lessons as well as instructions in all the things an officer of the Prussian artillery had to know in peace time.

The officer cadet course was certainly no vacation. Sometimes, there were sudden inspections of our rooms at 2:00 a.m., and the slightest infraction was noted. Once I was reprimanded for not having closed the top button of my undershirt and my punishment was the cancellation of a night out on the town and duty-watch. It was obvious that they needed someone for duty watch.

Oath of Allegiance

Near the closing date of the officer training course, we began to think about where we might be transferred. I heard of a newly formed division destined for Italy. The field artillery regiment of that division was still in the early stages of formation. I began to have dreams and fantasies of Italy. I was not thinking about the war nor the fierce battles at Anzio and Monte Cassino but only about 'O Mia Bella Napoli', and 'O Sole Mio', and many other well known Italian folk songs. I decided it would be much better not to think about it anymore. A transfer to Italy would be too good to be true.

While walking across the parade square one day, I noticed someone coming from the opposite direction. At first, I saw only the insignia of his rank and I prepared myself for a sharp salute. Then I noticed the Hand to Hand Combat medal in silver, and the Iron Cross First Class on the side of his uniform which gave more reason to present a smart salute. Suddenly, in a boisterous voice and typical Bavarian dialect, he lifted his arms shouting out, "Oh, kiss my arse! Where do you come from? I thought you were dead. Oh, bless thee God." It was a most unusual *Wiedersehen*. To my surprise, it was none other than *Wachtmeister* Gössl whom I realized had been promoted, and was now an *Oberwachtmeister* W.O.2.

Oberwachtmeister Gössl was, like myself, a survivor of the 10th Battery in Russia. He already had his orders for Italy. He was ready to travel to Pola via Trieste to join the 12th Battery of the new 278th Artillery Regiment, the artillery unit of the 278th Berlin Brandenburg Grenadier Division. The 12th Battery was commanded by Captain Berger, the former commander of the 12th Battery of our dissolved unit in Russia.

Hauptmann Berger had a good reputation. The Bavarian *Oberwachtmeister* insisted that I should get into his unit. I told him to forget it. I would not be that lucky. He asked me in which barrack I was quartered. He cursed and swore for no apparent reason. He was happy, I presumed. He walked straight toward the office still saying to himself in his dialect, "Oh, kiss me arse, he is still alive!" In fact, I had the same thoughts about him. The following day while on parade and inspection, the sergeant major called out my name. I was to report to the office where I was given my official transfer to Italy. The date of my transfer was set in the future, after the completion of cadet training and a short leave at home. This affair caused some envious remarks by a few of my comrades who thought that I must have good connections somewhere. I responded cynically, "I'm just in demand."

I think anyone who did time in Russia longed to get out of there, especially if it meant going to the west, be it the French coast or the Adriatic coast in Italy. Everyone realized that the sun and the water, the wine and the women would be more plentiful and more attractive in France and Italy than in Russia. However, the chance of getting killed was certainly no less. The Americans did not fire with pea shooters, the Tommies did not run away when they saw us and the Canucks certainly did not change their underwear when they met us. In fact, the material superiority was so great that I came to the conclusion that because the air in Italy would show a much higher contamination of iron, the chances of getting killed would be that much greater. But there was one consolation; the grave would be in holy grounds, with saints Francis, Benedict, Peter, and Catherine all holding vigil.

Meanwhile, I enjoyed a few nice days at home after completing the course. My recent promotion brought me a new popularity, especially with the *Damen-Welt*. I found this rather amusing since on my previous leaves home they did not see me as particularly worthy.

Before I began my journey to Italy, I had to return to my base in Küstrin to receive a new uniform. The dress for Italy was the same as the dress for the 'Africa Corps'. It was a tropical uniform and my new rank required that I carry a pistol on my belt. I was happy not to have to carry a rifle anymore. I traveled by train to Trieste by way of Prague and Vienna where I had to change trains and stay overnight in the *Soldatenheim* - an accommodation for soldiers. While in Vienna, I saw Bizet's opera Carmen at the Vienna State Opera with the Lipizzan horses on stage and the Vienna State Orchestra playing in the pit. It was a night not easily forgotten.

I was still in the world of dreams when I left the following morning. It did not seem as if I was on my way to another theatre of fighting. The ride was so pleasant - through the beautiful forests of Vienna, then rounding the mighty Austrian Alps into Innsbruck, through Bolzano, Udine, and, finally, into Trieste - that war was totally forgotten.

Trieste, in late April of 1944, was a fascinating place. I found its location on the Gulf of Trieste near the Istrian Peninsula beautiful indeed. The Emperor Augustus built the city as a Roman port in the first century. While I awaited my travel orders after reporting to the transport officer, I eagerly explored the ancient city. I came to understand why Trieste had changed hands so often in its history after I had seen all its rich jewels of architecture, the amphitheatre and the fifth century Basilica di San Giusto to name but two.

King Attila (better known in English history books as Attila King of the Huns) conquered Trieste. The Byzantine Emperors, the Lombards, as well as the Carolingian and the Frankish Kings, all took possession of Trieste until it came under Austrian protection in 1382.

As I walked through the ancient streets I felt more like a tourist than a soldier once again on his way to join the battle at the new defense line near Pescara. I did not give the impression that I had anything to do with the war until I was checked by the *Feldgendarmerie* - military police. When they looked at my papers and saw that I was a soldier waiting for transport to the front, they advised me not to walk around alone in such offbeat areas. However, it was not so easy to find a comrade who had the same interests as I, although had I been looking for the red-light district, I might have had some company.

The transport officer informed me that my battery was already on its way to Pescara. I was to remain a few more days in Trieste and take a group of ten late arrivals down to the new defense line near Pescara to the headquarters of the 278th division. I had two more days of sight-seeing, then I received my travel orders to leave with the group. Most of the men I had to take were older and more experienced hands which meant that I didn't have to be a baby-sitter. This made the travel much easier.

We went as far as we could by train. I remember our stops in Verona, Modena, and Bologna. While on route our destination to Ancona was changed and we were taken instead to Fano. I presumed this meant that the Ancona station had been bombed and was not yet operational.

Our next destination was Teramo. We traveled by truck and from there most of us made our separate ways to our respective units. I still had to take three boys with me to the artillery regiment. But how were we to get there? I approached an ambulance which was headed in the same direction as we. The driver was on his way to pick up wounded soldiers from the front, so I asked him if he would give us a lift. I was surprised to learn that the methods of conducting war were slightly different here than on the eastern front. The driver would not allow any armed soldiers in a Red Cross vehicle.

Examining our dilemma, I realized an imaginative solution was needed as to just how we were to get to our destination. We did not have many choices. We had been told to stay off the highways, especially along the coast, as they were constantly under attack by Royal Airforce (R.A.F.) fighter bombers. Even the roads leading over the mountains were no longer safe during the day. I asked one of the boys who came from an Austrian dairy farm how far an ox could walk. He simply replied, "Until it gets tired." After a short discussion, we decided to acquire an ox cart with a couple of oxen. Thus began our journey over the Abruzzi mountains. We did not consult any acquisition committee and nobody asked for receipts when we arrived, not even the sergeant in charge of the field kitchen.

Our sight-seeing trip over the mountains was quite an event. We were rather a funny looking sight, traveling over dusty roads, one of us wearing a straw hat, and someone else wearing a colourful shawl over the head and towels to cover the shoulders. We were perfectly camouflaged as a peasant family about to work in the fields below the Abruzzi mountains.

It was well known that the R.A.F. were sympathetic towards the Italian farmers and peasant-folk working in the fields and mountains, so I was certain they would not pay much

In an ox-cart over the Abruzzi mountains.

attention to a peasant family driving an ox cart on the mountain road.

Seppl, one of the three boys I was escorting, was even a yodeler from the south of Tyrol who not only spoke Italian, but also played the accordion. After we opened a bottle of wine we sang all the Italian songs we knew. 'O Sole Mio', 'Mamma Sono Tante Felice', 'Tiritomba' and many others filled the mountain air. Suddenly, Hansl, the Austrian farmer, cried out, "Holy Mary and Joseph, here come the Tommies!" Two R.A.F. planes appeared in the sky. As they turned toward us I shouted to the boys, "Get your towels and wave!" The pilots then made a circle around us, waved, and sped away. A minute later we heard them emptying their guns and then we heard a huge explosion. I looked through my field glasses which were a part of my issued equipment. About two kilometers down the road I noticed that they had just bombed two German army trucks. We could see it burning in the distance with some men running away from one of the vehicles. It was frightening to think that such an attack could have happened to us. As we saw other vehicles and motor bikes arriving at the scene of the explosion, we realized there was no need for us to give any assistance, especially since we could never have made it there with our slow oxen and cart.

We continued our journey into the evening sun, bypassing Gran Sasso mountain. We felt relaxed and Seppl played his accordion, automatically changing from his happy song 'Tiritomba' to the sad and sentimental Italian, 'Montanara.' By the time we arrived at the village where our regimental headquarters was located, Seppl was asleep with his accordion still in his hands, Toni was singing while still clinging to his bottle, and Hansl continued to shout "Avanti" at the oxen, using the long end of a rope as a whip. I was lost in thought, thinking what battles lay ahead.

I reported to the adjutant of the regiment, and when the captain informed me that my battery had just made a change of position, I quoted my old Latin teacher once again, "Doch Scheisse im Trompetenrohr, kommt Gott sei Dank nur selten vor."

I was given my new *Marschbefehl* (marching orders): to go back 18 kilometers in the direction from which I had come. I had to report to the 12th Battery before daylight. I saluted the adjutant and the oxen and shook hands with my Three Musketeers and wished them *Hals und Beinbruch* - break your neck and leg. I started marching *per pedes apostolorum* - as the apostles did. Happily, my knapsack was not as heavy as it had been in Russia where I had to carry winter gear. Nevertheless, although it was not such a pain in the arse, there was some weight on my back.

I reached my destination when, just before sunrise, I entered the little village in the vicinity of Penne, where the boys of the 12th Battery were just beginning the morning ritual of cleaning and feeding the horses.

The *Oberwachtmeister* in charge of the group pranced up and down shouting and cracking his whip. When he walked in his riding attire, he gave the impression that he was still on his horse. He was so bow-legged that there seemed at least 30 centimeters of space between his knees. He looked like an unsympathetic character and I felt a Kaiser Wilhelm moustache would have suited him well. However, *Oberwachtmeister* Wanke, a Berliner, was the *Futtermeister* - feeding master - and as such was an important figure in the battery's operation. He was also the person who had to supply me with a riding horse. So I put down my baggage, went over to him, and saluted smartly. My awareness of his importance seemed to make an impression on him.

When I told Oberwachtmeister Wanke who I was, he asked me how I, as a Rhinelander - he had recognized my accent and knew I was not a Berliner -, ended up in the Berlin Brandenburg Grenadier Division. He spoke in a typical Berliner dialect. What he really meant by his question was to infer that Rhinelanders were nothing but a bunch of softies, and were out of place in a traditional Prussian regiment.

As it happened, the Berliner, Wanke, and the Bavarian *Oberwachtmeister* Gössl argued from the very first day they met. They always referred to each other as *Verdammter Sau-Bayer* - damn Bavarian pig, or *Verdammter Sau-Preuss* - damn Prussian pig.

A lance corporal arrived with my official companion, a beautiful riding horse. The creature was young and nervous, perhaps because of his new master, or because of the sound of the artillery shells exploding not too far from us. I nearly flipped when I was told his name, *Robert der Teufel*. Robert was the name of my Irish Patron Saint who was a successful exorcist, and was therefore called, 'Robert the Devil'.

It looked as if we were going to have a beautiful day. It was warm, and the sun stood high as one of the stable hands held the horse for me to mount. I was told by the sergeant major I could find the Battery Commander, *Hauptmann* Berger, only a few kilometers away. He cynically remarked, "If you get lost just ask for the house with the best wine cellar." He then added a word of caution, "Ride close to the trees; there's a lot of air activity."

As soon as I left the village behind me, I started talking with my horse. I explained that I had to rename him, *Roberto*.

Robert der Teufel was too big a mouthful, and since we were in Italy, I felt I should speak to him in Italian. When I called out, "*Avanti*" he immediately began to trot but he changed to a gallop whenever a motor vehicle passed by us.

Up in the hills I could see the village, and over to the side there was a farmhouse surrounded by a vineyard. I concluded that since the captain was a connoisseur of wine, then that was where he would have his command post. Suddenly, two very low flying airplanes came down towards the road. There was no time to argue who had the right of way, when I saw lights flashing from its machine guns. It all happened so fast I did not get time to jump off my horse. Neither was there time for my rear end to relax. I called out, "*Mamma Mia!*" and tried to gear down my galloping horse. But he did not understand human language anymore and went practically berserk.

We were both shaking when we arrived at the courtyard. The captain stood outside with field glasses in one hand and a wine glass in the other. He had watched the entire scene. I jumped off the horse, the water in my arse still boiling, saluted him and reported what had happened. He handed me his glass saying with a big grin, "Are you that brave or did you not get time to take cover?" I replied that there was no hole big enough for me and my horse to jump in.

He laughed and when he refilled the glass of wine for me I added, "To tell you the truth, *Herr Hauptmann* I did not have time to be a coward."

With another glass of wine, we sat down and reflected upon our experiences on the Russian front when we of the 10th Battery had lost three battery commanders in one day. But the captain survived the ordeal with his 12th Battery and that was why he insisted on taking the 12th again.

And after yet another glass of wine, Captain Berger and I continued to talk for awhile until his batman came in to report that he had checked the horse and put a bandage on his lower right leg where it had two scratches, probably from the close call with the fighter planes. My horse deserved a medal for having received his first wound in battle.

Thanks to all the wine we had consumed, I felt quite

Oath of Allegiance

tired at this point. Captain Berger was still talking with me when the field telephone rang. The sergeant who answered suddenly shouted into the room, "*Stellungswechsel, Herr Hauptmann* - change of position!" The place immediately turned into a beehive of activity. Everyone was on the move packing and loading materials into vehicles. Thank goodness my things were still packed but where was my horse Roberto? My head was spinning like crazy. I sat down for awhile until someone came with my horse. But every time I tried to climb on top of Roberto, he gingerly moved away from me. He seemed to sense that I was not in any condition to be riding. I apologized to Roberto for not being my orderly self, but he stubbornly continued to avoid me. Finally I got a hoist from one of the gunners, only to slide off the other side. The captain who had been joined by one of the battery officers, stood in the doorway laughing at my clumsiness. *Unteroffizier Dietz,*" he howled, *Sie sind ein Stück Scheisse.*" Referring to my drinking episode he said, "I thought you had front experience." I had to admit I felt like a piece of shit, as he had said.

How I made the all-night, 24 kilometers retreat I don't know. I must have actually passed out at some point because when I regained consciousness, I found myself lying between the steel trails of a gun carriage as if in a coffin at a state funeral. The gunners told me later that the captain ordered them to place me there. I barely remember hearing the sounds of planes flying overhead followed by explosions and men screaming. There, between the steel trails of the 15 centimeter field howitzer, I probably was in one of the most secure and best protected positions.

When the battery commander finally came looking for me, I figured that I would be sent straight to the detention battalion. However, all he said was, *Mann muss den Wein mässig trinken, aber regelmässig* - "One must drink the wine with caution, regularly but with caution." Perhaps his down to earth attitude was what made him such a popular battery commander.

June 6th, 1944

As I said earlier, the ordinary soldier who obeys and executes orders is only interested with that which concerns him directly. Most of the time he does not even know his senior officers. When I was in Ukraine I became aware of the name of our divisional commander when he was replaced. He was of Prussian nobility and felt himself to be destined by divine providence. Our commander in Italy, a major general, was known by every frontline soldier. He wore short pants, had bowed legs, wore the Knights' Cross around his neck and spent more time in the front line than in his command post. He took over the command of a company when they were about to run away. This reminded me of Frederick the Great when he chastised his fleeing soldiers by screaming, "Come on you scoundrels, you don't want to live forever."

The invasion of Europe - D Day - took place June 6, 1944, while I was on my way to Pescara. I had just arrived in Porto Recanati a few kilometers from Ancona. In the distance I noticed a procession of people moving up a road leading to a church on top of the hill. At first I presumed they were people evacuating Ancona in anticipation of what might soon be coming. I looked through my field glasses and noticed children carrying banners. Suddenly I understood what was going on. The church was the famous place of pilgrimage, Loreto, where the *Litaniae Lauretanae* originated. I was very anxious to see the place myself and was able to persuade my companions to join me.

We left our baggage at the *Soldaten Heim* and began our pilgrimage to the shrine high on top of the hill. I remember it was a hot day for June. When we finally arrived at the church, we noticed a guard house at the entrance of the little town and cloister. There was a military policeman standing outside next to a poster which said that the place was under the protection of the Vatican, and according to the rules we had to deposit our weapons before entering the holy halls of the Franciscan community. It was from a guard at Loreto that I learned of the invasion which had taken place a few days earlier. When we entered the ancient basilica filled with pilgrims, the congregation had just started singing the Litany - *refugium peccatorum, ora pro nobis*, - Refuge of the sinners, pray for us - At the end of the vesper service the cantor gave the tone and we all sang the beautiful chant, *Salve Regina*. This whole scene brought me right back to the monastery where I spent three of my school years as a young boy.

The days continued without much change. I was sitting in our observation bunker on a hill overlooking a valley watching the grenades exploding from an enemy mortar company. I tried desperately to locate their position as their bombs were targeting our infantry company. The view over the Gran Sasso, the highest mountain in the Abruzzi, was actually quite fascinating, while to the right of us was the most beautiful sunset in the mountains. I told the lieutenant who had just arrived a few hours earlier that the magnificent scenery of the valley was not quite appropriate for our fighting position.

The lieutenant was to be the new forward observation officer. I took out the map to show him where the infantry battalion command post had taken shelter, since he had to find it early that morning. He stretched out in the corner for awhile to rest and collect his thoughts before sunrise. He had to plan the counter attack against the enemy positions on the other side of a dried up riverbed. A couple of hours later a phone call came from the regimental adjutant. He said that Lieutenant Goerdeler was to report immediately to regimental headquarters.

We began to wonder what in hell was going on. The lieutenant had just come to take over his post and before he started they were already calling him away. The battery commander soon arrived after a session with the commanders of the infantry regiments. He spread out a map to show Lieutenant Goerdeler where to go early in the morning. I informed Captain Berger about the phone call and he shook his head in disbelief. Then he ordered me to get ready. He showed me the positions on the map and told me to leave right away so that *Oberwachtmeister* Gössl could get a chance for an hour of sleep before the attack. I was to relieve him for a few days after the attack.

The 'Roving Gun' at night
Oil sticks on paper
R. Dietz

Chapter Fifteen

What the Germans did not destroy when they moved out, the allies destroyed when they moved in.

As I prepared to leave on my assignment, the captain added, "This is your chance, but tomorrow drink water, not wine. It will be a hot day." I packed my necessary equipment, grabbed my automatic pistol, saluted the captain, and shook his hand. He wished me *Hals und Beinbruch* saying, "There will be a lot of iron flying around tomorrow."

With a "Jawohl, Herr Hauptmann," I was on my way. By the light of the bright shining moon, I sneaked through fences, bushes, olive trees, and vineyards. I passed a platoon of our infantrymen who were filling the ammunition belts of their hungry MG 42s, the best weapons the infantry had on hand. I had heard tanks along the way and I asked the soldiers where they were. They laughed at me, saying those tanks belonged to the Tommies. I did not realize that we were so close to the front line. I found it extraordinary that we who were about to attack had no tanks. The other side was not yet aware that today was their turn to be on the defensive, to be attacked by a worn out, unenthusiastic, disappointed, and under-equipped Panzer corps that had hardly any tanks left.

Finally, I found *Oberwachtmeister* Gössl of the 12th Battery on whose knowledge, experience, and audacity our attacking infantry battalion would succeed or fail. As far as I could see, there was no other support than the heavy and light field artillery.

The *Oberwachtmeister* smiled when he saw me coming.

After all, my artillery know-how and experience I learned from watching him on the Russian front rather than from reading the artillery instruction manual. I recalled that he used to make fun about his position as forward observer when we were retreating. He said he felt like, "the red light on a caboose." In any case, I always felt better and more secure beside him than with anybody else. I was his apprentice in Russia, and he could depend on me.

While we were studying our maps, a tough-looking *Oberleutnant* joined us to go over details. I was surprised that he was in charge of the infantry battalion. The last time I had seen a major at the head of a battalion was in a garrison. Then, the battalion was at full strength with about 750 men. This *Oberleutnant* commanded only the 160 men left.

I wondered what the casualty count would be during this 24-hour period. It was now past four in the morning. Most of the men were lying around chewing on a piece of salami which they ate with some stale bread. They sipped from the canteen which hung from their belts. Some canteens were filled with ersatz coffee, others with vino.

There were four of us artillery men, including myself. We were lying behind an ox cart loaded with empty barrels and could still smell their former content. There was no danger the straw lying on the ground would catch fire because it was wet and smelt as if a few nervous bladders had been emptied over it already.

Our observation officer, *Oberwachtmeister* Gössl gave us final instructions. I was to follow him and his two radio operators as backup - in other words, to take over if he were to fall. I pointed out the spot on the map where I had seen the enemy mortar position which was to be our first target. Just as we finished our briefing session, the man-made thunder and lightening from our own artillery started.

We tightened our helmets and hit the ground while the grenades and shells flew over our heads. Some came so close that I worried they would end up striking our own infantry lines which were in front of us.

We radioed back for corrective action. The enemy responded to our artillery fire with the same vehemence and their shells came quite close to the ox cart behind which we were hiding. Gössl ordered us to move ahead so that we were positioned right under the arch of shells from both sides flying by us. He did this because the best protection is to move as close as possible to the enemy infantry line. (Attacks were normally preceded by heavy artillery preparations not only to keep the opposite infantry in their holes but also to create shell craters to provide cover for the attacking assault troops.)

About 100 meters to the right, one of our infantry platoons was ordered to spread out. Their battalion leader was shouting at the sergeant in charge that his men were huddled together like a bunch of scared chickens under the mother hen. I could hear the platoon leaders shouting orders amidst the confusion. We were now directing the fire of our heavy field howitzers into the mortar position and to the spot where the tanks and armoured vehicles were hidden.

Finally the artillery barrage died down and while the *Oberwachtmeister* gave new orders to move the artillery fire 500 meters ahead, the signal for the 3rd Company came, "*Sprung auf, marsch, marsch!*," and the whistles of the platoon leaders shrilled through the dusty and smoke filled air.

With astonishing speed a pathetic looking lot of worn out boys moved through the dried up river bed, at first on foot, then on their knees and finally on their elbows and stomachs to avoid the cross-fire of bullets from the enemy machine guns.

With every command of, "*Auf, marsch, marsch!*" fewer soldiers jumped up and more remained motionless on the ground. I was terrified. It was more my fear than the orders which made me run. When I used my automatic pistol, it was as if it was meant for the one who invented *dulce et decorum est pro patria mori* and not for the one I was aiming at. Our brave 3rd Company led by a young lieutenant barely 20 years old made it into the vineyards where we were pinned down by heavy machine gun fire while the enemy tanks moved further down from us across the river, an area infested with mines. The second platoon got into the mortar position almost before we stopped firing our howitzers. They were no longer scared chickens but fierce fighting cocks. Then suddenly, we heard the roaring, deafening, demoralizing noise of the *Nebelwerfer* rocket launchers. The allied forces called them 'Moaning Minnies.' They went over our heads into the tank area. At first I thought the *Stalinorgel* was here. The rocket launchers spit their deadly rockets right into the crossing point of the tanks which kept on moving with our mines exploding underneath them and our rockets firing above their heads. Not too many tanks were left behind. The mines were exploding, but not the tanks. Even with shrapnel whizzing by us, we managed to gain almost two kilometers of ground when our weakening infantry was stopped by fierce fighting enemy units. I believe it was the Polish division that was on the other side.

Le dejeuner sur l'herb (after Monet).
Gun Leader with gun crew.

Our situation became hopeless when the tanks got across and moved right up to our backs. There was dust, smoke, and fire in front of us when the battalion commander asked for cover for our retreat. This was now easier said than done, especially when the enemy tanks were already blocking the road to safety. It was only the degree of invisibility, through the dust and smoke which gave us a chance to slip through a small section of the river that was not yet mined.

I carried the radio equipment for one of the operators on my back. His arm was bleeding badly from a wound he had just received. I was suddenly knocked to the ground by a big bang. As grim as our situation was, *Oberwachtmeister* Gössl jokingly accused me of using expensive equipment to protect my backside. The set was completely destroyed but I only received a minor injury. Had I not carried the radio set, I would be in a wheelchair today. We managed to find some shelter in a ditch where I tore off the sleeves of my tunic to wrap around my elbows which were, by this time, in pretty bad shape from crawling on them. There was hardly any skin left.

At nightfall, we descended into the next valley, taking with us whatever we could carry. We took as many wounded as we could, but many more were left behind. Our infantry regiments suffered heavy losses. The 3rd Company led into battle by their young lieutenant was eventually led out by their old staff sergeant. I doubt there were more than 20 men left. After the heat of the battle I took a horse and carriage and went to the rear echelon to have my back and arms checked by a medical officer (M.O.). Along the way to the mountain village where he was located I picked up another wounded soldier. The M.O. used the rectory beside the church where he flew the familiar Red Cross flag for protection.

I was amused to see that the sergeant major located his battery office next door to the M.O.'s quarters. It seemed obvious that he was protecting himself by being so close to the Red Cross flag.

After the doctor examined my back and bandaged my elbows, I went to the village fountain where I washed and shaved. I even managed to replace my old, tattered uniform with a new one courtesy of the sergeant major. The battery commander then scheduled an inspection for the rear echelon personnel. He was in a miserable mood, not because of the losses from the previous days' battle, as I would have expected, but because of some incredible news he was about to read to us. The message from the High Command of the Armed Forces said that there was an attempt to assassinate our Führer. It went on to say that the attempt had failed and all the criminal elements amongst the German nobility and generals of the army had been captured and executed. This had happened a few days earlier, on July 20th.

I did not learn until much later that Dr. Carl Goerdeler, the former Lord Mayor of Leipzig, was one of the prominent figures they had executed. Our former observation officer, Lieutenant Goerdeler was a close relative of his. No one dared mention his name or ask questions about his early departure from our ranks. He probably met the same fate as the rest of the Goerdeler family. The army was now under the command of the powerful Heinrich Himmler, the SS leader of the Reich. This was a big blow to the professional officers corps. It was then that Himmler introduced the Nazi salute called, *der Deutsche Gruss*, the German salute. This, of course, was an insult to the Officers' Corps. Many high ranking officers were dismissed, some were executed, while others took their own lives.

Some front officers tried to avoid the new salute in interesting ways. Some just avoided saluting altogether, others combined the Nazi salute with the traditional German officer's salute by stretching out their arms in the air and on the way down stopping with their hand at their hat for the salute.

We also received another message from the High Command; anyone who fell into the hands of the enemy without having been wounded first, was to be considered a deserter. Next of kin would be held responsible. This was both new and extraordinary. It was clear that only if we were prepared to die would we be worthy to live - to sacrifice my life as a brave soldier. – Oath of Allegiance.

Oath of Allegiance

While I was recuperating at the rear echelon, in a charming little mountain village in the Apennine, I was not on holidays, but not yet fit for frontline duty. The sergeant major had an opportunity to place his fit N.C.O.s and other men for duty elsewhere. One of my first assignments was to supervise the digging of a few trenches for reinforcements around the village and facing the frontline which would be useful for protection if retreat was necessary. I made the village men do their work at night under natural moonlight to avoid detection by air.

One of our corporals had some problems with his team when a local parish priest appeared. The priest apparently persuaded some of the villagers to run away. When the priest tried to do the same thing the following night, I told the corporal to arrest him and give him a shovel too. The priest put up a fuss and demanded to speak to the person in charge. With my modest knowledge of Latin, I could make out that he insisted as a man of prayer that he could not be treated like this and forced to work. I reminded him of the rules of Saint Benedict - *Ora et Labora*.
What was good for Saint Benedict was good enough for the priest, too. But he would not give up. He insisted that today was a day of rest, it was Sunday and no one works on Sunday.
E un giorno di riposo, il settimo giorno, la domenica, non lavoriamo, he kept insisting. I ignored his demonstrations and told him to get to work or else. After that, nobody ran away and that was how I persuaded the community to follow the rules of Saint Benedict.

My next assignment was to assemble a troop of 12 armed men on horseback and two men ready to operate a MG42 machine gun from a double-wheeled carriage. I carried an automatic pistol strung over my shoulder. We were to check out partisan activity somewhere in the mountains, but my principal orders were to assist some men of the organization *Todt* - work crews - in rounding-up cattle from the neighbourhood villages for the army's slaughter house. An army needs a lot of food, and the supply for the German Army in Italy came almost exclusively from Italy. I now became an official 'cattle rustler'. I found it disgusting that I had to stand by and see the peasant folk being robbed of their precious cows and oxen. These were heartbreaking scenes. I just was not made of the proper stuff to handle over-emotional Italian peasant women who had all the saints mentioned in the *Litania di tutti santi* on their side. I was glad when after a few days, the job was done. I was assigned to the battery post to take over the second gun.

I can't say that my new posting was an ideal job either, especially as the battery was on the march to a new destination and under air attack. It wasn't easy to hold together a gun carriage and a barrel carrier when eight horses were attached to each vehicle. While fighter bombers dove toward us like hungry hawks, we shouted at drivers, gunners, and all the horses until we reached our new post.

I experienced quite a few disasters as a gun leader. On one occasion, as soon as we were set-up, the enemy artillery showered us with what seemed to be every shell they had on hand. I could not figure out how they had detected us so quickly, but thank God, we had only a few casualties.

We would normally relocate our gun post during the night in order to avoid enemy air observation during the day. As it was, however, we moved out under the light of flares which were dropped by Britain's Desert Air Force[17] before the bombings.

It was about this time that the unified allied command (Canada and Britain), introduced the use of searchlights on their front lines. We were helpless because these lights were located out of ordinary field artillery range. We had no long-range artillery nor any air force that could challenge them. This had a demoralizing effect on us and the element of surprise often caught us with our pants down. As it happened, the relocation of our battery became a *disastro dopo il terremoto*. –disaster after an earthquake.

I remember quite vividly how my heavy howitzer - some 6.000 kilos - flipped over with the heavy horses dead or wounded lying there as if still in tow. The drivers screamed in panic

The Gun Leader, heavy field artillery Gun carriage, Horse drawn, 8 horses, 4 drivers, Barrel carrier, horse drawn, 8 horses, 4 drivers; 5 gunners. Riding horse for Gun leader.

"Haaah...avanti, ...aaa..vanti!" as they beat the dead and half dead horses. The cursing and swearing of the battery officer and gun leaders echoed throughout the night while everyone passed the blame as they shouted to the next person down the line. It became a hopelessly chaotic situation in which nobody was unable to untangle anything at all. I realized then that I had been much better off a few days earlier in my role of 'cattle rustler'.

There is no ideal place free of danger in a war zone, be it on the front line or in the rear echelon. A passport to heaven or hell comes with every assignment and the position one is in when one leaves this world does not really matter. The soldier grows to care not. I was now a gun leader without a gun, without a heavy field howitzer. I was a warrior at large but not for long, not when one is a *Fahnenjunker Unteroffizier*.

As a *Fahnenjunker* (officer cadet) one is often in a disadvantageous position. First there is the matter of age. An officer cadet is young, and has difficulty gaining the proper respect when put in charge. He is expected to fill any position held by a non commissioned officer with the exception of administrative positions such as Sergeant Major. Sometimes, in cases of emergency, they are assigned to replace junior officers; for example, the platoon leader in the infantry, or the forward observation officer in the artillery. Either one of those positions requires frontline experience and is no place for those who might experiment or make mistakes. The latter privileges are reserved for Generals. Even with frontline experience, the *Fahnenjunker* is not always popular with his men who often think of officer cadets as snobs, mainly because they have had a higher school education. There are naturally exceptions.

Still, after a few assignments, and in situations where one man must depend on another, the tension between officer cadet and the lower ranks drops and respect for the 'leader' is established. But there is no room for cowards, especially in a situation where an officer cadet must replace a non commissioned officer previously decorated for bravery.

The officer cadet's relationship to non commissioned officers is even more difficult. After perhaps two years, the officer cadet may take over a position for which the non commissioned officer has trained for as long as ten years. Such a non com knows his army instruction manual inside out and does his job well. Without the support of the non commissioned officers, any cadet, ensign, or junior officer will get into trouble. Non coms usually earn their decorations long before the actual medals are awarded. A cadet fighting beside such a non com cannot afford to be a wimp or a yo-yo.

I was again sent to an observation post to replace a forward observer, of another battery this time. It was our light field artillery. The difference was that being light they were able to move around more easily. I was temporarily attached to them, 'on loan'. Everything else remained the same, even the odds of being killed.

It was another hot day following a rainy week, and with a heavy load of equipment on our backs, we tried desperately to get behind the new lines. We were mostly crawling on our knees and bellies with artillery shells exploding behind and in front of us. From where they actually came was difficult to establish. We had to take cover no matter from what direction they came. Whatever part of your body was sticking out from the rest of you, was shaved off.

Our new lines were established in the next valley. As usual, the line was positioned on the other side of a little river. In this case, it had more water than we had expected because of the recent heavy rainfall. Guided by the engineers of our Pioneer Company, who were already in the process of mining the river and its banks, we got across.

No sooner had we crossed the river when we came upon a group of medics bent over a young chap who had stepped on a mine. It must have been a mine which had had its marker removed by the strong current of the swelling river. The wounded man twitched and twisted on the muddy ground, moaning and crying out for his mother.

I looked around and when I saw that nobody from my troop was missing, we dashed toward a farm house surrounded by trees and bushes. It looked like an oasis in the desert.

But there was already a lieutenant preparing to put his antitank guns in position. Therefore, we kept running toward a small elevation quite suitable for a new observation post. I wiped the sweat from my brow with the torn sleeve of my shirt just as a new barrage of shells came whistling above us, tearing tree trunks and branches to shreds. Some exploded in front of the stone wall of a stable. They flung up clouds of rocks, dust, roots, and earth leaving behind white and yellow clouds and the peculiar smell of a close-by explosion. It was like the touching of two live electrical wires.

As the shelling eased, I had thoughts of night or death hoping to embrace me soon, but then again, I did not want to die. Perhaps I could exchange an arm or a leg for a bed in any army hospital at home. Then I remembered having read in my last letters from home how they had begun bombing the smaller towns, destroying churches and cultural monuments. I read how they aimed their bombs at heavily populated areas. Are they so inhuman? I wondered. I had forgotten about Rotterdam and Coventry and London. I had forgotten too about our own treatment of prisoners, especially those from the Slavic nations, those Hitler considered less than human. Slavic - slaves.

But there must be a way out. Perhaps the new secret weapon, the V-2 would end it all. Rumour had it that the V-2 was more effective than the V-1. It was the effectiveness of this new weapon that provoked the hope that the war must be over soon.

These were my thoughts as we reached the steps of a small house. It turned out to be occupied by a middle aged couple and their two daughters. They were evacuees from a nearby city.

Three of us went inside while the others kept watch outside.

The youngest girl, I believe her name was Tina, gave us water and bread. Her mother brought a few grapes, and the father, to my surprise, brought out a long stick. He poked up and down, around the chimney, and then withdrew a decent sized salami. I could not believe it! I thought I was dreaming. He said, "This is our last salami," and began cutting a slice for everyone of us including the boys outside. I noticed one of my boys eyeing the one left-over end piece of salami. I knew he wanted it, so I looked at him sternly. He understood that I meant business and did not attempt to touch it. Our padrone also caught on and smiled.

I noticed too that the older of the two daughters sat in the corner with her arms clenched around a box covered with dark brown canvas. She held it as if she were guarding the crown jewels of Emperor Vittorio Emmanuele himself. When I approached her and touched her arm, she said in a trembling voice, *Per favore, per favore, non tocchi il mio violino.* She was frightened, and continued, *Non rompa il mio violino, lei puo far male a me, ma non al mio violino!*

I understood her plea - "please don't touch my violin, you can hurt me, but not my violin." I embraced her and assured her that no harm would come to her or her violin.

Her passion and love for her instrument brought tears to my eyes too and when we left, I made sure I was the last. We embraced each other one by one, and Pina, the owner of the violin, whispered a few words to me which I did not understand and kissed me.

I was thrown off balance. When I reached the door, her father pulled at my arm and pointed to a cover on the floor which lead to what looked like a cellar. *Noi vi nasconderemo qui fino alla fine di guerra!* - "we will hide you here till the war is over!" he said.

I was stunned, shocked. For a moment I didn't know how to respond. He was lucky no one else was within earshot, he took a terrible risk. He could have been shot for inviting me to desert.

In this short moment, I faced my situation. I found myself at the crossroads with no sign pointing the 'right' direction. Again there were two souls in my breast. '...the one which robust love desires clings to the world with all his might. The other fiercely rises from the dust to reach sublime ancestral regions.'

I was aware of the fact that for some time now I had been fighting for a cause in which I did not believe. I had different ideals. I thought of my Oath of Allegiance. "I swear by God..." But even God did not seem to know what he had gotten himself into. Surely I would be forgiven for not keeping this oath. Hitler was now in the process of sacrificing the whole youth of Germany for his cause. Nor was I interested in dying for the generals who had not received as yet the Swords to the Oak Leaves to the Knight's Cross of the Iron Cross, or even the Marshal's staff. None of that was good enough reason to go on fighting. But I did think of my comrades who were fighting with me and beside me. I could never let them down. I could not let them remember me as a deserter or as a coward even though I was perhaps cowardly, though no more so than others who take the credit for being heroes. And there was also the matter of Hitler's latest order - *Sippenhaft* - to punish the families of deserters.

I had to make a decision at that very moment. I looked into Pina's eyes. They made my heart accelerate, but even she would not play her violin for a deserter. I then saw the eyes of my comrades. Their eyes were like those of animals waiting to be slaughtered. No, no there was no choice other than to remain and help my comrades.

So, with the usual, *"Grazie, Signore,* for your hospitality and kind offer."

"Arrividerla, signora, arrividerla, signorina Pina e Tina."

I left hurriedly to catch up with my B crew feeling ashamed about the thoughts and doubts I just had.

We reached our destination at midnight without further incident. We arrived with detonations of artillery shells. I found a corner in a deserted hut which I selected for my crew for the night. I took off my boots, used my rolled up blanket for a pillow, covered myself with my uniform jacket, and fell into a deep sleep.

When I awoke, I thought again of the wonderful family I had met. I could not understand why they would offer me

Oath of Allegiance

shelter, a soldier of the nation that was responsible for all the misery and destruction that was taking place. I had to change my mind about the Italian people whose military accomplishments were not their forte. They had big hearts. They saw their two-thousand-year- old cultural heritage being destroyed by war. The Germans on one side claimed to defend their - the Italian - *cultura* against the evil of the invaders. The allied forces, on the other hand, were liberating the Italian people from the evil of fascism. In the process, death and destruction became the order of the day. Both parties came up with the most legitimate excuse to blow up bridges, buildings, or whatever else was in their way. Entire communities were destroyed. One called it, "the scorched earth policy." Every bridge in the Abruzzi mountains and in the valley was blown up to delay the advance of the Allied divisions. It didn't matter if the bridge was a thousand years old. Bombs were planted like land mines on narrow, winding, mountain roads. The explosions left yawning craters and cut one village off from another. What the Germans did not destroy when they moved out, the allies destroyed when they moved in. The ones that suffered most were the poor Italian peasants, the farmers and the vintners. Their work was interrupted for months until their rivers, roads, and fields were cleared of mines, debris and live ammunition. Of course the bridges and the roads had to be rebuilt.

Rocket launcher, 'Moaning Minni'.

Observation post near San Marino.
Observation officer without shirt. Fhj. Unteroffizier, top right.

Chapter Sixteen

The Major asked, "Are they wearing pants or skirts?"
The General replied, "Rifles and grenades."

One did not need to be a military expert to see what was building up in the area of Rimini, Riccione, and the tiny Republic of San Marino. Although I was only an ordinary 'rabbit' in the field belonging to the 12th Battery of the 278th Artillery Regiment of the 278th Berlin Brandenburg Grenadier Division of the 76th Panzer Korps of the 10th Army under Colonel General Heinrich von Vietinghoff, I could see that the battle of Rimini was soon to commence. In preparation for this battle, several artillery observation posts had to be established. The most advantageous position would be located in one of the medieval towers in the little town of San Marino on Mount Titano's triple peak some 740 meters above sea level and only six kilometers from Rimini, once one of the most beautiful, medieval towns on the Adriatic coast.

San Marino, with its population of some 20,000 (4,000 in the town itself), is said to be the oldest republic in the world. Free and independent since 1291, San Marino's neutrality had been respected, and it looked as if this would continue to be the case. As a result, our observation post was located outside the town, on the slopes of Mount Titano. From this vantage point, I had the most fantastic view. I could see the Adriatic coast, around San Martino, and along the Martino and Ausa rivers. I could also see all the troop movements. I felt as if I could win the whole Italian war by myself if only I had .... But I was not a general, and had no airplanes and long range artillery.

It was not long before I saw three figures approaching our post. One of them wore short pants and had awfully crooked legs. As I observed him through my field glasses, I realized who he was. "*Himmel Donnerwetter,*" I called out to the Observation Officer, "*das is der Herr Kommandeur, der Herr General!*" Before we were able to pull ourselves together and straighten out our little bunker, he had already appeared. "Carry on," he said as he walked over to the telescope without waiting to listen to the lieutenant's report. He explained to the two accompanying officers, one a lieutenant colonel, the other a major, the situation taking place some 700 meters below us. The two officers were the commanders of two of the three infantry regiments of our division. I overheard the general explain what we might expect within the next few days. At the foot of the mountain was the 46th British division coming from Montescudo. To their right was the 56th and the armoured division with the Gurkha brigade, the first Canadian Corps was between Corriano and Riccione with the Greek Mountain Brigade at the shore. Between them were one or two regiments of *Neuschottländer* - Nova Scotians.

The Major asked, "Are they wearing pants or skirts?"

The General replied, "Rifles and grenades."

I recall the general saying, "*Meine Herren, das ist kein Kinderspiel!*" (Gentlemen, that is no child's play!)

Even I could see that there was more steel and iron packed into a small area at the foot of this mountain than throughout the rest of the Italian front. It certainly was *kein Kinderspiel.*

I thought of the poor people of Rimini who were still making their way up the mountain in large processions to seek refuge within the borders of the neutral Republic of San Marino.

Oath of Allegiance

There was a lot of tension in the air, but the weather was good, a nice change from all the rain we had lately. When I looked through the donkey-eared telescope as the general had earlier, I noticed two destroyers some distance away in the blue waters of the Adriatic. I also saw a reconnaissance plane circling around. It worried me a bit. I was confident, however, that the English would respect the neutrality of the Republic of San Marino as we had done. At least I thought we did because we were not staked out in a church tower within the little town. We were on the slopes of Mount Titano. In any case, who could blame our field commanders for taking advantage of the situation. I thought as long as the Desert Air Force respected the neutrality, I would stay alive.

I noticed some movement taking place around the Republic of San Marino close to the Adriatic coast. I suggested to the observation officer that we were too exposed and should disguise our position much better than we had. I ordered the rest of the crew not to step out anymore without proper camouflage.

Naturally I could not give orders to the lieutenant who simply told me, "Don't shit in your pants, *Herr Unteroffizier.*" To which I replied, "That would not be possible since I emptied myself only a half hour ago." He made me furious so I took out my frustrations on the crew, shouting at them all the things I wanted to say to the lieutenant. I even threatened to shoot anyone who went outside without a proper disguise. At least that made them, and the lieutenant, look for their shirts and other gear. At 20, I was the senior man in the group who had the most frontline experience and had already been wounded three times.

Soon the cannonade of the artillery facing each other down below grew fiercer. The continuous shooting was frequently mixed with the dreadful noise of the 'Moaning Minnies.' The *Nebelwerfer* 18 were usually placed at critical points of action which, in our case, was to our left where the parachute division was in position. It was an elite unit under Major General Heidrich. While the crew kept themselves busy with improving our bunker, I was preparing the map and entering the positions of troop gatherings, tanks and other vehicles. I especially noted artillery. I had never before seen so much from any observation post. We were able to observe many activities around us: troop movements, tank hide-outs, artillery going into position, and clearly marked ambulances that usually gave away the places they came from and the places they were headed.

There was a lot of traffic towards San Martino where the *Kanacken* - Canucks - gave our 29th Panzer and 1st Parachute Division a hard time. Both divisions were there because, as one of our divisional commanders expressed it, *die verdammten Kanacken müssen im Schach gehalten werden.* (The damn Canucks have to be kept in place.) I learned this from a conversation between the commander of our division and the commanders of our infantry regiments.

It was said that one of our Grenadier Regiments had to be moved into the *Brennpunkt* (burning point or point of action) to prevent the Canucks from cutting us off. We were quite happy that the Canadians were not in front of us. At that moment, I definitely preferred the Tommies of the 46th Armoured Division, but when night fell, the activities below and in front of us became no *Kinderspiel* either.

Illuminating flares went up on both sides, and the snap and scream of high velocity tank gun shells coming from built-in Tiger turrets on our side, and tank cannons from the other side, pierced the evening sky. Explosions of artillery and mortar shells provided a symphony of 'sound' in this fantastic battle in which the rattling of machine guns made us aware that there was also a part orchestrated for the infantry.

Our observation post became a busy place. Certainly, it was not big enough to accommodate the traffic within.

We tried to locate new enemy artillery positions while sending our light and heavy field artillery shells in irregular intervals to points we had discovered during the day. (Irregular intervals in order to surprise the enemy.) This went on throughout the night, and at sunrise, fumes, and clouds of dust caused by all the explosions covered the terrain in front of us. It became a shell-riven battlefield.

It was impossible to observe any moving vehicles such as tanks and armoured cars. Only smoke and dust clouds could be seen. But to our surprise, there was nothing moving around the San Martino area. When I brought this to the attention of the observation officer, Lieutenant Schultz said, "It fell into the hands of the Canadians." I believe it was September 19th when Colonel General Heinrich von Vietinghoff recorded "...*eine Materialschlacht von grösstem Umfang*...". "(...a battle of materiel of the greatest magnitude....)"

The lieutenant took charge of the telescope and I gave him the distances. He was waiting to hear from the battery post, *Batterie Feuerbereit!* - (Battery ready to fire!) In order to avoid detection, we stopped using our radio and used the field telephone instead. While another observation officer looked through the telescope, I peered through my field glasses waiting to see where our first salvos would land. The explosions of the infantry weapons grew stronger with the rattling of the machine guns mixed with the sounds of the *Nebelwerfer*. I don't know why, but I had a confident feeling when I heard the dueling of machine guns with our Mg 42s shooting much faster. We would have had a greater advantage if only we had our air force and long-range artillery. Suddenly, one of the crew pointed to the sky as two airplanes approached. They turned toward Rimini and turned again, perhaps avoiding our 8.8 flak anti-aircraft cannons below. Finally, the message from the gun post came through loud and clear, "*Batterie Feuerbereit!*"

Before I realized it, one of the aircraft made a steep dive toward us. Flashing lights, a black dot getting bigger, shells, explosions, explosions......

When I first regained consciousness I was groggy. I thought I was once again laying on an ox cart, listening as someone calling "Avanti! Avanti!" But as my head cleared, I found I was laying on a bed of straw beneath which was a stone floor.

As it turned out, I was not in a stable but in a little village church. I could hear other casualties moaning and groaning all around me as I watched medics bringing in the wounded and taking others out. When I saw a chaplain closing someone's eyes, I shivered beneath my blanket. *Requiescat in Pace.* There was no organ playing but there was the roaring sound of artillery firing in the air.

    I tried getting the attention of a medic, and it was then that I realized I could not speak - I could not make a sound with my voice! I was laying close to a side altar which had a statue of Saint Francis of Assisi. He was depicted in the traditional pose, that of Saint Francis preaching to the birds and animals. He had such a kind, plain face and looked as if he was content to be poor. Since he appeared to be talking to the animals, I pretended that he was talking to me as well. After all, I was laying on straw and could not speak.

    I must have passed out because when I again awoke I was in another strange place with an intravenous tube in my veins and a young nurse leaning over me. She introduced herself as Dottore Fanfani. She was a doctor, and she tried to talk to me but I could not give her a coherent answer. I was becoming very worried about my condition, and wondered if my inability to speak was a temporary or permanent condition.

    After the doctor left, I looked at my chart hanging above my head, in order to find out my diagnosis. It said - *Aphasia, commotio cerebri.* Applying the little I learned in school about the ancient languages, I had no difficulty in figuring out that I had a loss of speech as a result of a shake-up of my brain. I could not find out what had actually happened to me.

    A few days later I tried to walk a bit through the corridors of the field hospital, but I found that I was just as insecure walking as I was speaking. I made it to the end of the hall where I sat down on a bench in front of the statue of another Franciscan monk, Saint Anthony of Padua. The field hospital was outside of Padua where Anthony, the Portuguese monk, was buried in 1231. Anthony was known for finding lost articles. I thought that perhaps he could help me find my ability to speak. I recall my mother saying to me once when I lost some coins, "If you pray to Saint Anthony, you will find it." At the same time my father would mumble under his breath, "If you

Oath of Allegiance

bend down and open your eyes, you will find it sooner." Perhaps both answers were right.

I don't know why I became so religious all of a sudden. I could not have had a loss of memory because I still was able to remember all kinds of prayers and poetry, especially parts of Goethe's Faust which I had to memorize in school.

> "....Why are humility and lowliness the finest
> gifts of loving bounteous nature...."

Perhaps it was my state of depression, or was it a kind of weakness as in catching a cold when one is without proper immunity and therefore more receptive to diseases? It was perhaps the same with my psyche - there was no resistance. I guess I was in the ideal condition to be brainwashed if taken prisoner.

Whatever was wrong with me, I became a great admirer of Saint Francis, not because he was poor, but because he was rich and embraced poverty. I admired his simplicity and the many wonderful canticles he wrote. I was in search of peace and inner contentment.

> "O' Divine Master, Grant that I may not seek
> - to be consoled as to console
> - to be understood as to understand
> - to be loved as to love."

I have no idea how long I was in this field hospital, but I started to talk soon after I had a terrifying dream. It was a dream about the two planes approaching our observation post on Mount Titano. I woke up screaming from my nightmare, my whole body in a sweat.

At the same moment as the explosion in my dream occurred, a bomb exploded near the railway yard not far from the field hospital. In some strange way, my dream mixed with reality and cleared my head. When I awoke from the sounds of the explosion, I could speak again.

Luckily, I would be soon well enough to go on the hospital

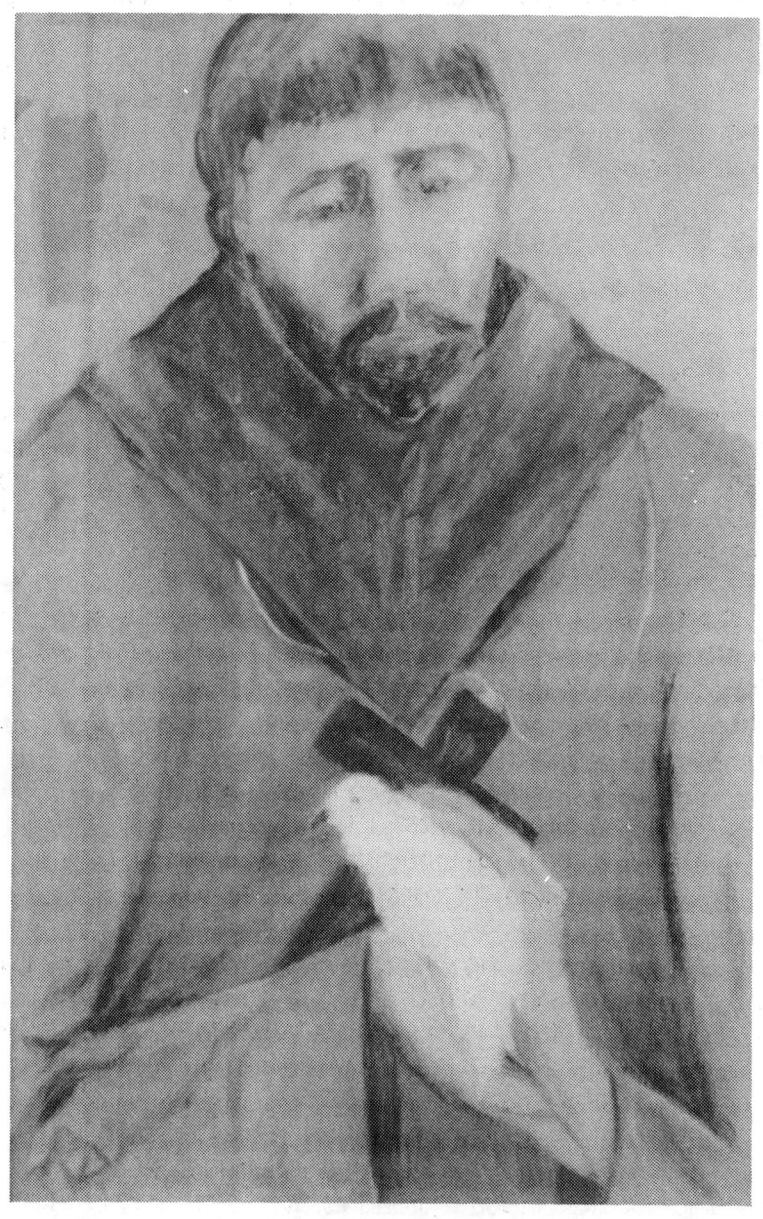

'Saint Francis of Assisi'
R. Dietz
Oil on board
Photo: George Georgakakos
Collection: Dr. Earle and Judith Bain

Oath of Allegiance

train. When we rode near the Brenner Pass along the Austrian-Italian border, I spoke with Goethe again:

"O gentle moonlight, how I wish that you could see the end of all my misery."

I remembered Dottore Fanfani. When she gave me the last glucose injection, she put her hand on my head saying, "*Buona fortuna, Roberto, il sole si leva ancora.*" - Good luck, Robert, the sun will rise again. I remember now how beautiful she was. I wasn't sure who helped me recover the most, Saint Francis, Saint Anthony, or Dottore Fanfani.

I don't remember too much about the train ride through the Italian Alps. It was a subdued atmosphere in the slow moving *Lazarettzug* (hospital train) and with the knocking of the wheels when rolling over the rail joints I hummed without interruption Verdi's chorus from his opera Nabucco:

Va, pensiero, sull'ali dorate;
Va, ti posa sui clivi, sui colli,
Ove olezzano tepide e molli
L'aure dolci del suolo natal!
Del Giordano le rive saluta,
Di Sionne le torri atterate...
Oh, mia patria si bella e perduta!

(Go, my thought, on golden wings;
Go, and lay on hills and valleys
perfumed with the sweet air of my native soil!
Salute the Jordan shores,
The towers of Zion in ruin...
Oh, my fatherland so beautiful and lost!)
Of course, I was thinking of my own fatherland.

The train wound its way through a long tunnel, but at the end of the tunnel there was still darkness. We were entering *Die Ostmark* - Austria, now a part of *Gross Deutschland.* There were no happy and joyous people at the station waving and shouting *Sieg Heil* as they had six years ago when the Austrians returned home to the Reich. Rather, there was an atmosphere of gloom and doom. Large placards announced that Germany would be fighting to the *Endsieg* - to the final victory. They had no idea how many casualties filled this long train moving slowly through the mountain tunnels under the sign of the Red Cross.

I had been in Italy for a period of five months. It was no *Kinderspiel*, no vacation provided by Hitlers *Kraft durch Freude* - strength through joy organization. Neither was it, 'O Sole Mio'. It rained bullets, bombs, and grenades most of the time. I ran, walked, and crawled on my belly, and rode my horse from Pescara to Rimini. Every defence line from the Gustav to the Gothic line was a rendezvous with death. Before they were surrendered, those lines were defended by taking two paces forward and three paces backward through the Abruzzi and Apennine mountains.

Our Brandenburg Grenadier Division with its crest of Frederick the Great met them all: English, Indians, Gurkhas, Poles, and Canadians. At first, we met them face-to-face, and then we had them on our backs chasing us across the Metauro, the Foglia, and the Concha rivers. Sometimes we retreated at the last minute, sometimes the rivers were already seeded with our own mines. I was wounded twice in Italy - my third and fourth injuries out of six during the war.

The defence of the Gothic Line and the Battle of Rimini seems to be remembered only by those who were there. The 76th Panzer Corps of the 10th Army on our side, and on the other side, the 1st Canadian Corps and the 5th British Corps of the 8th Army. When we came home we were asked: how was it in sunny Italy and on the beaches of the Blue Adriatic Sea?

The Germans who fought in Italy were the D-Day, *Drückeberger* and the Canadians were honoured likewise as D-Day Dodgers. According to a former lieutenant of the Cape Breton

Oath of Allegiance

Highlanders, Duncan Fraser, (now a retired professor at Acadia University in Wolfville, Nova Scotia):

"The war in Italy was cruel and dirty. Under-equipped with everything but spirit, guts, and determination, the Canadians in Italy made a reputation as tough and courageous fighters. They slugged victoriously northwards against an implacable, efficient, and seasoned enemy army, through the most difficult and heart-breaking terrain encountered by any army in the Second World War."

According to Volume II, of **The Canadians in Italy**, the 10th Army's condition report for the week ending 25th September reveals that of its 92 infantry battalions, only 10 were classified as 'strong' with more than 400 men; sixteen were said to be 'fairly strong' with 300 to 400 men. There were 26 'average' battalions of 200 to 300; while 38 had less than 200 in all ranks. Two were unreported. These figures provide a striking commentary on the cost of the Gothic line operations to the German 10th Army whose 76 Panzer Corps on 15th September, when the Battle of Rimini still had seven days to run, had reported a total of 14,604 casualties suffered since the begining of the 8th Army's offensive.

Also in the official history of the Canadian Army of the Second World War, Volume II, the Canadians in Italy.

With reference to the battles of Rimini and San Marino, it says:

.....rising more than 740 meters above sea level. It would have been surprising if the Germans had refrained from using such heights to watch the course of the battle and direct the fire of their artillery.

(A 76th Panzerkorps map of 16th September, 1944 shows the enemy's 'Rimini Line' cutting obliquely across the miniature state, and subsequent situation traces reveal the 278th Infantry Division holding positions inside the Republic's boundaries.)

During the early stages of fighting, Colonel General von Vietinghoff reported to Field Marshal Kesselring: "I am told that the 5th Canadian Armoured Division was excellent....though not strong in numbers, the Canadians are right good soldiers."

Field Marshal Albert Kesselring tells us, "....the fighting lasted eight weeks, four to six of them involving big battles in country difficult for the attack. The weather conditions were variable and ran through the whole gamut of northern Italian autumn.

"The fighting was very costly, supplies insufficient, and our resistance for the most part stubborn. Where the attack came up against good divisions, the enemy's efforts and losses were out of all proportion to the result. Supported by technical weapons undreamt of by us and magnificent fighters as they were...."

"THE BATTLE OF THE APENNINES CAN REALLY BE DESCRIBED AS A FAMOUS PAGE OF GERMAN MILITARY HISTORY."

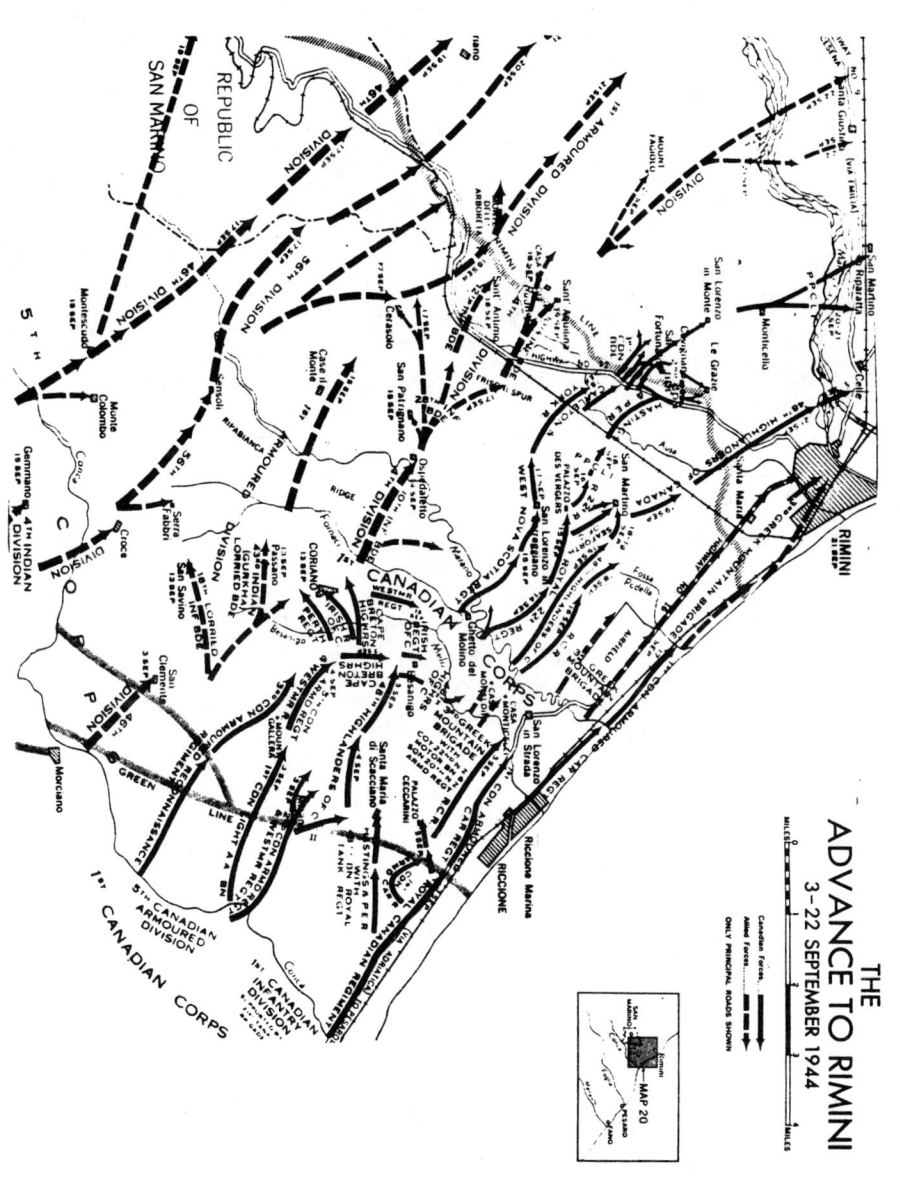

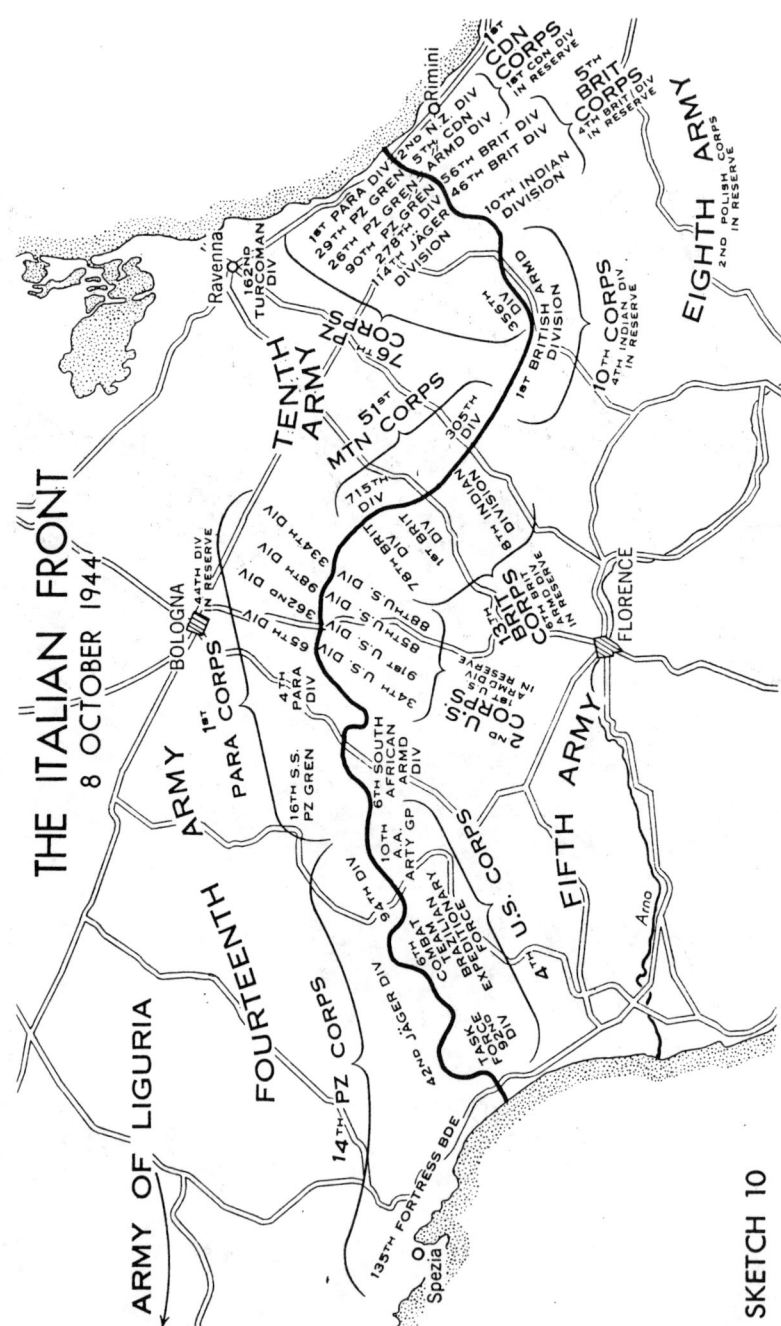

Part Two
Back In The Fatherland

Chapter Seventeen

"There is a higher court before which we all must stand."

After leaving the Brenner Pass, *the Lazarettzug* - the hospital train - moved slowly without interruption through the Austrian Alps. There was little chance of air attack because since "D" Day the area had not been a priority for the allied airplanes. It was rumoured the train was destined for a hospital in the area of Augsburg. I must have been dozing during most of the trip since I have no recollection of the beautiful landscape which so impressed me several months earlier when I made the trip going in the opposite direction. I vaguely recall, however, stopping at Innsbruck where ambulances transferred some of the wounded to the local army hospital.

When the station master lifted his signal to proceed, I thought of Heinrich Isaak's beautiful melody *Innsbruck ich muss Dich lassen* - Innsbruck I must leave you. I must have completely shut myself off from the outside world because I don't know which route we took. I do remember that we did not take a detour through Vienna and Salzburg to get to Munich.

As we approached the Bavarian Plateau, the long train began to travel faster. At Rosenheim I saw the results of the destruction caused by Allied bombers, especially the effort to hit railway stations. The closer we came to Munich, the greater the destruction, and the greater the destruction, the more nu-

merous the victory signs. *Wir kämpfen bis zum Endsieg* - We will fight until the final victory.
Similar signs and posters lay on the rubble heaps where the pride of baroque architecture once stood. The more hopeless the situation looked, the greater was the belief, at least for many, that any time now a secret weapon would be used. There had to be an effective bomb since the V-1 and the V-2 were not quite what they were promised to be.

I remember the train turned south at Augsburg. We arrived at a convent school recently converted to a military hospital. As usual the nuns, most of whom had medical training, provided convenient nursing and administration personnel. Many of the new arrivals were placed on the floor of the gymnasium while I was put into a small room with a lieutenant who was screaming with irregular seizures. I guess I must have been in bad shape too since I ended up in a 'semi-private' room. At the time I did not really understand what was wrong with me. I must have had what one calls 'invisible battle scars' which were until then hardly recognized by any military medical authority. If a frontline soldier cracked up and became hysterical and ran away, he would be executed for 'cowardice before the enemy'.

When everything was settled and calm, I began to have the same thoughts and misgivings about the comrades I had left behind in Italy, as I had about those I left behind in Ukraine the previous year. I constantly thought of the observation post in San Marino and who might have survived. I found out after the war that the lieutenant who had shrapnel wounds in his upper leg and chest died of pneumonia in an Italian hospital. His parents, who lived in my neighbourhood, told me of their son's death. They were desperate for me to tell them everything I could remember about their only son. I found this awkward because I did not know him very well. However, I told them that he was a brave soldier and a good comrade, an example for all of us to follow. I painted a wonderful picture of their son so that the elderly couple could go home in peace and full of pride. What else could I have done?
'De mortuis nil nisi bene.'

During the first two weeks of my stay in the hospital, I

had incredible headaches which prevented me from reading. I was able to enjoy walks in the convent garden, despite the miserable November weather and the gloomy atmosphere created by the graves of nuns from centuries past. I had already seen enough of graves and death.

One day I met the sister superior who said how delighted she was to see me attend the early mass. When she realized I was quite familiar with ecclesiastical matters and enthusiastic about Saint Francis, we met more often to discuss these things. I talked to her about our youth group back home and all our secret activities with my friends. She trusted me enough to tell me all about the student uprising at the University in Munich the previous February. I was, at that time, on the Russian front and unaware of what was happening in Germany. She told me a most shocking story about the young Scholls - Hans and Sophie and their friends. The students printed and distributed leaflets among the university students telling about the horrible war situation and asking their colleagues to resist tyranny and engage in sabotage. All of them were arrested. During their interrogation by the Gestapo, Hans tried very hard to shift the entire blame to himself. His sister, Sophie, displayed the same kind of heroism, trying to save her brother. Her interrogator appeared to show kindness by offering coffee and cigarettes and suggested that had she been aware of the wrong she had done, she would not have engaged in such reckless activity. "You are wrong," replied Sophie. "You are wrong, Herr Mohr. I would do exactly the same thing all over again. It is you, not I, who has the mistaken *Weltanschauung* - political belief."

Hans and Sophie Scholl, together with their friend Christoph Probst, were executed by guillotine. It is recorded that the father of the Scholls leapt to his feet during sentencing and cried out, "There is a higher court before which we all must stand." Sophie was the first to be executed. As recorded, she was stretched out on a wooden rack with her hands tied behind her back. Her brother was the next to be beheaded. Guards remembered how he cried out, *"Lang lebe die Freiheit!"* - Long live freedom. Probst was next in line.[19]

The German historian Golo Mann wrote that their efforts were doomed from the start. "If German resistance had consisted of nobody but the Scholls and their friends, their actions would have been enough to save a little of the honour of those whose tongue is German."

After the sister superior told me about the Scholls I began to understand what the journalist member of our youth group back home tried to tell us when we went into the woods to take our Oath of Allegiance. I realized now too how dangerous it was for my friend Lothar and I to have distributed the pastoral letters of Count Clemens of Galen, the Bishop of Münster. This tragic story about the Scholls and the disappearance of Lieutenant Goerdeler, my former observation officer, really shook me up. From then on, every time I had to lift my right arm for a salute, I felt pain. There must be justification for tyrannicide.

A sister, working as a lab technician, asked me if I would like to help her in the lab. She had been overloaded with work since the arrival of the last train. Of course I was willing to help because she was so friendly and happy looking that it was difficult to refuse. It was better than getting an assignment from the sergeant major. I went and helped her for a few hours each day. I found out that she played the organ during the evening church services so I offered to turn the pages of the sheet music for her. I was surprised by the kind of music she played. I had no objection to Mozart's music, but I tried to bring to her attention the sacrilegious text of the arias in <u>Don Giovanni</u>. She simply said, "God only listens to the beautiful music, we should do likewise." She doubted that any of the sisters had ever read the text of the opera. I finally gave up on her strange theory and thought, "What is good enough for God, is good enough for me."

The few hours a day which I spent with Sister Veronica made me realize that life was worth living, so my revolutionary thoughts had to be put on the back burner for awhile. I thought of Goethe's Faust, "Two souls, alas, dwelling in my breast, each seeks to rule without the other."

I did not see too much of the area around the hospital

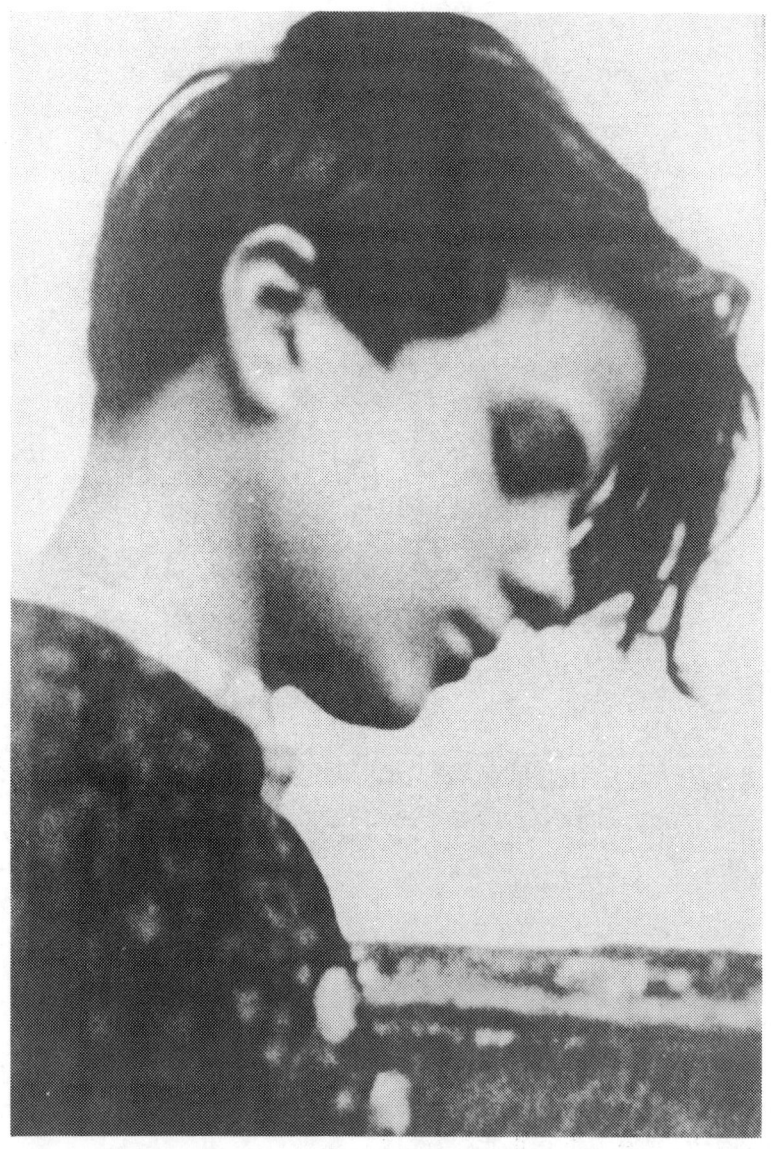

Sophie Scholl, the 'Resistance'

and because of the miserable weather, I stayed inside and made myself useful. My medical records now showed that I was no longer fit for frontline duty so I thought that here was as good a place as any to await the end of the war. Surely, I thought, it cannot last much longer. If I had known what had taken place on the eastern and western fronts during my weeks in transit and hospital, I would not have had these illusions.

Chapter Eighteen

Until then I thought that only Hitler could think of such cruelties.

While the public awaited the introduction of some secret weapon, all the rumours and the ear-to-ear whisperings were quite different. In October, 1944 the Russian armies had invaded East Prussia. They murdered, plundered and raped. It was their way of taking revenge.

One day a special commission of three senior medical officers appeared at the hospital. As I recall, they appeared unannounced. Every patient was commanded to be at the foot of his bed either laying, sitting, or standing, depending on his condition. When asked, he was to present his record chart. The visit was an inspection as well as a re-assessment of the soldiers' fitness for frontline duty. There were two good reasons for such an inspection. First, men had to be sent back to the front where they were badly needed and second, beds were required for the constant flow of new casualties from the front. We used to call this type of commission, *Raus-Schmeiss-Kommando* (Throw-out-commission).

When it was my turn, I remember the *Herr Oberstabsarzt* saying: "You've had enough vacation, fresh air will do you better". So I went from "unfit for front duty" to "fit for front duty under condition", which means one can be sent back to the front but is not expected to fulfill 100 percent of the job requirements. In my case, as it said in my papers, they recommended that I not wear a steel helmet for a long period. This, of course, was nonsense. I used my steel helmet only when there was enough iron in the air to merit its use, and when I slept outside in a dug-out, I always put the steel helmet on my face. I guess it made me feel more secure. Why, I don't know. Perhaps I was scared most of the time. To be perfectly honest, I was scared all of the time, even when I tried to encourage new arrivals who were put in my care. In this case I gave the impression to the younger men that I had no fear. But unless one is brain dead, someone ready for an assault spends the last seconds before he goes over the top saying, "God help me, don't let me down."

I was allowed a few days at home before returning to my artillery unit in Küstrin. The timing was perfect - just before Christmas. But it was not at all what I hoped it would be. I was not aware that a small medieval town like Mayen had become a target for the allied air force. Nor did I know that our town was in the area from which the last great offensive was about to begin.

When I arrived at the Koblenz *Hauptbahnhof* - main railway station, the sirens sounded and bombs just dropped everywhere. There was no difference between military or civilian targets. It was *Totalkrieg* - total war. I grabbed my personal belongings, (coming from a hospital I had no weapons) and ran as fast as I could away from the railway station which was the worst place to be during an air raid. While I was running, I passed by a mother with two little children. At that point I forgot my own problems and could not afford to be a coward. I wrapped one child in my overcoat and kept on going until an army truck stopped and gave us a ride to the next village where the mother and her two little children found shelter at their grandparents' home. I did not accept the invitation to stay and take a rest because I was too anxious to get home and see how things looked there.

It was almost dark. Only the moon gave light not only for me but also for the tanks and trucks that were on the road going west toward the Belgian border. I had almost forgotten what a heavy field howitzer looked like. But these were not the horse-drawn variety, but rather mechanized and motorized heavy field artillery, even self-propelled artillery. I noted that it was a newly outfitted SS Division with mainly new equipment. Where did all this new equipment come from?

When I finally arrived home, I noticed hard lines etched in my family's faces, and I especially noticed my sister Waltraud. These were lines of wear and tear from all they had to go through. I became aware of the fact that the war was no longer at the front but was now at home, in Germany. It became quite obvious that the war would be over sooner if soldiers on the front were demoralized by news of the bombings at home. They would be worried and uncertain whether or not their loved ones were alive or dead.

The following day started with sunshine and soon after it snowed. It covered the roads, the tracks, the tanks, and all the other vehicles left behind. It was December 16, 1944, the beginning of the Ardennen or Rundstedt Offensive.

I don't recall exactly what took place. All I remember was the fact that I had to return soon to my reserve unit east of Berlin, to the fortress of Küstrin where Frederick Wilhelm I once held his own son prisoner.

At Küstrin the situation was doom and gloom too. When I reported my arrival to the garrison sergeant major who was at one time my battery sergeant major, he hardly gave me any time to get settled. He immediately had a new job for me saying, "I always look after my boys."

I had to report to the garrison commander's office to work with the adjutant on an evacuation plan for the civilian population which was kept secret for obvious reasons. It was not my most interesting job but I was told that it was an important part of my career and that a promotion would follow. In any case, I was allowed a short leave for New Year's. Perhaps I would have been excited about a promotion a year ago, in December of 1943, but 1944 was no time to consider a military career.

I was overjoyed to go home again, especially at a time when leave was only granted to a very few. My papers were even signed by the *Kommandeur* himself. I thought I was lucky, and my father could not believe that I was home again. But my luck was soon to run out. The air raid sirens sounded

on New Year's Eve.
We all ran for shelter, taking with us a few necessities, such as food and milk for my baby sister. Waltraud had spent most of that day going from one farm to another in our neighbourhood looking for some milk. She was able to get some in exchange for pieces of her clothing or linen from our inn. I realized that it was Waltraud who made great personal sacrifices to keep the family going.

The population of Mayen had plummeted from the original 18,000 to somewhere around 9,000 by this time. The younger people were drafted and in uniform while others moved to neighbouring villages to avoid air raids on the town. The remaining population, mostly those needed to keep the town functioning, either sought shelter from air raids in their cellars or went to the common bunker - a shelter built underneath the castle in the middle of town. Shafts were driven into the slate stones of the castle hill from three directions. The technique was similar to drilling a mine. There was an average of 17 meters of protection. It was a safe haven designed to adequately accommodate 1350. Usually more than twice that number would run to the bunker during an air raid. I spent one night in there and nearly fainted from lack of air. It was a place where babies were born and old people died. It really shook me up to see what our civilian population had to endure. It made me angry to see signs placed in the bunker proclaiming, *Wir glauben an den Endsieg* - We believe in the final victory. It seemed obvious that the Führer declared war on his own people and anyone who did not want to follow him had no right to exist. I was so outraged that I couldn't take it anymore.

The following night I slept in an abandoned house outside the town. There was no food or heat. It reminded me of the time my mother told my father during supper, "Do not eat so much that you cannot sleep." Of course he always had a fitting answer to my mother's comments - "I prefer not being able to sleep on a full stomach than on an empty one."

I lay awake on this cold night in the middle of winter. I forgot all about the New Year. That was yesterday and I didn't even remember anyone saying "Happy New Year." I must have eventually fallen asleep in the cold room because I finally woke up to a bright, sunny day. I don't know what reminded me of my departure from the hospital in Italy, but I thought of the words Dottore Fanfani spoke as she put her hands on my forehead, "*Buona fortuna, il sole si leva ancora*".

The water tap in the house was still functioning and the cold water which I splashed on my face quickly woke me up. I was very hungry by this time. I went into town to look up my friend, Marlies. Her parents had a butcher shop and, as a result, many other things to eat also. Her mother suggested that we pack a lunch and make use of the sunny day. We soon arrived on top of a hill overlooking the town. We were happy to be alive!

While we were standing on the hill, we looked down toward Mayen where chimney smoke indicated there was still a lot of life - it looked almost as if it was business as usual. As we continued our walk we noticed a swarm of airplanes coming from the west. We started to count these flying fortresses, the name we used because they were huge and had four engines. These planes caused much death and destruction - more to the civilian population in the large cities than to military installations. We wondered where they would drop their load of bombs. Would it be Cologne or some city in the industrial districts? Then two light flares and a few seconds after bombs hailed from the sky towards our town in the Nette Valley.

We were stunned and speechless as we ran toward the clouds of dust and smoke. Each one of us hurried in a different direction toward our home. It was a scene beyond description, watching people running around in a state of panic and shock. Mothers with their children and the elderly climbing over the rubble-strewn streets and sidewalks with the stone walls of houses still collapsing all around them. Our own house, in the middle of town had partly collapsed. By this time I was really frightened. What if my family hadn't made it? I anxiously ran to the large bunker underneath the castle not far away. As I approached the entrance, I came across soldiers and others digging out bodies beneath the rubble, bodies of people who didn't reach the shelter in time. Thank God I found everyone in my family

*"Ite missa est", The mass is over.
My parish church in January 1945.
St. Clement 13th century.*

alive. I later learned that some 5,000 people were in the bunker designed to hold 1350. It withstood seven heavy caliber bombs.

While my sister took charge of the family situation, as she always did, I left the bunker to help look for survivors. We were able to save many who only had time to take shelter in their cellar corners. But many were not alive. When we found a mother's body with her baby still alive in her arms, I broke down. I ran away thinking that had to be worse than anything I saw at the front.

One entire clean-up crew got killed by a bomb that exploded as they were digging for survivors. What I had heard to be rumour, I found out was actually true - that the allied air force dropped bombs with fuses set on delayed action.

They exploded while clean-up crews were out digging for survivors. Until then I thought that only Hitler could think of such cruelties.

I did not get permission from the military authorities to overstay my leave to help in the emergency, and so I prepared for my return to Küstrin. Our family drove east, across the Rhine, in a truck which my father arranged with another family for the evacuation of all of us. When I asked my father exactly where we were going he just replied, "As far as we can. I don't want to look back anymore." The truck we had operated on wood gas so we didn't have to worry about running out of gasoline.

We made it across the Rhine River on one of the few bridges still intact. I remember how we expressed a sigh of relief. Our family of six sat on the back of the open truck while the owner's family of four squeezed into the front cabin. On the other side of the Rhine my father lit a cigar to express his satisfaction that we were safe. I never knew how he was able to get his supply of cigars during the war. My mother was all cuddled up sitting on a box with her rosary beads in her hands and tears streaming down her cheeks. Waltraud had our youngest sister, Evi asleep on her lap. Evi was still sucking her thumb to console herself. Our brother, Hans Werner, sat next to her with a blank look on his face. He didn't understand what was happening in this cruel world.

I then set off to return to the base - the artillery garrison in Küstrin. One could not risk being late or being anywhere without a *Marschbefehl* - order to travel - at the time. At every station the *Feldgendarmerie* - military police - checked travel orders and passports. If there was a day not accounted for, one would be in deep trouble. They were constantly on the look-out for soldiers 'adrift'. Whenever I missed my train connection, the first person I went to see was the military station officer for a stamp on my sheet explaining the reason for having missed the train.

No sooner had I arrived at one of the many train stations in Berlin, when the sirens roared their deafening sound. The nearest place I could run to was one of the underpasses. They provided at least some protection from flying debris but in a direct hit, hundreds of casualties would result. That is exactly what happened not more than 50 meters away from me. That day became another night of digging for the dead and wounded. There were no more train departures from this station.

In order for me to continue my journey to Küstrin, I had to walk for almost an hour to find another railway station with trains still running eastwards that would take me to my destination, *Festung Küstrin* on the Oder River.

Once I made it to the garrison I noticed things had changed a lot since I had left three weeks earlier. The barracks were filled with new recruits - they were younger, almost children averaging about 17 years of age. They had to be trained in a hurry. They were under the impression they would be drafted into the artillery. But without guns there was really no artillery. And so they became infantry men.

I was immediately put in charge of drilling the recruits of our *Ersatzbatterie* (Reserve Battery) in the usual routine on the parade square. I also taught them how to handle a *Panzerfaust* grenade and how to knock out a tank.

Without being aware of it, I was given the responsibility of *Fahnenjunker Wachtmeister* - cadet, master of the watch - while I was home on leave. An infantry first lieutenant, minus his right arm, and two experienced sergeants looked after the infantry training which had to be completed in two weeks. The reason that I was part of the training staff was because I was not yet considered ready for frontline duty. The same applied to the other two training officers. The Russians were pressing harder and harder against our forces. Soon we would not have to worry whether we were fit or not. We all became fit enough to carry a rifle as attack and counter-attack became the order of the day.

Some of the young soldiers became very disillusioned and depressed for they could not understand or digest the hard methods used in drilling recruits. I remembered my own recruitment training. I thought I had a bunch of sadists making my life miserable. I must admit, I had behaved with a similar resentment as these young men. But when a young recruit tried to tell me that he was a Hitler Youth leader and already knew all the drills, I made use of the authority I had at the moment. I asked that all Hitler Youth leaders step forward. I then let them know, since they knew so much already and had such an advantage over the others, they would not need to participate in every routine which the others had to follow. I then detailed them to clean out all the latrines <u>after</u> duty. In other words, after their regular daytime routines and drills. After that episode, no one dared admit he was a Hitler Youth leader, not even an *Abiturient* - a student with senior matriculation.

I explained to everyone over and over how important the next two weeks of tough drilling would be. I said, "You may not understand now but you will in a few weeks time when you are face to face with the Russians." I was surprised how seriously they took their infantry training after that. They also took seriously the instructions on how to handle a *Panzerfaust* - grenade. It was used to knock out tanks but one risked one's own life if the slightest mistake was made. The two infantry sergeants were very experienced instructors and they had the medals on their chests to prove it.

Within the next few days there was another company of one-time happy youths full of ideals, whatever kind they were, ready to be slaughtered. *Dulce et decorum est pro patria mori.* They had no idea. It did not take long before the barracks were filled once again with another group of what seemed to be younger and younger boys.

The situation on the eastern front began to look alarming about the middle of January when the Russians began their big push toward the fortresses on the Oder River: Stettin, Küstrin, and Frankfurt-on-the-Oder. The main pressure was on the old fortress of Küstrin, not far from Berlin, the 'Terminal'. The famous old garrison city of Küstrin was made up of the *Altstadt* and the *Neustadt* - the old and new town. The *Altstadt* still had the character of the old fortress with its *Kasematten* - casemates of four to six meter thick walls facing east. This was the direction from which the enemy would attack the fortress. At least that was the presumption some 250 years ago.

Since Küstrin was also an important road and railway junc-

Oath of Allegiance

tion between the capital of the Reich, Berlin, and Königsberg, the capital of East Prussia, one could assume that all the arrows on Marshal Zhukov's strategic maps were pointing towards Küstrin with its garrisons. I remember that there was one garrison in the *Neustadt* and that the artillery garrison with its long standing tradition was a part of the *Altstadt*. The artillery garrison, however, was on the west bank of the Oder so that town and garrison were, in fact separated. In all, there was almost one Division, approximately 12,000 in uniform trapped in the fortress.

According to my diary, which I kept though it was *verboten* to do so, the Russians had already established a bridgehead south west of Küstrin and with all the military and more than half of the civilian population still in the city (both the old and new towns), an inferno or a major disaster was predictable. However, the 25th Panzer Grenadier Division which was joined shortly by the 21st P.G.D., two elite units, tried desperately to push back the Russian bridgehead and open up the encirclement for a few days during which many of the civilian population and wounded soldiers were evacuated.

We heard many horror stories from the refugees from the east who continuously streamed by on their way west. They said rape, arson, and murder were frequent occurrences. This type of news sifted through to the troops and had a terrible demoralizing effect. Some soldiers, thinking what might have happened to their wives and children, just couldn't handle it and fell apart. They never received treatment for their invisible battle scars. They were simply shot by the notorious drum head court martials - executed for insubordination and cowardice before the enemy. I don't think that one could imagine the horror of the time without having been there to get a proper picture of the situation.

As reported by the fleeing civilian population - the cruelties committed at that time put everything previously experienced in the shadows. Rape and mass murder of innocent people are images and experiences permanently engraved into the memories of the people who lived through these horrible months. Those who were formerly the judges and executors only a few years earlier now became the ones to be judged and executed. But many were able to run away and escape their executioners leaving behind innocent people to take their place. There was no time for pardon. No one said, "Stop! It is enough!" *Vae victis.*

One of my lasting impressions during the final stages of the war was of mothers fleeing with their children. They carried them in their arms, wheeled them in carriages and dragged children still hanging onto their mothers' coats along snow-covered roads often caught in the cross-fire of the fighting troops. I saw them standing at the railway stations, shivering in the freezing cold and waiting for the trains to take them away. Waiting for trains which never came. Waiting with motionless babies in their arms, babies already dead from exposure. All this took place in and around the battle lines at the Oder front which was held by the 3rd Panzer Army under von Manteuffel, and the 9th Panzer Army under General Busse. They were the nation's last real hope and Küstrin was the last fortress before Berlin.

The only reinforcements were children. Columns of Hitler Youth squadrons on bicycles with Panzerfaust grenades tied to the front of their bicycles and rifles over their shoulders drove towards the frontline. Often, with smiles on their youthful faces, they hurried past retreating soldiers. Many of these young boys distinguished themselves and received the Iron Cross for bravery, but many of them died, not old enough to understand what it was all about. Using them was an exploitation of innocent children's loyalty to the Oath of Allegiance.[20]

Except for a few ancient cannons and some other museum pieces, the fortress artillery did not exist in Küstrin. There were several flak batteries (anti-aircraft) and a few cannons of Czech origin for which there was no ammunition available. But Tiger turrets were set up and built into the ground on every strategically important point in the city.

I now belonged to a combat unit, an infantry assault group of 110 men with a 1st lieutenant as commander. An infantry lieutenant was put in front of the first platoon and I, the Fähnrich - ensign, was put in the back of the second platoon. My primary task was to keep the group together and prevent the 17-year-old boys from running away at the

Oath of Allegiance

'Legibus Obsequimur'

Robert Dietz
Oil on canvas

Photo: George Georgakakos

first sight of the enemy. I could rely on my sergeant and two corporals. They were old hands and would do what ever was necessary and in the way they were used to doing things.

'Der Einsatzbefehl'   R. Dietz
Move into position   Oil Sticks

We were still waiting for our *Einsatz-Befehl* - order to move into position - when we received new weapons for our group. It was brand new equipment which lifted our spirits a bit. Two M.G. 42s for each platoon, a new assault rifle for most of us, lots of hand grenades, Faust grenades, and some received adapters for firing rifle grenades. At least we looked like a special assault group even if we didn't exactly feel like one. I guess that is what we were supposed to be; an assault group, a combat unit.

Now that we had all of our equipment we waited for the field kitchen to arrive. Dinner was a watered-down beef soup but horse meat was substituted for the beef. We were so hungry that we didn't even care. We also received half a stick of salami with *Ersatz* butter - substitute butter - to share among three starving men. (Margarine and artificial honey was made of coal at that time.) But we had no bread and when the others complained I told them to put the butter on the salami and pretend they were eating bread. I told them to shut up and stop complaining because it was likely going to be their last meal anyway. Such cynicism was a sign of desperation.

At this moment one of the young lads pulled on my sleeves and pointed with his salami stick up to the tree. My God! I nearly dropped my mess tin with its precious hot, 'horse bouillon'. There were two soldiers hanging from a tree limb with a sign across their chest which read, *Ich habe geplündert* - I have plundered. They had probably been caught entering one of the deserted houses looking for food, and perhaps put something else into their pockets. That 'something else' was enough for the execution commando to act in the name of the Führer and the authority of the Commander-in-Chief, Field Marshal Schoerner.[21]

While we were standing around and joking about the "donkey salami" which was as tough as leather, one of the corporals brought to my attention a scene that was just developing across the street by the banks of the Oder River. An over-officious *Kreisleiter* - district party official - had just stopped one of the covered refugee wagons. Women and children were crying because the over-officious *Schweinhund* had taken their grandfather off the wagon, handed him several Faust grenades and assigned him to a fox-hole. When the veteran of the Great War pointed out that he had an artificial leg and would not be able to do the job, he was told he would be very suitable because he could not run away.

That was too much even for the combat unit commander who was attracted to the scene because of the commotion. While he argued with the *Kreisleiter*, we hoisted the old man back onto the wagon and with a slap on the horses arse, the wagon wasted no time getting away. It was a heart-breaking scene that turned out well.

The *Kreisleiter* was furious and pointed out that the Führer, in a special order, had transferred the defense of the fatherland over to the *Gauleiters* and *Kreisleiters*. The *Oberleutnant*, our unit commander, replied sarcastically, "He has not told me as yet!" The *Kreisleiter* walked away like a dog with his tail between his legs. We could still hear him cursing at some men of the *Volksturm* company. About a half hour later, the Russian artillery sent a few salvos our way, and one of my corporals saw the *Kreisleiter* sneaking away.

"Himmel, dieses feige Schwein, - this cowardly pig, chase him back,"- I said to the corporal.

"With pleasure," he replied.

A few minutes later the Kreisleiters body was floating face down on the Oder River. It was a case of tasting one's own medicine.

While still awaiting the *Einsatzbefehl*, - order to move into position, I heard some rifle firing about 100 meters to our rear. It was like a firing party at a state funeral. I sent a man to check it out. When the young soldier returned, he was shaking and stuttering these words, "They are shooting our own men, they kill us!" The poor boy had just witnessed what would happen to him if he ran away. It was the 'Execution Commando' which picked up stray soldiers or those who had been court-martialed as showing 'cowardice before the enemy.' This was another one of the orders that came from the *Führer Haupt Quartier* and was executed behind the *Kasematten* of the old fortress.

I was stunned, I felt almost sick to my stomach. The shooting continued throughout the night. I even thought I heard a young soldier screaming for his mother to help him. I could not help saying something to the desperate-looking boys around me who were waiting for a few words of encouragement. They did not realize that I had a feeling of hopelessness myself.

I guess one doesn't have much choice. "Death is in front of us, do your best and make sure 10 Russians go with you." I did not have the guts to remind them about the death by execution squad that awaited behind us nearby. However, I reminded them that "Ivan" does not take prisoners. "Think of that," I told them, "before you throw your last hand-grenade."

In this tense situation every leader from the combat unit

commander down to the platoon leader tried to say some encouraging words to the team over which they were given responsibility. But whatever was said was mostly meaningless. We could only think about *unsere Lieben daheim* - our loved ones at home - what will happen to them? That was our final motivation for fighting: to prevent these murdering, raping, and victory- drunk hordes of revengeful berserks from falling on our families at home.

At that moment, the combat unit commander passed by with another officer. "We will be moving shortly," he announced. But with the artillery shells exploding around us, I thought it would be a good idea to get out of there soon.

But when we were ready to proceed, a tank came unusually fast toward our direction. It scared our young boys who were about to receive the *Feuertaufe* - baptism of fire, first action. It was not until the platoon sergeant told them not to worry, "It's only a Tiger (one of our tanks) ," did they return to normal. The tank really is a dangerous looking machine and at night time it gives the impression that a noisy monster is approaching in the shadows of the night. When it came to a halt an *Unteroffizier* shouted from his turret, "Is there an ammunition depot somewhere?" We could not answer his question, but I suggested he roll another 100 meters further down the road where he would find a built-in Tiger turret. They would know where he could go, because they use the same kind of ammunition. He was grateful for the good news and cautioned us that the road was blocked by a caravan of fleeing civilians and a column of supply trucks moving in the opposite direction. Russian planes had just attacked them. He pointed to the direction where we saw the sky lit up and could hear the explosions that probably came from the burning ammunition trucks.

When we eventually reached the area, ghastly scenes met our eyes. The road was completely blocked with horse drawn wagons filled with fleeing civilians. There were terror stricken mothers and children, burning trucks with infantry ammunition still exploding, shot-up vehicles with struggling horses shrieking through the night, and sporadic Russian artillery fire to complete the horrific scene. Naturally, at the time I did not know anything about Picasso and his famous Guernica painting, but looking back I wonder how he might have painted that scene. After the Polish campaign Hitler had said, 'Mit Ross und Mann und Wagen hat sie der Herr geschlagen' which translated freely means, 'Men, horses, and trucks were struck by the Lord.' Now it was our turn. We were unable to help because we had orders to proceed.

We moved silently further down the road between some farm houses into position while more and more Russian airplanes dropped incendiary bombs over the city. From several corners we saw fire and smoke in the early morning sky. We heard the engines and the tracks of the T-34s spinning around which psychologically prepared us before we put our hands onto the Panzerfaust, an anti-tank weapon which was effective from only 30 meters away. I thanked God we were not that close as yet. Although we practiced our manouvers over and over, we never practiced getting that close to reality. God help us!

We soon arrived at our assigned position near a farm where a row of freight cars were left on the tracks across the road. I believe our engineers moved them into that position to hold up the tanks. I felt very reassured when I saw a PAK (anti-tank gun) in position. I hoped they would get them first from a distance of 1000 meters before we would have to try with 30 meters.

When I looked into the sky, I saw the red glow of the rising sun. I could not help but think of the song:

> "Morgenrot, Morgenrot,
> Leuchtest mir zum frühen Tod"
> (Morning red, Morning red
> provide the light for my early death.)

If anyone had looked into my face, they would have seen me crying. I had just lifted my arm to wipe away my tears when a cannon from a T-34 blasted into the farm house roof behind us. It knocked us down. Some were carried away. A piece of shrapnel lodged in my shoulder and a smaller bit caused bleeding above my eye. That was the sixth time I was wounded during the war. But these wounds were not serious enough to seek help. Besides, there was no medic around at that moment. A year earlier, I would have been happy to seek refuge in a sheltered area. But not now, not after looking into the desperate eyes of the baby-faced soldiers around me. How could I ever desert those boys? Deep down in my conscience I would have felt guilty of murder. There was no more allegiance to the Führer. I had written him off a long time ago because he had declared war on his own people. My allegiance, therefore, went to those entrusted to me. I almost believed I had courage.

Two low flying planes coming at us from a distance forced us to quickly take cover. They looked like Stukas. Yes, they were Stukas, our own Stukas, Colonel Rudel's dive-bombers equipped with anti-tank cannons. They suddenly dove down between the Russian tank units as in the olden days and when we saw the smoke of the burning tanks, we became almost jubilant. When we discovered that only one T-34 had made it to the freight cars, we waited for the Pak (anti-tank cannon) that was giving its all from a camouflaged corner of the farmyard.

We all took cover from our own gun-fire and iron that was flying around. As usual, though, the corporal of our platoon, the machine gun troop leader, knew when it was his turn to spit out the bullets with his MG-42 into the withdrawing Russian assault troops. Now we showed them what our small combat unit of infantry men could do. We had two Paks and an 8.8 Flak behind us. They would have to try again.

My runner looked at me and with a twinkle in his eyes said proudly, "Sir, we stopped those bastards, didn't we!"

The Russians came at us again and again all day with more tanks and men. They did not even wait till morning but instead continued on the same day at sunset. Now there was more artillery activity coming from the Russians, but I thanked God there was no Stalin Organ as yet. The use of that weapon would have been a disaster due more to the moral effect it would have had on the boys, than the physical damage it would have done.

When the sun went down the Russians came back. While they had to look into the sun, we were at an advantage because we could make out every tank and man. They were lit-up by the sinking sun rays and the whole assault on our position started all over again, but this time our men were better prepared. Out of the five Russian tanks that supported the attack, three of them made it. They broke through the barrier but inside, between the burning farm buildings, they came to a halt again. Two were immediately blown up by our platoon with Faust grenades. The last of the three had lost one track because of a well aimed Pak grenade. While it spun around, we hit him broadside with a *Panzerfaust*. And again, the corporal, with his MG troop from our platoon's right and the MG troop on the left, blocked with their cross-fire any further penetration by Ivan. The Russians withdrew beyond the railway tracks behind the burning tanks. With night-fall, and the guns and MGs given time to cool off, the cries of the wounded became audible and the stretcher bearers crawling on their stomachs busied themselves with carrying back the wounded. There was no time to bring out all the bodies. We knew if we wanted to survive another assault, we had to be prepared.

Before the next sunrise, the combat unit commander was crawling around giving orders. I considered myself lucky that I was not with the 1st platoon which had to go over the top first. Instead, he ordered my platoon to attach the adapters for the rifle grenades and fire, on his signal, into the freight cars where Russians kept hiding.

I busied myself crawling around checking the rifle grenade adapters. I noticed one boy doing it with his rosary beads in his hand. I told him to wait with the Rosary until tomorrow. First, he must deal with the adapter. I guess he made me think though. "*Morgen ist es zu spät."* - Tomorrow it is too late. The lad was not present for the next role call. And neither were many others.

The arrival of the *Essenträger* - meal carriers made us feel much better. We did not care what we got to eat. That was not very important anymore as long as we got something to fill our stomachs. Soon we were ready and waited for the signal to fire our rifle grenades which were actually used in our case as a substitute for mortars.

The signal came, the grenades exploded. And with the command, "Sprung auf, marsch, marsch!", the young lieutenant ahead of his platoon, after throwing the hand grenades, moved into the freight cars that were occupied by a Russian unit outnumbering our first platoon at least 10 to one. We used illuminating flares to provide the light for the assault which was only successful due to its element of surprise. But as soon as the Russians recovered from the first shock, the surprise effect was gone and we were driven out again even faster than we got in to the position. We were just too weak to resist the pressure of a far superior force. The Russians immediately made a counter-attack but were stopped by the cross-fire of the second platoon's MGs and the fast action of the PAK, the anti-tank gun that aimed at everything that came our way. That, unfortunately, included some of our own.

The *Oberleutnant* and combat unit commander - gave me the sign to move in next when suddenly several tanks broke through the barrier. This, of course, called for withdrawal which meant falling back behind the first houses by the gates of the city, the old fortress of Küstrin - the last stronghold before Berlin. That was the reason for the order for the fortress commander to defend the bastion to the last bullet and the last man.

We withdrew, running as fast as we were still able with some of our wounded men in tow disregarding the grenades and bullets coming from behind us. Once in a while we stopped for a few seconds and looked around for the rest of the platoon. I was glad that I saw one of the corporals who, in turn, was looking for me. He told me that some of my boys were waiting for me further down the road. I learned that our commander got cut off from his party. "If he is still alive," he said, "he will be walking the other way." In other words, towards a prison camp.

Then the cannon of the Tiger turret started to fire towards two tanks approaching our section. Ivan kept pushing so hard we did not get a chance to take a deep breath. And the fighting continued,

> "The foremost fell, the next could stand,
> the third was ready, lance in hand;
> each took new strength a hundred fold,
> The slain lay heaped, unmarked untold."
> Goethe, Faust II

When we reached the first houses at the outskirts of Küstrin, I collapsed behind a heap of rubble. I was exhausted, starved and thirsty. I looked at my young soldier who stayed with me all along. Another one of our boys jumped over to us. Now two pairs of eyes were looking at me. In both I read and felt the same question: what now?

One of them asked, "Are there still miracles?"

But there were no miracles. Only Russians storming into the burning city with loud cries of, "Hurrah! Hurrah! Hurrah!"

We stood together and kept our heads down and waited for the first wave of victorious Russians to pass us by. We dropped our weapons, but I still held on to one hand grenade.

In these moments of fear and despair I learned that it takes much more to kill oneself then to kill somebody else. And so spiritual courage was gone and with it the drive for physical courage. We were waiting to be slaughtered.

Vae victis!

> "And so to be is nothing but a burden;
> my life is odious and I long to die."
> Goethe, Faust, Part I.

But we were not slaughtered. We became prisoners of war instead. My months as a prisoner, I prefer to forget.

Oil on board, 'It's Enough 1945' Robert Dietz

Part Three

Home Again

Chapter Nineteen

We called our mission, 'Operation Bernkasteler Doktor'

It was late into the summer when I arrived home. I don't remember a date or anything else except that Mayen was still a heap of rubble. No wonder, it was destroyed. Eighty-seven percent of the houses were ruined.

When I finally made my way through the streets where I could find my home or whatever was left of it, I saw Waltraud beside a mountain of bricks knocking off the concrete to clean them for re-use. I remember she was still wearing my hobnailed army boots. It seemed that she was waiting for me to come home, cleaning the bricks in anticipation. The reunion was a happy occasion. Everyone looked at me in shock. I was so thin that I believe I didn't weigh more than a 15 centimeter Howitzer grenade. My mother thought I badly needed some oatmeal porridge. My father, as usual, lit up a cigar. He thought the first thing I needed were proper papers. After all, I had escaped from a Prisoner of War Camp.

My father knew his way around the system. He had the proper connections. So the following day, with his cane in one hand and his cigar puffing away in the other, we went to the office of the *Bürgermeister*. Mayor Anton Schwindenhammer, a friend of my father's since school days, was delighted to see me. He had followed my previous political activities with admiration. He himself ended up in jail. (He was instrumental in rebuilding our town after the war, often with unconventional methods.) The mayor fixed me up with proper documents which he kept locked up in his drawer. They were all properly signed by the military government. He did the typing himself to eliminate a witness.

Now I was a properly dismissed prisoner of war with documents which showed I had been dismissed not from the camp I had escaped from, but from another prison camp which I never saw. After the two old friends exchanged cigars with one another, we all shook hands. As we left my father turned around to his friend and said, "I suppose, since there is no portrait of the Führer behind you on the wall, we do not have to salute *Heil Hitler* anymore." The mayor replied, "Peter, it was all a bad dream." "It was a bloody nightmare!" added my father with great bitterness.

The next few months were not the happiest in my life, although they should have been since I managed to survive the great slaughter. Many of us endured death and destruction and the ugliest, most indescribable, dehumanizing scenes as prisoners. But we lived on illusions and thoughts of home. After returning home, however, we experienced great psychological injuries because things really weren't what we expected. This phenomenon was so strong that had we known beforehand we would experience it, many of us would have lost the spiritual strength and energy to generate the physical strength so important for our survival. It did not take long to find out that nobody was waiting for us, we weren't needed and were often not even wanted. Those who managed to get home first got the best jobs available even if they had a questionable past.

But the war was over now and there was no time to reflect, mourn, feel sorry, or take revenge. It was time for reconstruction. One's own roof came first, then the churches and outstanding historical and cultural centres and theatres. These were the priorities of the day. Even in communist east Germany the minister of culture announced in 1945 that St. Thomas Church in Leipzig would receive the highest priority for reconstruction. This was a priority because in five years, the 200th anniversary of the death of Johann Sebastian Bach would be celebrated. It was obvious that their minister of culture had some cultural background besides sufficient economic foresight to recognize the public relations benefits of such undertakings.

I had thoughts of rebuilding too, but not until things were first cleaned up and certain people cleared out. This meant ridding the administration of people who gained positions not through personal ability but through political and unethical means. The military government, and later the Adenauer Christian Democratic Union, were great practitioners of patronage. I had a hard time accepting the fact that the people who caused most of the misery, and those who supported them, got so much consideration.

I thought of my own personal way of coping with disillusions. During that time, especially throughout the long nights, I thought of the time I stood on guard at the banks of the River Donets. I thought about the fear and suffering I felt and saw while in prison. I recalled my escape from the P.O.W. transport, when I walked along a road eating a few blades of grass just to have something in my empty stomach.

I had dreams about who would be waiting for me when I came home, about the kind of respect I would get for having experienced all the hardship and horrors of the war, and about being a student at the Gymnasium during a period one refers to as 'youth', if there was one for me. I felt that I missed that early and important period in my life. Most of us missed this period. We went from 'baby-face' young recruits to battle-hardened front-line soldiers almost overnight. From boyhood into manhood in just one step.

One of the most humiliating affairs was the fact that the new government would not recognize the senior matriculation diploma given to students who were drafted a half year before school was completed. I saw veterans on crutches who had difficulty squeezing their stiff legs behind desks designed for the young and the healthy. Many who had been awarded the Iron Cross for bravery a year earlier, did not earn a badge of merit for making the final exam. After experiencing war, many could no longer concentrate on academic subjects.

There was no sympathy for these men, no time given

over to sorrow. Even remembering or mourning ones friends was considered a waste of time. "You can't call them back anymore," were the words heard over and over again. The war was over. Except for a few million Prisoners-of-War.22

Whenever I visited the parents of my fallen school friends, I left afterwards with a feeling of guilt. "The best of us did not return," I would say. (I said it first, to prevent them from telling me). They would show me the family photo album with pictures of us in our school days. It upset me most when I saw myself in the same photo as their dead son. Then they would take me to the room where we played together - the bed was neatly made, ready for his return someday. These visits never took place without a lot of tears.

I tried to console myself by walking regularly to the monastery at Maria Laach. It was a two-hour excursion through a forest of huge oak and beech trees. I walked down from the hills, sometimes accompanied by the sound of the great church bells. The walk afforded a wonderful view of the abbey. Its romanesque basilica dating to the year 1025, would make me feel like joining the choir of monks singing inside, *Te Deum laudamus.*

It was a very special place to me. Nature, architecture, art and all of that under the benedictine motto, *Ora et Labora* - Pray and Work. Just to be in the abbey was an emotional experience. Famous figures from every walk of life either met there for important conferences or stayed there in retreat. Konrad Adenauer constantly held private meetings there with General de Gaulle of France and other French leaders or heads of state from other nations. Great musicians like Pablo Casals would sit for hours in the basilica listening to Dom Anselmus improvising on an ancient Basque folk tune. Dom Anselmus Ross was a world-renowned organist and a master of the art of improvisation. Benjamin Britten, Herbert von Karajan, Eugen Jochum, and Wolfgang Fortner were famous musicians and composers who regularly visited Maria Laach and collected their inspirations by walking through the dark, hallowed halls.

The basilica itself is an architectural masterpiece. To understand architecture, man's earliest art-form, one has to make use of all the senses. The feet that touch the floor, the hands that slide over the railings, and the rough surfaces of the walls. Even the sounds created by footsteps and the echoes that follow, all contribute to the understanding of architecture.

In a building such as this, no symbols are needed. The feeling of the structure makes one want to kneel and share in the spirit of the sacred hall and join the choir of monks in their singing: *"Ad te Domine levavi animam meam"!*

I thought if ever I should find peace, that would be the place. *Da pacem Domine* - Give peace, oh, Lord. This was the place where I could repent for all the misery I had caused others. This was where I could mourn my fallen friends - Lothar and Heinz - and all the other people who, like Sophie and Hans Scholl, and their friends, died at the guillotine. I never realized, until much later, how close our youth group came to meeting the same fate as the Scholls.

In order to prepare myself for the kind of inner peace I needed to find, I entered the philosophical and theological Academy in Trier. The Roman emperors referred to this ancient city as *Augusta Treverorum*. It was the capital of the celtic *Treveri*, and an *Episcopal* See since the early 4th century. The famous entrance-way called, *Porta Nigra*, and the ruins of the Roman baths are still visible.

The Benedictine Monastery of Maria Laach

I now became an enthusiastic follower of St. Thomas d'Aquino, the great doctor (teacher) of the church who organized the philosophy and knowledge of his time into the service of his church. He embraced the Aristotelian philosophy and called it, *Philosophia Scholastica*. In order to follow the lectures, I had to return to my studies of Latin since all the lectures in logic, cosmology, psychology, and philosophia moralis (ethics) were given in Latin. But after years of war, most of the students were not too keen to study Latin, Greek, Hebrew, and the other ancient languages all over again. We buried our heads so deep into the books that we did not notice what went on around us. What was happening outside these protected walls in a bitter world still recovering from the devastation of war?

Trier had also been an Archiepiscopal See since the year 815 and during the Middle Ages the bishops became powerful, worldly rulers - the Prince Electors. Besides the *Dom*, the Cathedral, was the Palais (residence) of the archbishop since the Middle Ages. The Palais of the Vicar General was adjacent to another church of no lesser historical importance. Many churches were destroyed during the war especially those in populated areas. The city, as did many other cities, suffered from the effects of carpet bombing by the allied air forces. It was the time when many civilians and families still lived in cellars and bunkers. Most of them were starving. The black flag was hoisted on one of the cathedral towers. Mothers were in great despair - their husbands still missing or in prisoner-of-war camps. Some committed suicide by opening the gas taps and then waiting to die with their children clutched in their arms.

I thought a lot about desperate mothers who struggled for their own survival and that of their children without losing their dignity. Nobody was there to help. There was no milk for their children, not even a slice of bread. Most of these people came from poor backgrounds, that is why they were still taking shelter in these cellars and bunkers. Because they were poor they had no jewelry to exchange for food. Exchanging jewelry for food was common in those days, and it made the farmers in the neighbourhood the wealthiest people

Oath of Allegiance

in the area after the war.

Things were so bad for the women that even if they wanted to, there were no fashionable dresses left to make themselves attractive for the soldiers of the occupation forces who could pay for their services with food, chocolates, cigarettes, coffee, and other commodities that had not been on the market for years.

All of this made me desperate too. I lay awake at night finding consolation by reading Rainer Maria Rilke's Book of the Hours from his monastic life.

"If sometimes, God next door, my knocking
on your wall at night disturbs you out of season,
I scarce can hear you breathing - that's the reason,
and know you're in your room alone.

"And when you grope about, there's no one there
to find a drink and pour it out for you.
I'm always listening.   Just a rap will do
I am quite near."

When I became aware of my very protected existence, I realized how good life was for us at the seminary. While others were crying for food outside, we were eating breakfast at 7:00, drinking coffee at 10:00, eating lunch at 12:30, having another coffee-break at 3:30 and a full supper at 7:00. The teaching staff, some of whom had as many as five doctorate degrees, joined us for the main meal in the evening. This did not agree very well with some of us, veterans of a miserable war whose wounds had not quite healed as yet. We organized our own revolutionary council at our table. When I lay awake at night I thought of my old high school Latin teacher who always provided me with the appropriate saying, *Quaerendo invenietis* - by seeking you will discover. I did some soul searching only to discover that I gave my Oath of Allegiance to a god who made me accept everything he delivered to us. A god incomprehensible, a god who could not be understood. Of course, it was easy to say, "I believe". But that did not make me sleep any better at night.

It was sometime after midnight when I heard the noise of trucks. I walked to my window and watched people unloading army trucks that came from the British occupied zone. Bags of potatoes and case after case of food were wheeled into the cellars of the seminary while cases of wine were loaded from our building to the trucks. It appeared like quite a deal - food for wine and wine for food.

I did not know that our seminary was the largest wine producer in the upper Mosel area. It also owned the best vineyards all the way to Bernkastel. But I did know that nearly every parish priest in the isolated Eifel parishes was an expert wine connoisseur, recognizable by their magenta coloured noses. I figured that perhaps they worked harder than the other priests, and celebrated more masses than others were required to do.

If I were to describe a scene with card-players in an Eifel village inn, the parish priest would be somewhat overweight with a red nose from a chronic overconsumption of Mosel wine, the schoolmaster would have a moustache and a Zwicker (pintzer) on his nose - those eyeglasses held on only by a nose pincher - and there would be a forester and doctor, if there was one around.

The peasants of the Mosel valley had slaved for the prince electors since the middle ages. They had built the castles high atop the hills and slopes of mountains, they had pruned the vines and harvested the grapes, and had brought the heavy barrels to Trier to be stored in the wine cellars of archbishops and princes. The wine was served during ecclesiastic or special occasions. The peasants got as little as possible for their labour but took as much as they could steal.

Karl Marx was born in Trier. As a young boy he witnessed the Napoleonic hordes mistreat and execute the peasants and burghers of Trier for not being able to meet their quotas of wine and agricultural production.

In spite of the fact that our meals were consumed under strict *Silentium*, I was able to pass along my night observations to my colleagues which we later discussed during the colloquium period in the afternoon. We were not going to sit by

Oath of Allegiance

and allow the poor to have nothing while the well-to-do had everything. I volunteered to work the following week in the wine cellar bottling the wine for the next "cultural exchange" with the British zone. In return, my friend Heinz had to do some Latin translations for me. I worked hard and took advantage of the situation to hide a couple of bottles of wine in my cassock every afternoon before finishing work. I also got a wax impression of the cellar key and acquired a piece of heavy wire. On my next day out of doors, I was able to obtain a small anvil and soon became an expert in making keys to fit all the locks in the medieval wine cellars of the Archbishop of Trier.

We called our mission, 'Operation Bernkasteler Doktor'. It was a most fitting name for one of the best wines of the Mosel valley and also for what we intended to do. One of our colleagues, however, got cold feet and thought that we should reconsider what we were doing. Oh, we sure thought it over, but with a good bottle of Bernkasteler Doktor.

We checked the night-watch routine of Brother Adalbert who was the official watchman of the portal, the main entrance of the seminary. Under the motto 'In God We Trust', we filled our bed sheets with food, soap, and towels. We didn't get too far before I realized that walking out with white bed sheets at night would be a mistake. The store room was nearby, so we wrapped everything up in dark woolen blankets. Now we were all set to take our 'bounty' to the poor. They got it all, and even a few bottles of *Bernkasteler Doktor* to celebrate the occasion. It was delivered right into the bunker. We were able to get away with doing this three times, but we got caught on the fourth. Poor Brother Adalbert was so upset. He begged us to return the stuff and said he wouldn't report us if we did. After all, he was a colleague of ours who had lost his left leg during the French Blitzkrieg.

We had a few other things to straighten out with the old-fashioned and pre-war administration and teaching staff. We were only allowed out for two afternoons a week. We did not mind so much the number of afternoons we had, but we didn't appreciate having to be back before dark, especially in winter when darkness came so early. We felt as if we were treated like children, "Make sure you're back before dark."

This did not allow us to attend any cultural events. We could not go to concerts, the theatre and other similar events which we thought were as important to us as eating. Surely the cultural events were more important than attending an afternoon soccer game. I learned that something other than sports forms character.

"Mens sana in corpore sano" is a great fallacy. It may train good soldiers or goons among university students, but it does not create human beings. After all, if we look at the great geniuses of the past 200 or 300 years, we will find that most of them had brilliant minds in an often very sick body. When we talk to people who listen to good music, read good books and appreciate fine works of art, we get the impression we are talking to people from a different world. We can judge people by their reaction to artistic and spiritual things.

One day we asked for an audience with the regent, Dr. Wehr. He was an extremely nice man, a saintly person. In fact, he would become Archbishop Mathias of Trier five years later. We confronted him with our problems. I told him that more than 80 percent of his candidates were mature people who were veterans of the war and served on each European battlefield including the 'Red Light districts'. If we couldn't be trusted to look at a woman without resisting the temptation, then we should not be here. In any case, when I was finished, the saintly regent was visibly upset. A week later he came out with new rules and from then on we could go to any cultural event we wanted. I survived two semesters before leaving the seminary.

Chapter Twenty

"*Komm lieber Mai und mache die Baüme wieder grün.*"
(*Come dear May and make the trees green again.*)

I was not very happy during the next few years. I became involved in political matters and was not successful in anything else I studied. I was told by several well-meaning friends to forget the war, it was over. I was bitter and upset about the government's leniency toward former Nazis. The memory of those who had suffered was still too fresh in my mind. I wanted revenge and did not want to forget what they had done to me and my friends. I got involved in tracking down former functionaries who lived in hiding. But when they finally appeared, they came up with the finest recommendations from the parish priest. I wondered if these priests ever thought about their colleagues who had died in concentration camps. In fact, many theologians died in camps. But now the audience for the church service had changed again.

My old Latin teacher would have said, *Qua mobilis est aurea popularis.* My father said to my mother when she questioned his absence from church, "There is no room for me anymore. All those crooks and hypocrites are back again sitting in their usual seats." Of course, my father was right. The front seats at church were filled with the same people who vacated them during the eternal Reich. While the clergy spoke of the 'Prodigal Son' who returned home, I spoke about our sons who did not. The attitude and conduct of many clergy after the war greatly disturbed me. I had forgotten that even 'Peter the Rock' had fallen. Perhaps I never realized that the exceptional people among the clergy were an exception themselves.

I did not give up. It took me two years before I was able to track down a former high-ranking Hitler Youth Leader who had been responsible for the misery caused to many people. I was prepared to confront him when I finally arrived at his place after marching 16 kilometers on a warm, sunny, spring day. I saw his wife sitting in the garden playing with their five children behind the house. They were playing the guitar and recorders and were singing and dancing with the neighbourhood children to Mozart's beautiful spring song:

"Komm lieber Mai und mache die Baüme wieder grün."
(Come dear May and make the trees green again.)

As the little children were dancing and singing happily in the garden I thought of my friends Lothar, Heinz, and all the others. But the war was over and those children were as innocent as were all the others who had died. No act of revenge on my part would ever bring them back. I wiped the tears from my eyes. I recalled the young, beautiful Dottore Fanfani and imagined her hand on my head, *Il sole si leva ancora*.

The sun did rise again for me on a snowy morning on the 12th of December in 1951 when I arrived in Halifax at Pier 21.

EPILOGUE

When the war finally came to an end, the world was quick to blame the whole German people for everything that had gone wrong, for every crime the Nazis had committed. But these were the same people that Hitler also tried to destroy at the very end.

The victors declared every German guilty, at least by association. Many accepted this guilt because they felt ashamed of the horrendous crimes a very powerful minority had committed. The fact that the nation had been held together by bloody terror and that there were so many who had not escaped to foreign countries but remained at home and sacrificed their lives, was hardly considered.

The responsibility for the situation and all the crimes committed rests on the shoulders of many people. In fact, those who stood by in other nations and let it happen are somehow also guilty. This may even include part of the German intelligentsia who were lucky and able to leave Germany in time to reach the United States and other countries which provided a safe haven for German scientists, artists, and architects. They were then able to live and work well protected against physical and psychological abuse. Unfortunately, quite a few of these people participated after the war in a general criticism of their brothers and sisters who withstood at home all the perils of war of both the enemy and their own government.

As the historian Golo Mann states in his, History of Germany Since 1789, "The Germans now lived between two terrors, enemy attacks from the air and people's courts which passed sentence of death on Hitlers' Germans." Mann then speaks of resistance, "If history is worth telling because of the noble things which people have done or tried to do then it is worth telling the story of the last years of the war because of the German resistance. In the darkness it was a shining light."

Hitler's intentions were well known through his book, *Mein Kampf* which was published long before he came to power. Responsibility rests on the shoulders of all those who recognized his goals at a stage when something could and should have been done about them, instead of signing pacts and treaties with him as the major European statesmen did. Ironically, Cardinal Pacelli, later Pope Pius XII, was the first who signed the 'Concordat.' Therefore, can one not say that every one who did not fight the Nazis is guilty also?

After most military conflicts the common goal is to weaken the former enemy and not to try and live with him. I am speaking of the two great wars and also about the conflicts in the Middle East. We will never settle for understanding as long as we do not look into the development of these conflicts with an open mind and heart. We must be willing to learn to live and let live. We must accept the fact that our God is not necessarily their God nor anybody else's God. We must learn to accept the fact that our religion has been invented to suit our culture and not other people's culture. The God we like, the God we have created for ourselves, is a creation of the human intellect. Therefore, imperfection is as possible as to err is to be human. If we can accept this, then we do not need to waste any time excusing our God for tolerating the murders of the children in Bethlehem, the Auschwitz gas chambers, and the bombings of Rotterdam, Coventry, and Dresden. And of course, one of the most criminal undertakings - the explosion of the atom bombs in Hiroshima and Nagasaki.

We have already forgotten the massacre of Armenians by the Turks, the massacre of the Polish officers at Katyn,23 the eradication of Lidice, and the brutal killing of the Vietnamese peasants at My Lai. But these are only minor events when compared with what we find in our history books. The names of Nero, Diocletian, Galerius, and Maxentius are synonymous with the martyrdom of early Christians and even Emperor Constantin, who put an end to the killing of Christians, plundered and burned the settlements of the Germanic and Frankish tribes in the Rhine area and delivered his prisoners to the circus in Trier to be used as food for the wild animals. But soon the tide turned and the 'civilized' Christian nations applied the same cruelties they had suffered to others.

Whose religion can justify the Crusades for the defence of Jerusalem and the protection of the Holy Land where arson, rape, murder, and plunder were the main attractions for the participating knights? And all that took place under the sign of the Cross and under the sign of the Half Moon that made the bugles of the Christian nations of Europe call for assembly in the defence of Vienna and the Christian Occident against the 'Godless Turks.'

These battles continue today and under the pretense of *Gott mit uns!* (God be with us) or in any other language we might express. In the name of God, or with God's blessing we think we are doing the right thing and we take it as a license for offensive actions that cause the death of not only hundreds, but often the death of thousands or millions of innocent people.

If one looks at the fighting between ethnic groups in Yugoslavia, it seems that the whole world is nothing but a torture chamber - an ocean of blood and tears in which a few peaceful periods are floating like lonely islands.

When I began writing this book, there was hope for a long and lasting period of peace because of Perestroika, arms reduction, the tearing down of the Berlin Wall, and so on. I tried to make a contribution to the new era by showing how ugly the world can become if we do not count our blessings each day. But we so easily become complacent. We think war is something of the past, something that provides us with a day off on Remembrance Day. While our politicians publicly declare war on war, they are already making preparations for the next war to come. And like little boys, they compete with one another for who would come first like in a backyard soccer game.

But war is no "Kinderspiel".
War is no football game.
War is where soldiers die who follow orders.
War is where mothers and children die;

The innocent die by accident because they were too close to important strategic points. Then they die in order to prevent the prolongation of the war; cities have to be bombed, and in order to demoralize soldiers, one has to kill their families. Of course that was only for the sake of bringing about the end of the war.

Politicians manipulate us into war. They declare war and send others to do their fighting. And when the war becomes uncomfortable for them, they call for peaceful action and take the credit for having wanted peace all along. Then on Memorial Day they show up and recite for the next generation:

"DULCE ET DECORUM EST PRO PATRIA MORI!"

NOTES

1a Who is a hero?

When Johann Wolfgang von Goethe spoke of heroes, he made reference to those who distinguished themselves through acts of extreme bravery and sacrificed their lives for a cause thus setting examples for others.

Nowadays the name hero applies to anybody who distinguishes him - or herself in almost anything, be it in sport, commerce, politics or even crime. With a very few exceptions, our youth has not as yet experienced any examples worthy of being looked up to. In fact they have had too many disgraceful examples in sports, politics or other fields who have let our young people down badly. They were mainly people, often with Million Dollar contracts, who became heroes through cheating, drugs and through other dishonest means. But when they, the so called heroes were caught in the act (Olympic Games), they presented themselves as the most pitiful creatures to the T.V. audiences.

Perhaps we may not agree with Goethe when he says: "Three things one recognizes only at a certain time:

> A wise man in rage,
> A friend in need,
> And a hero in war."

In the military the word hero is only sparingly used. In fact War Veterans who distinguished themselves feel often uneasy even embarrassed when referred to as heroes. It should be applied to the battlefield only. One makes a sharp distinction between those who distinguish themselves on the battlefield or on the parade square.

We had a typical example in our unit in France while in training and in Ukraine while fighting in the Donets Basin in the First Panzer Army.

'Gunner Willy' was the most impossible and the most useless creature one could imagine. He was just hopeless during our training period. When the drill sergeant shouted "Right turn".

Willy made a left turn.

When marching, he was not able to co-ordinate his arms properly. In fact, he swung his right arm together with his right foot and his left arm with his left foot. When there was an inspection by a senior officer, we hid him. So he spent most of his training time in the battery kitchen pealing potatoes, or cleaning the latrines and stables.

In spite of all the mistreatment Willy received from us, he did everything with a smile. In fact he always had some kind of innocent and stupid smile on his face.

When, during the great offensive against the German First Panzer Army in the Donets Basin (July 17-30, 1943), Russian assault forces overran our battery post. Gunner Willy put us all to shame. With a howitzer shell in his arm, ready to load the gun once again, he was bayoneted by the attacking Russian soldier. Perhaps, it was as always, with a smile on his face. We did not see it. He was still facing the enemy, while we were running in the opposite direction.

Gunner Willy did not receive the Iron Cross for bravery, not even a wooden cross to mark his grave.

¹ Die Machtergreifung.

The way that Hitler and his party took power on January 30, 1933, was without comparison.

At first the situation looked as if it would produce another coalition government in the long succession of coalitions that characterized the Weimar Republic. No one worried. Those who opposed Hitler felt that with all the safeguards in place, Hitler would be finished in a few months. Not even in the last free election on March 5 had Hitler obtained a majority. Only together with the *Deutschnationale Volkspartei* were they able to form a majority in the *Reichstag*. But with two of his chief lieutenants in the proper positions - Göring as Prime Minister of Prussia in charge of police, the largest force in Germany, and Goebbels soon to be placed in charge of propaganda, directing (or ordering) the media - it turned out that nothing could go wrong for Hitler.

There was no time to correct the mistakes. Those who were put into place as safeguards were soon guarded safely by the ones they were to guard. The public had confidence in the old Field Marshal and the military behind him, but Hitler already had the support of the heavy industrial sector headed by Krupp with an election fund of three million marks backing him, an amount until then unheard of. Hitler was quite underestimated.

The Nazis went immediately to work. Hermann Göring dismissed undesirable senior police officers in Prussia, replaced them with his own men, and deputized the *Sturm Abteilung* S.A. - Storm Troopers - as auxiliary police officers. Any tramp off the street was welcome to join. This power was now used and abused by some vengeful comrades-in-arms.

When the Reichstag building went up in flames on February 28, 1933, the Communists were immediately blamed. It was rather a strange coincidence that on the very same day, the Reich president had already signed a new law for the protection of People and State which outlawed Communism. Could it have been prepared in advance? Hindenburg was already more than 80 years old.

The signing of the new law also gave the green light to the establishment of concentration camps. Anyone who resisted went to Dachau, the Bavarian town where the first concentration camp (K.Z.) was established. The people in Dachau initially were not sent there because they were Jews, but because they were deemed enemies of the state. Many were members of the intelligentsia, many of whom happened to be Jewish. University professors, Communist leaders, Social Democrats, the leaders of the *Zentrum* Party, and finally union leaders, were sent to Dachau, the first, and at the time, only concentration camp.

2 Germany after Versailles

As a result of the Versailles Treaty (1919), Germany lost all of its colonies and some of its territory. The armed forces were reduced to a peace time strength of 100,000 men called the *Reichswehr* (Reich Defence Force). There was hardly any navy left and no air force.

The German people always thought that the treaty of Versailles was harsh and unreasonable. They did not actually believe they had lost the war. It was an armistice signed on the soil of the victor.

A slight economic upswing occurred early in 1924. The German government was able to convince the Allied nations, its former enemies, that the destruction and dismantling of factories could not pay the debts and reparations from the previous war. The enemy was now invited to invest in Germany, and with the help of the Americans, the bankers of the world, factories were modernized and the economy was soon booming. Everything else flourished as well, especially in the world of entertainment.

There was a similar situation after World War II, with the dismantling of the German factories, fear of Communism, the

Marshall Plan, recovery of German industry, and Dr. Erhard's Economic Miracle of the 1960s.

Soon after the economic upswing caused by modernization, low unemployment and high productivity, the world economic crisis of 1929 caused a great collapse in the marketplace. The stage for chaos was set. This great economic crisis caused political and social tension in the fledgling 'Weimar Republic'. It was under this cloud of economic depression that many people followed the more radical movements to the Left, while the better-situated middle class moved to radical parties on the Right. Others who had suffered and still had some national pride also moved to the Right. The emerging party furthest to the right was the Nazi-party. They promised to restore national honour and regain national dignity.

3 Jud Süss

The movie was a story about "Jud Süss" and a masterpiece of manipulation and demagoguery of Dr. Goebbels' propaganda offices. Some of Germany's best actors and actresses including Ferdinand Marian, Kristina Soederbaum, Heinrich George, Albert Florath, and Theodor Loos were engaged for the production.

One could not help but become incensed at the way Ferdinand Marian was made-up to characterize a Jew. His face and manner created hatred against this caricature and, ultimately, the Jewish race. The film was under the direction of Veit Harlan who was tried in a Hamburg court after the war for "Crimes against Humanity."

«Ὦ ξεῖν', ἀγγέλλειν Λακεδαιμονίοις ὅτι τῇδε κείμεθα, τοῖς κείνων ῥήμασι πειθόμενοι».

⁴ King Leonidas I

Although the date of the King's birth is unknown, he was the King of the Spartans from 490 B.C. until his heroic death in defence of the pass of Thermopylis in 480 B.C.

Leonidas withstood the Persian invasion for two days when Ephialtes, a traitor, showed Xerxes a path over the mountain. When Leonidas learned about the attack from the rear, he sent most of his troops to safety and defended the pass with his 300 Spartan warriors.

The Spartan King did not enjoy the same popularity as did Frederick II, the Prussian King, but he was an important figure - more mythological than historical - for any student attending the Humanist Gymnasium. The story of Leonidas and his 300 Spartans was always held up as a great example for heroism: "Oh wanderer when you happen to Sparta...." And when the German 6th Army was encircled and about to surrender, Hitler promoted von Paulus to field marshal and ordered him to defend Stalingrad as Leonidas defended the pass of Thermopylis.

But von Paulus was not Leonidas, and his army was no band of Spartan warriors. This order was given throughout the war but without the expected success. There were a few exceptions. Soldiers died at the barricades without their leaders most of the time. Even the 'great' SS Panzer Division leaders were not quite as great in their own last performance. They had no difficulties preaching to the young 17-and 18-year-old soldiers to fight and save the last bullet for themselves but they did not apply the same rule to themselves. They raised their hands because it was easier than to shoot themselves. Sepp Dietrich, Kurt Meyer, and all the others knew very little about King Leonidas who died with his soldiers. They did not learn in school: "Wanderer, kommst Du nach Sparta...."
They sang:

"Es zittern die morschen Knochen...

The rotten bones of the world
Tremble before the great war.....
....
....

Though the world will be a shambles:
For today Germany is ours
And tommorrow the whole world!"

They understood how to exploit their young soldiers' loyalty to the oath.

5 The Spanish Civil War, 1936-1939

Since the invasion of Abyssinia (Ethiopia) in October 1935 and the proclamation of Victor Emmanuel III as Emperor of Ethiopia in May 1936, Mussolini's pomposity grew steadily, especially with pecially with his involvement in the Spanish Civil War. Hitler, on the other hand, took advantage of the situation and saw it as an opportunity to test new weapons for a war that was still on the drawing board of the German General Staff. These weapons included the very effective 8.8 cm Flieger-Abwehr-Kanone, (Anti-Aircraft Cannon) called FLAK.

The new dive bombers, the Ju 87, the Heinkel bombers of the German 'Condor Legion' were used in the attack on the ancient town of Guernica, a Basque cultural centre. Generalissimo Franco, the German government, and the Holy See, denied that Guernica was actually bombed. They claimed that the town was dynamited by retreating republican hordes.
The Spanish artist, Pablo Picasso, memoralized the tragedy of Guernica in his mural called "Guernica".

The Canadian government did not wish to get involved in this war. Prime Minister Mackenzie King was content to sit on the fence because the Cabinet in London did not want to upset the 'Balance on the Continent'. However, a passionate Canadian youth was of a different opinion, especially since 'God' was on the side of Generalissimo Franco.

The Catholic press reported that the rebels (Franco and his associates) were saving Europe and the world "from the menace of Red Spain." Likewise, the 'L'Action Catholique' stated, "His victory will be that of Christian Civilization against Marxist savagery."

The other side of the debate was not less vociferous in supporting the Republican government. "Every man of decent feeling can only hope that the government will prevail", reported the Canadian Forum. Canadian students demonstrated. In Montreal, McGill University students invited Republican speakers while students of Loyola University promoted the other side. There was only one group willing to invest in more than words. They were prepared to sacrifice their lives. One of them was Norman Bethune, a medical doctor. He said, "It is in Spain where the real issues of our time are going to be fought out...."

Dr. Bethune and other communists, liberals, socialists, and idealists went to Spain to set up a mobile blood transfusion service for wounded soldiers and civilians. They were joined a few months later by about 600 volunteers from Canada. By mid-1937, they formed the 'Mackenzie-Papineau Battalion'. It was a unit of 1250 men, a part of the 'International Brigade'. Only half of them returned home. They died fighting against Fascism before the rest of the world took action.

These heroic soldiers never received proper recognition by the Canadian government, a government which was later quick to provide shelter to known Nazi war criminals.

There was also the American contingent, the Lincoln Battalion, which was numerically larger than a regiment; it had approximately 3200 men of which less than half survived. Both the Canadians and Americans returned home to a certain amount of persecution because they were seen as communists, though not all were.

Then, of course, there was the German group called the 'Thälmann Brigade' which was a very unfortunate contingent of not much more than 500 volunteers. They were young anti-Fascists and Jews who had nowhere to go after the Civil War was over. Some went underground in France. Only a few survived. Less than twenty.

The leader of the 'International Brigade' - volunteers from 57 countries - was Hans Beimler, a former member of the Bavarian Parliament who was sent to Dachau in 1933. Beimler was one of the very few people to ever escape the concentration camp. He was killed in Spain in 1936.

6 The Polish Campaign

The war began with the invasion of Poland. It was a 'Blitzkrieg' that was over within three weeks. The Germans invaded Poland from the west and the Russians moved in from the east. How little we students knew of what horrendous crimes were committed by both invaders. Having been taught history only from the German or more accurately from the National Socialist point of view, we did not realize that Poland was raped by two giants at the same time. Nobody came to her defence. Hitler was triumphant. He quoted in his victory speech one of our patriotic poets who said, after Napolean's retreat from Moscow, "Mit Ross und Mann und Wagen, hat sie der Herr geschlagen". (With horses, men and wagons, the Lord defeated them.) The Führer also made sarcastic references about their outdated equipment.

I recall the media reporting a Polish cavalry squadron charging a German tank unit. No matter how senseless and stupid this attack appeared to everyone else, it was, indeed, an act of heroism. It was not until six years later that Hitler's army and the German civilian population experienced a bitter revenge.

There was a general victory atmosphere all over. While the cinemas, theatres, and dance halls were all closed during the campaign period, all of these places were now open again and filled with people. Soldiers were on leave with their friends, and officers were in the company of young ladies of society where rank became, once again, a measurement of acceptance. It was for some socially conscious parents a replay of a fairy tale film from the days of Kaiser Wilhelm II. It gave many students something to laugh about and others something to dream about.

7 Der Volksempfänger

Today, the Volkswagen is well known in our society and many people are familiar with its background. But few recall the 'Volksempfänger'. As was the case with the "People's Car", the Nazi's also produced one of the cheapest radio sets in Europe. The 'Volksempfänger' - the people's radio receiver - was known as the V.E. The aim was to have one in every home and that was nearly realized.

In a matter of a few years, the radio audience in Germany

quadrupled. The Nazis not only provided the radio sets, but also the programs which were strictly controlled by Goebbels. The listeners soon got used to certain signature tunes applied to certain politicians and events, especially during the war when normal radio programs were interrupted for important announcements - the so called, 'Sondermeldungen'. They were preceded with fanfares, cymbals, and tympani rolls of Franz Liszt's 'Les Préludes' and reported one of Rommel's victories in North Africa or U-Boat Commander Prien's sinking of another ship at the entrance of some British harbour.

There was a similar situation regarding the German movie industry. Goebbels was known for his connections with the cinema, especially with the town of Babelsberg and its actresses - he was, in other words, 'The Stud of Babelsberg'.

The personnel of the German movie studios of UFA were made in May 1934 to take an oath similar to the one sworn by the civil servants. The German motion picture law also came into effect. From then on all proposed film projects had to go through the office of the Reich Drama Film Advisor to prevent such subject matter from running 'counter to the spirit of the time'.

One of Dr. Goebbels' great accomplishments was his art of manipulation. With his demagoguery he kept the whole German nation, the military as well as the civilian population, fighting even long after any hope of victory was gone. Many people believed, until the very end, in a secret weapon and final victory, the 'Endsieg'. Only a few weeks before the end, Goebbels had said, "I firmly and unswervingly believe that ultimately our cause will be victorious..."

When the victorious Russian troops stormed the burning city of Berlin, he and his wife followed the example of their 'Beloved Führer'. They killed their six children by lethal injection and then they themselves committed suicide.

7b Ministerium für Volksaufklärung und Propaganda

Only thirteen days after the Reichstag fire on February 27, 1933, the 'Ministry for Popular Enlightenment and Propaganda' was established by the government. Dr. Joseph Goebbels was put in charge. It became Hitler's most important ministry; it was a powerful institution like the SS and one of his most effective weapons.

The Nazis did as Frederick the Great had done 175 years earlier - they looked upon information and misinformation as a very important means of keeping peace or stirring up war. It was like a musical instrument with which one could play on the emotions of people on either side of a given issue, with the military, and with other powerful institutions. Now it is more accurately called "psychological warfare". It can be most effective and can be used either to boost the morale of the people or to demoralize them.

Whenever Hitler appeared to speak, the offices of the Propaganda Ministry made the most of it. They ensured that in all places where people gathered, loudspeakers were set up to give as many people as possible the opportunity to listen to the Führer's speeches. The loudspeakers appeared first in the schools so that the nation's youth - 'Germany's Future' could participate in writing the nation's history. Next they appeared in places of work and recreation; they even appeared in the worker's favourite pubs. All were turned to one of the Reichsender (the state-owned radio network) stations.

The ideal place for such speakers was the town or village square, where the masses gathered. It was easy to install a powerful loudspeaker for the occasion of a speech. People were encouraged to listen in groups and these groups were infiltrated by what we might call, 'cheer leaders' who, at the appropriate moment would shout and lead others in shouting, 'Sieg Heil!' When Hitler appeared, following the usual Wagnerian introduction (his appearances were always proceeded by the music of Wagner), he addressed his audience with 'Meine Parteigenossen, Volksgenossen' - My fellow party members, fellow citizens. It sounded as if he spoke directly to each individual. Nearly everyone who heard him reacted promptly with 'Sieg Heil' to the Führer.

The people looked upon Hitler as a Messiah. The market square was just an extension of the *Sportpalast* where he delivered all his major speeches. These speeches were a far cry from Roosevelt's famed Fire-Side Chats to the Americans. Hitler did not talk to the nation or chat. He sent his hysterical screams about the Jewish-Bolschevist conspirators via the air waves into every meeting hall and home.

The Propaganda Ministry became a most important war machine even before the war. The public, who did not actually want war, were prepared for war. Goebbels constantly used the phrase, 'Lebensraum' - room to live; in other words, expansion to the east was vital for the existence of the German nation and hence a justification to make war.

[8] Rosenbaum

The name Rosenbaum was well established in our area, as was the name Rosenstock. During the Nazi regime, the Rosenstock family began investigating their heritage since many of their neighbors believed them to have Jewish ancestry. In the end, it developed that there were two families with the name Rosenstock. One was an integrated, intermarried family of Jewish origin, and the other was entirely gentile with no Jewish heritage whatsoever. During the war, Rosenstocks of Jewish origin perished in camps or fled the country, and at least one Rosenstock of gentile origin was a high ranking S.S. officer.

Ironically, prejudice and the search to discover the family origin brought members of the two families into contact and they continue to communicate on geneological matters to this day.

Experts on German patronymics suggest that at the time last names were being acquired, some Jews who worked for gentiles as rent collectors took the name of the gentile family for whom they worked or perhaps chose the name of someone they admired. In any case, German gentiles with Jewish sounding names were subject to questions and sometimes prejudice. They were often placed in the position of having to prove they were not Jewish.

[9] The Russian Campaign

The actual numbers, which we did not know at the time, according to The World War II Almanac by Robert Goralski, Putnam's Sons, N.Y., 1981, pp.164 are as follow:
"One-thousand-eight-hundred mile front -as the crow flies- from the Arctic to the Black Sea. Three million troops, 600,000 vehicles, 750,000 horses, 3,580 tanks, 1,830 planes."
These figures are verified by both Russian and German records.

[10] Scorched-Earth

Scortched-earth is the description of a state of destruction of a country or region left behind by retreating armies. It means total destruction of food, shelter, road and transportation media - anything essential or useful for the survival of the invading armies.
In Russia for example: The Russian troops burnt down whole communities before retreating. The German armies did likewise before they gave up the territories a few months later.

[11] Der Lebensborn

The 'Lebensborn' was established for the preservation of the Nordic race. Although many of the uninformed believe that these institutions were homes of pleasure (SS brothels), they were actually established for stock rearing.
Nothing was known about the 'Lebensborn' before the war, but sections in Hitler's 'Mein Kampf' and Rosenberg's 'Mythos of the Twentieth Century' indicate that at least the planning of these institutions may have started during the pre-war years.

It became widespread knowledge after the 1941/1942 Russian winter campaign when the German army received heavy losses and during which the ranks of the participating SS units were almost decimated. The system was made available to any healthy looking, blond, blue-eyed German girl, who would be willing to meet a young SS man with the same physical features to "make a gift to the Führer". These young, specially selected women could then stay in such 'Lebensborn' homes until the SS fathered children were born.

One can imagine the reaction in high schools and universities when this project became known. In school yards and corridors, during break periods, students put their heads together and joked about the newest in the program of preserving the German 'Superior Race'. It also created a furor among students with religious ties. In addition, it contributed to the growth of resistance movements. Thus the program did not become a success and was perhaps the reason that the stories of blond and blue-eyed children abducted from occupied countries such as Poland and Czechoslovakia turned out to be more than just rumours.

[12] Dr. Goebbels - see [7b], page 225

[13] Frederick the Great

Can a monarch be called "Great" when his greatness is based mainly on military accomplishments?

As a high school student and history enthusiast I had always admired Frederick the Great. During the war, after my first encounter with battle and the cries of death, my admiration started to lean more toward Frederick the philosopher, the composer, the flutist, the architect, and the art collector, rather than the soldier and strategist.

As soon as he followed his father, Frederick Wilhelm I to the throne, he did away with torture and he recalled all the artists, philosophers, and scientists expelled by his father. He criticized Generals for their brutality. "Humanity and intelligence should be put on an equal level with bravery and aggressiveness," he once said. In spite of this statement, it is safe to say that most Germans admired Frederick for his military prowess.

In 1740, the first year of his reign, he was attending a costume party at the Berlin Royal Palais. He greeted ambassadors and other foreign dignitaries who were not aware of the young King's priorities.

After a most jovial conversation, it is said that the king left the party via the backdoor. He dropped his costume and already in battle dress jumped on his horse to join his troops marching toward the Silesian border.

He did badly in his first battle, the battle of Mollwitz, and he never forgave General von Seydlitz for having won the battle for him, but he was grateful to his horse on which he had escaped. The horse was decommissioned and received a lifelong 'pension'.

From then on, Frederick prepared for his wars and introduced methods no one else had used before him.

"In war one has to change his fur as required," he said. "one day you put on your lion's fur, and the next day that of a fox, because tricks often succeed where strength fails."

At a later date, Frederick changed his mind about most of his newly introduced improvements and slowly adopted some of the methods that had made his father, the 'Soldatenkönig,' the soldier King, so unpopular. He even enlarged his army with an additional 16,000 men. It was, in part, the politics of the day, the politics of expansion. He only tried to get ahead of many of his royal counterparts.

Frederick the King, already highly intellectual, now became a master of intrigue and disinformation. Even Dr. Goebbels, Hitler's Propaganda Minister, could have learned a lesson from him.

Frederick introduced 'sleepers' in the Viennese Court.

The Old Fritz

These were people who gained trust and were only 'activated' to duty when Frederick required information or wished to spread false information. He arranged for faked secret messages to fall into the hands of his enemies.

It was also Frederick the Great who originated the 'Blitzkrieg' strategy. He was as controversial a statesman as he was a strategist. He declared the writings of Machiavelli dangerous, but followed them in his own actions.

He introduced the basic principle of eastern German politics - that is, to stay on friendly terms with the Russians. This led, at the time, to the first division of Poland.

I saw Frederick II as a man with two souls. One was the soul of a Monarch as hard and cold as steel. The other was the soul of an aesthetic human being. In the end, he caused great misery, death, and destruction to millions of people. One in 10 Prussians died for his cause.

14 Latrine

Something about rumour: Latrine, Latrinengerücht

'Latrine' is an expression used by the more educated members of the armed forces: those who eat in the officer's mess. The rest of the military would eat from their mess tins, sit on benches, and door steps and would use the words *Scheisshaus* - *Scheisshausgeflüster* - shit house - shit house rumour.

While 'Latrine' derives from the Latin word 'Latrina' or private bath used by the officer ranks, 'Scheisshaus' is the German word for the same thing but without the elegance of a bath. Both institutions have always been favourite places for rumours. They are called 'Gerücht' - smell in the latrine and 'Geflüster' - whisper in the common man's shit house. Both words describe the same activities in different words.

15 The Second Gun

The Company is the smallest unit in an infantry regiment. The battery is the smallest unit in an artillery regiment which consists of 12 batteries. (pre-World War !!.

A battery has four guns (howitzers or cannons) of which the second, the number 2 gun, is the main gun, called the Richtkanone (the gun that gives the direction). The Gunner I of the Richtkanone, called Richtkanonier, sets up his gun first and the number I gunners of the first, third and fourth gun adjust their guns accordingly.

The second gun is also called the Arbeitsgeschütz (the working gun or work-horse). It is the 'roving' gun and is always on alert and ready for single commitments such as moving in and out of the battery post and firing from alternate positions to make the identification of the battery location more difficult. For this reason the number 2 gun, unlike the other guns, is normally not dug in.

16 The People's Tobacco

Machorka was known as the tobacco for the poor people. Made up of strings and bits of papyrossi, it was smoked only by making a cone of newspaper in which the "tobacco" was deposited.

A Ukrainian peasant once told me, "The smell is the result of the combination of both the literary content of the newspaper and the tobacco that goes into the cone."

As the Russians would say, "Cigarettes made of Prawda newspaper smell most Machorka-like."

17 The Desert Air Force

This was the name of the Air force unit attached to the Allied Forces in North Africa. Since the troops which invaded Sicilly and later the Main Land were under the same command, the name 'Desert Air Force' applied also to the units that fought in Italy.

18 Stalinorgel

The Stalinorgel (orgel = organ) was one of the Red Army's Fearsome weapons. It was the truck-borne Katyusha rocket launcher. It did not sound like an organ; but it produced a roaring, thundering and frightening noise caused by several projectiles launched in succession of four seconds and exploding in a smalll area. It had a great moral effect when experienced in battle for the first time.

The Nebelwerfer

The German Nebelwerfer or Do-Gerät, called 'Moaning Minnies', by the allied forces was a similar rocket launcher. They consisted of six tubes and were mounted on a two-wheeled carriage with a split trail. An electrical firing contact was at the end of the barrel. To escape the blast, the firer took cover in a split trench about 15 metres to the flank, using an electrical switch.

19 The Cost of Freedom: Something about Resistance

The people of every country Hitler conquered and occupied formed resistance movements as soon as they experienced the brutalities of the occupying forces. Colonel General von Blaskowitz expressed it well - after the Polish campaign - when he complained about the "bestialic and pathological instincts" that were running rampant behind the lines; he was speaking of the "S.S. Sicherheitsdienst" (S.S. Security Forces), with their clean-up operations.

The fact that Germany had an active resistance movement since 1933 had been a well-kept secret. Only occasionally were the names of traitors and saboteurs publicly announced on the so-called 'Litfassäulen' (concrete columns bill-boards) in the form of red posters with the heading 'Im Namen des Volkes' (in the name of the people) in large letters.

The resistance movement grew out of many segments of the population: Trade Unions and professional associations, different 'Weltanschauungen' (political beliefs) like Communists or Socialists, and especially the German nobility which was well represented in the military. German church leaders such as the Catholic Bishop of Münster, Count Clemens August von Galen, and the Protestant theologian Pastor Martin Niemöller became thorns in the side of the Nazis because they spoke out publicly from the pulpits of their churches.

There were intellectuals, artists, and generals active in planning the assissination of Hitler. There were high school and university students who distributed Pastoral letters, leaflets, and other literature calling for resistance and sabotage despite being aware of the consequences: the guillotine, or death by hanging.

These possibilities, or the firing-squad were still no deterrent for the unsung hereos who made contributions to the great struggle in shaking off the yoke of dictatorship. An outstanding example was the "White Rose" organization made up of a group of Munich University students: Hans and Sophie Scholl, Christoph Probst, and their friends and associates. The White Rose was not a political organization, as it stemmed from the Catholic Youth Movement.

As Golo Mann states in his history of Germany since 1789: "....if German resistance had consisted of nobody but the Scholls and their friends, their action would have been enough to save a little of the honour of those whose tongue is German."

Several attempts were made to assassinate Hitler. One occurred in 1938 before the invasion of Czechoslovakia, another in 1939, and yet another in 1942 after the catastrophic Winter Campaign. Other attempts failed due to unfortunate circumstances.

With the growing intensity of cruelties, crimes against humanity, and Hitler's strategic failures, the spirit of resistance grew among military leaders, politicians, and church leaders. Thus, there was again another attempt on Hitler's life on July 20, 1944. Colonel Count von Stauffenberg placed a briefcase filled with explosives in Hitler's headquarters at Rastenburg, but the assassination attempt failed and it resulted in the elimination of the entire leadership of the resistance and many others, including family members of those in the movement. Those executed were Dr. Karl Goerdeler, the Lord Mayor of Leipzig, Field Marshal von Witzleben, along with many generals and politicians, and the members of their families.

In all, according to the "Mordregister" (registry of murders or executions), 11,881 executions were carried out between 1933 and 1944, and until the day of capitulation, an additional 12,500 executions were scheduled.

There were numerous soldiers and civilians killed by the so-called execution commandos; the estimated figure is between 32,000 and 33,000. Estimated figures for last minute political executions were 7,000 to 8,000. Günther Eisenborn states in his book, 'Der Lautlose Aufstand', (Silent Resistance): "In the struggle for freedom, in the fight against Hitler, our people sacrificed a whole army."

On May 7, 1945, the German army capitulated without condition. World War II came to an end with the cost of 30 million lives among the civilian population. Ten million soldiers died in various war theatres all over the world. Thirty-five million were wounded and three million were missing.

Freedom does neither provide nor does it give,
it demands the utmost of sacrifices.

20 The Children's Crusade

When German troops had had enough of it, children took over. These groups of young fighters were called, 'Werewolves'. On the eastern front, 15-year-old boys of the Hitler Youth equipped with bicycles and *Panzerfaust* confronted Russian Tank Regiments, and in the Ruhr and Weser districts, and in the heart of Germany the 'Werewolves' took over when the regular troops fled or surrendered. But while the regular army quit, Goebbels still managed to keep unsuspecting and innocent young people going underground to fight. The 'Werewolves' were supposed to keep the flames burning and even fight against their own people who did not wish to be sacrificed any longer. Underground fighters everywhere were considered to be heroes, provided they fought for the 'right' cause. Some of the 'Werewolves' were executed by U.S. firing squads.

The following is an account by a former member of such a group who considers himself lucky:

On the morning of April 10, 1945, when the sirens signaled, 'enemy alarm', I was one of 450 fifteen-year-old boys hurrying to the edges of the town of Lebenstedt to defend it against the approaching American forces. Before the day was over we would be shot at by artillery, strafed and bombed by fighter bombers, fired at by a tank, and finally by an infantry outpost from just across the country road. But by then it was pitch dark and we were flat on the ground, too surprised by the event to be able to shoot back.

We should have been well prepared, though. For three weeks we had been in a pre-military training camp. Under the guidance of experienced sergeants we had learned to handle anti-tank weapons and rifles, and how to use camouflage by putting mud on our faces. We wore new fur-lined camouflage jackets, carried a 'Panzerfaust' to use against tanks, and we were equipped with a variety of rifles, even some of .22 caliber. I had a short Italian-made carbine with a collapsible bayonet, which was not very safe and reliable, as I found out much later.

So decently equipped, we followed our sergeant to the edge of town. Initially we were placed in house basements, where we knocked out narrow windows in preparation for defence. When the first shells hit the buildings we were ordered out into the fields, just in time to escape a wave of bomb attacks.

We then took up positions on the side of a dam, with ditches in front of us, and a low plain and gently rising hills in the distance. There we saw enemy tanks, one of them burning, probably it was hit by our 8.8. flak. Fortunately, these tanks did not come our way. Maybe the ground was too marshy, not because I think we scared them off.

We found shelter from the next wave of fighter bombers in a prepared dugout, which had a flimsy earth-covered roof. Our troop now consisted of about 10 boys and two old men of the local 'Volkssturm'. The Americans entered the town from the rear. We heard a lot firing and saw smoke bellowing from burning houses. One tank roared out and turned its turret towards the open entrance of our dugout. The first shot fell short, the second went wide, and since we kept our heads low and the tank did not see any movement, it reversed its engine and drove off. When dusk fell, the old men prepared to go home and advised us to do the same. But at that moment a lieutenant appeared to collect us and lead us on behind enemy lines, to join our troops still fighting in the Harz mountains, as he believed.

A silent march through the dark spring night was followed

by the encounter with the outpost. None of the boys remembered to shoot back, but the lieutenant gave a couple of bursts from his submachine gun, firing right over my head. I could feel powder burns on my neck. I had the pleasure to hear one American running off, after which we withdrew into the forests. We stayed in uniform and kept our weapons for a few days, carefully making our way past American camps and hordes of former forced labourers, who roamed around the countryside loaded with plunder. When we found out that there were no German units in the mountains we buried our warm jackets and guns. Our lieutenant, who was actually a Hitler Youth leader with officer's rank, did not look as dashing anymore in ill-fitting civilian clothing, but he declared, that we were now part of the 'Werewolves - the resistance movement. In that role we would hide weapons laying around the fields, and he would cut enemy field cables and set fire to a small depot of oil drums. Eventually, though, our leader was persuaded to, 'let the kids' go.

I was one of the kids and after two days of walking I reached my home village. I was lucky not to have been captured, starved, or executed for being a member of the 'Werewolves', like others in my group.

In February 1946, the British Occupation Forces arrested me and many other of the so-called, 'Action Nursery', suspecting that we were involved in dangerous activities. I spent time in jails and an internment camp. Some of us were slapped around a little bit to prepare us for interrogation, and we were kept on a scarce diet, but generally the treatment by the British was fair and humane. After two months I was released, and that seemed to be the end of the affair.

— Horst Deppe

(Horst Deppe is a professor at the Nova Scotia College of Art and Design in Halifax. He came to Canada in 1955.)

21 Execution Kommando - Drumhead Courts-Martial

To explain this procedure, one need only tell the story of Hitler's last Field Marshal, Ferdinand Schoerner, who attained his promotion on April 5, 1945, exactly four and one half weeks before the end of the war.

Schoerner was the most ruthless of Hitler's senior army officers. To quote S.W. Mitcham's book, 'Hitler's Field Marshals', "... he dealt as harshly with his own men as he did with the Russians whom he considered subhuman."

Schoerner was the son of a Munich police officer. He distinguished himself as a junior officer in the Great War and received the Imperial Army's highest decoration, 'Pour le Merite'.

When Hitler appointed Schoerner in January, 1945 to the command of Army Group Centre, on-the-spot executions became the order of the day and were visible everywhere. Soldiers were hanging from trees and light poles. Usually there was a placard round their neck saying, "I was a coward", "I was a deserter", or "I was a looter." I remember one couple - a sergeant and a young girl. They were 'caught stealing food'.

Field Marshal Schoerner had the reputation of shooting down a colonel as cold bloodedly as he would execute a private. One of his most despicable deeds was to appoint Lieutenant General Niehoff defence commander of the city of Breslau because the General had five children who could be executed under the law of 'Sippenhaft' - collective family responsibility. It is said that he sent Niehoff to his new mission to defend the city by saying, "If you fail, you will pay with your head." The defence of Breslau, in which about 250,000 civilians and approximately 35,000 soldiers were engaged and trapped, lasted longer than the defence of Berlin.

Lt. General Niehoff and the ruthless Nazi Gauleiter Karl Hanke did not surrender until May 7, 1945 despite the daily bombing and constant artillery barrages by the Russian troops surrounding the city.

It is known that Field Marshal Schoerner deserted his troops at the end in order to save his own neck. He committed the same 'crime' for which he personally executed others.

After the war, the German Prisoner of War Society was instrumental in having him charged for manslaughter for the murder of thousands of German soldiers.

As Sam Mitcham Jr. states in his book, "He (Schoerner) will go down in history as a good defence commander and a thoroughly despicable human being."

22 Program of Elimination

There is no doubt that Hitler was successful in many things he did. Some were well done and beneficial to the masses, but the people were soon blinded by his success. In spite of the fact that he announced his elimination program publicly, often and early, not many people took him seriously. In fact few believed that a human being could be that evil.

Hitler's elimination program had two categories. His first were his political opponents. These included the intelligentsia: academicians, clergy, and artists. Second were the Jews! When I write secondly, I do not mean that the Jews were not a priority, but it was important to first eliminate those who could have interfered with the big program, the total elimination of the Jewish people. Hitler did not stop there. He even included other non-Aryan minorities such as Gypsies and the so-called, 'inferior' Slavic race. After the invasion of Poland, Hitler ordered all representatives of the intelligentsia eliminated. He said, "...two masters side by side cannot be tolerated."

If we talk of cruelties, then the most incomprehensible action is the one against his own people. Already, in the earlier stages of the Russian campaign of November 1941, before the beginning of the Russian counter-offensive, the Danish Foreign Minister, Cavenius, records in his diary the following brutal statement which Hitler made in his presence: "...when the time should

Oath of Allegiance 241

come that the German People will not be strong enough anymore and willing to sacrifice and give its blood for its own existence, then it should disintegrate and dissolve and be destroyed by a stronger force and I will not shed any tears for the German people..."

This cruel statement was made a reality in 1945 when Hitler, during the last two months of the war, gave the order:"...whatever still stands should be blown up and destroyed in order to take away any possibility of survival." Shortly before the collapse, after he had converted all of Europe into a slaughterhouse and sacrificed the whole German Youth, he even intended to punish his own people when they refused to go down with him.

If one were to assess Hitler's military accomplishments one could easily put him on the same level as Alexander the Great, Frederick the Great, or Napoleon. There is, however, a difference. In many wars, the conqueror does not spare the blood and lives of his defeated enemies. Hitler killed not only soldiers, but millions of innocent helpless people: the Jews, the sick, and children. This makes him a mass murderer, almost on the scale of the modern factory assembly line. All of this and his actions during the last few weeks of the war assure him a place in hell. Meanwhile, there are many other candidates who deserve a special place down there, too. We followed their actions and their fate via the media in our own living rooms.

According to the Canadian writer, James Bacque, in his book, <u>Other Losses</u>, General Dwight Eisenhower has also earned himself a prominent place down there since he may have been responsible for the death of one million German prisoners. This destruction took place not during the war but after the war after May 1945.

When the German Army finally laid down their weapons and surrendered on May 8th and 9th (the official date was midnight May 8th), the Allied Forces were suddenly confronted with masses of German prisoners. Approximately four million soldiers were left mostly without food or water. When supplies came, only very little was available for distribution. Scenes took place that looked more like the throwing of a hip of lamb into a large pride of hungry lions, rather than the feeding of human beings. Men almost killed one another for a little bone with no meat left on it.

Some of the soldiers had been held in camps since March when they were taken prisoner during the fighting west of the river Rhine, in the Eifel mountains. But most of them surrendered to the Americans after May 8th. What is difficult to understand is that some who suffered were children and old men. Of the 630,000 who came under French supervision, 250,000 died. Approximately 750,000 German prisoners died in American prison camps. James Bacque's findings are horrifying. His account of the situation is not only shocking, but unbelievable for any one who has not lived through those days of hunger, horror, and cruelty.

There are people, some of whom associated with great responsibilities, who deny the existence of such situations, like some who deny the existence of Auschwitz Gas Chambers. There is, however, a difference: the witnesses of the Auschwitz Death camp and the other camps have spoken up, since 1945, while the witnesses of the Eisenhower Death Camps have remained silent since 1945, partly out of shame and guilt, no doubt about the Concentration Camps and the behaviour of the SS security soldier Kommandos behind the lines. It is no more a secret today that German authorities participated with the Americans in covering up, and, fama est, many documents disappeared in German Archives.

I saw an American POW Camp at Sinzig on my way home. I passed the town on tip toes. How else would one walk after a second prison camp escape and with no papers in my hands? I couldn't take any chances. Only another 30 kilometers to walk before I was home. I still remembered all the short cuts through the fields and woods which passed the famous Benedictine Monastery of Maria Laach. How I would have loved to visit the Basilica and kneel down to thank God for allowing me to survive the war. But I was even afraid to stop at the gate to ask for some bread and water. I was extremely hungry

Passierschein

Der deutsche Soldat, der diesen Passierschein vorzeigt, benutzt ihn als Zeichen seines ehrlichen Willens, sich zu ergeben. Er ist zu entwaffnen. Er muß gut behandelt werden. Er hat Anspruch auf Verpflegung und, wenn nötig, ärztliche Behandlung. Er wird so bald wie möglich aus der Gefahrenzone entfernt.

Dwight D. Eisenhower
OBERBEFEHLSHABER
der alliierten Expeditionsarmee

Englische Übersetzung nichtzutreffend. Sie dient als Anweisung an die alliierten Vorposten.

SAFE CONDUCT

The German soldier who carries this safe conduct is using it as a sign of his genuine wish to give himself up. He is to be disarmed, to be well looked after, to receive food and medical attention as required, and to be removed from the danger zone as soon as possible.

Dwight D. Eisenhower
SUPREME COMMANDER,
Allied Expeditionary Force

and thirsty, but the French military vehicles were parked in the court yard. They were in the process of taking the district over from the Americans.

Judging from what I heard and saw, things nobody at the time would believe, I was almost glad I did not make it to the American side on time at the end of the war. Willi K. Michels in his documentation: 'Heimat in Scherben' - Our Home in Rubble - reports that 120,000 prisoners were kept in an area of 3000 metres by 800 meters. No cover, no food, no water, and no sanitation. Only sickness, cold, and rain in March, April, and May, and a burning sun in July and August.

Bacque quotes one prisoner: "I thank God I am in this camp. Nowhere else would I have been so lost in my thoughts

or seen humans in their total nakedness. Nor would I ever have believed the victors to be capable of such cruelties."
We like to forget such cruelties because we can't bear thinking about them.

Perhaps it should be mentioned here that many young and inexperienced soldiers were lured into desertion with the so-called, 'Passierschein' - safe conduct sheet, dropped by airplanes in the combat area. It said: The German soldier who carries this leaflet is using it as a sign of his genuine wish to give himself up. He is to be disarmed, to be well looked after, to receive food and medical attention as required and to be removed from the danger zone as soon as possible."

It was signed, 'Dwight D. Eisenhower', Oberbefehlshasber der alliierten Expeditions - Armee"

There is nothing illegal about the methods used to win a war. It all falls under propaganda, misinformation, and psychological warfare. But what a shocking experience to end up in a "Death Camp" after one has been given safe passage by an honourable General. The concept of elimination was not unique to Adolf Hitler.

23 The Forest of Katyn

Immediately after the Invasion of Poland, Hitler ordered the elimination of all representatives of the Polish intelligentsia. This included the officer corps. He said, ".....two masters side-by-side cannot be tolerated..."

Since Hitler's stand towards the Eastern, especially the Slavic races was known, the Russians had no difficulty in making the world believe that almost 5,000 Polish officers were killed by the Nazis, or more specifically, by the SS Security commandos. Even I did not have any problem accepting this theory. However, Stalin must have feared the Polish intelligentsia even more than Hitler did because they wasted no time in eliminating them. Only after the exiled Polish government asked for the release of the Polish officers to have them serve in General Anders' Polish Free Army, did the Russian authorities declare them missing. The Russians later reported that the Poles had been assassinated by the SS Security forces.

According to Dr. Stanislav Swianiewicz, a former professor of economics, the officers had been transported by train in April 1940, believing they would join the Polish Free Corps. Instead of arriving somewhere at the Baltic coast, they were unloaded in Katyn, not too far from Brest Litovsk, marched into the woods, with their hands tied behind their backs, forced to kneel, and then shot, one-by-one, into the back of their heads.

When the German authorities discovered the mass graves in 1943, the Russians immediately blamed the Germans for the assassination of the Polish officers. The German authorities, on the other hand, invited an international medical commission to investigate the case. The commission agreed unanimously that the bodies were in graves since 1940. (This opinion is based on the clothes - winter uniform and boots - letters from families, entries in diaries, etc.) During that time the territory was still in Russian hands.

In the past 50 years, many testimonies from various sources proved Russian culpability; but only recently did the Russians admit guilt by blaming Stalin, the easy and fashionable way nowadays.

Dr. Swianiewicz was perhaps one of the very few officers who escaped the massacre because he had been taken off the transport by the Soviet Secret Police and was incarcerated in the infamous Lubyanka prison in Moscow for having criticized in an academic paper the Russian Kolkhoz system (collective farm system). Dr. Stan was prepared to meet his death as many others did at the Lubyanka prison. He survived, his collegues who thought to join the Anderson corps, were murdered in the woods of Katyn.

When the elderly gentleman told me this story in the fall of 1978 during dinner together, he had just returned from Sweden where he presented a paper on Katyn. When I asked him what was the reason for his scratched face and black eye, thinking he may have been in an accident, he told me that he had just survived an assassination attempt at his London hotel. He was found unconscious on the floor of his hotel room. Dr. Stanislav was more than 80 years old at that time.

+ Stalingrad

Although I do not consider myself an expert in the history of World War II, nor any other history, I would like to give a short account of what I learned and remember about Stalingrad, the 6th Army, and its leader, General Friedrich von Paulus.

From my high school days I remember that Tsarytsin (named after a nearby river) was originally built as a fortress in 1589 to protect trade and the shipping of goods down the Volga River to the Caspian Sea.

In 1917, during the early stages of the Russian Revolution the city was taken by the Bolsheviks and later, in 1925, renamed Stalingrad, in honour of Joseph Stalin who played an important role in defense of that city against the White Russians. Because it was an important industrial centre, Stalingrad became an important strategic objective during the war. A large German force, the 6th Army, consisting of 20 Divisions, began an assault against the city in August of 1942.

In the middle of September, during a short lull, the commanders of both the Russian and German forces had a briefing session with their Commanders-in-Chief. Marshal Zhukov with his Chief-of-Staff Vasilevsky and General Chuikov met with Stalin while von Paulus met with Hitler. Zhukov and his Generals argued with Stalin about how to save the city and how to surround the German forces. Stalin's ideas were rejected and he withdrew, leading his Generals to understand that his concern was that Stalingrad should not fall. Von Paulus, on the other hand, took his instructions without objection or criticism. The great battle which became the turning point in the war started.

The fiercest hand-to-hand battles occurred during a period of 80 days and 80 nights. J. Keegan's, World War II, quotes a German soldier who wrote: "....Stalingrad is no longer a town. By day it is an enormous cloud of burning, blinding smoke, it is a vast furnace lit by the reflection of the flames. And when night arrives, one of those scorching, howling, bleeding nights, the dogs plunge into the Volga and swim desperately to gain the other bank. The nights of Stalingrad are a terror for them. Animals flee this hell; the hardest storms cannot bear it for long; only men endure."

General Chuikov reporting from the other side on October 14th wrote: "The Germans struck out; that day will go down as the bloodiest and most ferocious of the whole battle. During the day there were over 2000 Luftwaffe sorties.... After four or five hours of this stunning barrage the Germans started to attack with tanks and infantry and they advanced one and a half kilometers and finally broke through to the tractor plant."

By the end of October, according to Chuikov, both armies were left gripping each other in a deadly clutch. The Russian troops were inspired to fight as if there was no land across the Volga. They ferried thousands of wounded across the river and returned with twice as many replacements.

General von Paulus still had a few successes, such as reaching the Volga in the south and encircling the city. But then winter arrived together with 'Zeus' (General Voronov with his 2000 guns) and the thunder and lightening started on the other side in the north of Stalingrad. Zhukov began his counterattack and von Paulus was soon trapped. Field Marshal von Manstein tried to persuade Hitler to order von Paulus to break out and connect with his (von Manstein's) forces, which were attacking from the outside. However, Hitler could not be persuaded. Soon the supply lines were cut off, and the main airfield was overrun by the Russians. Voronov and Rokosovsky asked von Paulus to surrender. After he refused, the Russians started a bombardment with the largest concentration of artillery in history, some 7000 guns. In order to make sure von Paulus would not surrender, Hitler promoted him to field marshal. No German field marshal has ever surrendered to the enemy.

By the end of January, about 20,000 wounded soldiers were lying in unheated houses (makeshift hospitals). The outside temperature was minus 30 degrees celsius.

After von Paulus' headquarters were overrun, on January 30th, the 6th Army finally capitulated on February 2, 1943. At the time, I was about 200 miles further to the west, marching to the east, in the 333 Infantry Division of von Manstein's Army Group and experiencing a cold Russian winter for the first time.

There are slightly differing figures as to the losses at Stalingrad. According to the senior lecturer at the Royal Military Academy at Sandhurst, England, out of the original 280,000 who had been encircled, 70,000 died, 42,000 had been evacuated, and 91,000 had surrendered. The remainder managed to find their way back. Of the 91,000 who were captured, it is reported that only 6,000 returned home.

Those men took and kept their Oath of Allegiance, but von Paulus did not keep his Oath. He became a member of the National Committee for a Free Germany organized by German Communists in the U.S.S.R. Many of the other 24 generals who were captured at the time suffered for their allegiance.

IMPORTANT DATES OF EVENTS

September 1939 - May 1945

1939

Sept. 1	Invasion of Poland
Sept. 3	England and France declare war on Germany
Sept 17	Russia invades Poland
Sept 29	Germany and Russia divide Poland

1940

April 9	Germany invades Denmark and Norway
April 15	Small British force lands in Norway
May 10	Invasion of Holland, Belgian and Luxembourg
May 14	German troops move into French territory
June 4	Evacuation of British and French forces at Dunkirk
June 10	Mussolini declares war on Allied Powers
June 25	France surrenders
Nov 14	Coventry bombed

1941

Jan 5	British troops attack Italians in North Africa
Feb 12	Rommel arrives in Libya
March 9	Italians invade Greece
April 6	Germans invade Yugoslavia and Greece
May 24	Sinking of the "Hood"
May 27	Sinking of the "Bismarck"
June 22	German troops invade Russia

1942

July 1	Rommel captures Tobruk
Aug 19	Raid on Dieppe
Oct 23	Montgomery defeats Rommel at Alamain

1943

Feb 2	Field Marshal Paulus surrenders Stalingrad
May 13	Germans surrender in North Africa
July 10	Allies invade Sicily
Sept 3	Allies invade Italy
Sept 8	Italy tries to surrender

1944

Feb 15	Allied bombers dropped over 450 tons of bombs on the monastery of Monte Cassino
June 4	Fall of Rome
June 6	D-Day invasion
June 13	First V1 bombs fall on England
July 20	Assassination attempt on Hitler
Sept 13	Battle of the Gothic line in Italy
Dec 16	Ardennes offensive

1945

Jan 17	Russians capture Warsaw
March 7	American troops at the Remagen bridge
April 30	Hitler committed suicide
May 2	German troops surrender in Italy
May 8	Unconditional surrender of Germany

BIBLIOGRAPHY

Bacque, James. Other Losses. Toronto: General Paperbacks, 1991.

Dancocks, Daniel G. The D-Day Dodgers: The Canadians in Italy, 1943-1945. Toronto: MacClelland & Stewart Inc., 1991.

Dresler, Dr. Adlolf. Deutsche Kunst und entartete Kunst. München: Deutscher Volksverlag, 1938.

Friedrich der Grosse. Vom Dienst des Herrschers. Jena: Eugen Diederichs Verlag Jena, 1941.

Gall, Lothar. Fragen an die Deutsche Geschichte. Stuttgart: Verlag W. Kohlhammer GmbH., 1974.

Goerlitz, Walter. History of the German General Staff. Trans. Brian Battershaw. London: Hollis & Carter Ltd., 1965.

Goethe, Johann Wolfgang von. Faust, Part I. Trans. Peter Salm. New York: Bantam, 1985.

Haffner, Sebastian. Anmerkungen zu Hitler, Kindler Verlag GmbH Copyright 1978 München.

Gombrich, E.H. Ideals and Idols, essays on values in history and art. Phaidon, Oxford, 1979.

Johann, Ernst and Jörg Junker. Deutsche Kulturgeschichte der Letzten Hundert Jahre. München: Nymphenburger Verlagshandlung GmbH., 1970.

Kesselring, Albert. The Memoirs of Field-Marshal Kesselring. Trans. William Kimber. Novato: Presidio Press, 1989.

Lotz, Jim. Canadians at War. London: Bison Books, Ltd. 1990.

Mann, Golo. History of Germany since 1789. Middlesex: Penguin, 1987.

Manstein, Field-Marshal Erich von. Lost Victories. Novato: Presidio Press, 1982.

Michels, W.K. Die Heimat in Scherben, R.Z. Dokumentation 1985 Mittelrhein-Verlag GmbH, Koblenz I.

Mitcham, Samuel W. Jr. Hitler's Field-Marshal's and their Battles. London: Grafton Books, 1989.

Nicholson, Lt.-Col. G.W.L. The Canadians in Italy 1943-1945 (Official History of the Canadian Army in the Second World War). Ottawa: Minister of National Defense, 1956.

Rovan, Joseph. Germany. Trans. Margaret Crosland. London: Studio Vista, 1964.

Staatl. Realschule Mayen. Auf den Spuren der Juden in Mayen und Umgebung. Mayen: Stadt Mayen, 1987.

United States War Department. Handbook on German Military Forces. Baton Rouge: Louisiana State University Press, 1990.